UNIX® System Security

Addison-Wesley Professional Computing Series

Brian W. Kernighan, Consulting Editor

Ken Arnold/John Peyton, *A C User's Guide to ANSI C*
Tom Cargill, *C++ Programming Style*
David Curry, *UNIX System Security: A Guide for Users and System Administrators*
Scott Meyers, *Effective C++: 50 Specific Ways to Improve Your Programs and Designs*
Radia Perlman, *Interconnections: Bridges and Routers*
W. Richard Stevens, *Advanced Programming in the UNIX Environment*

UNIX® System Security

A Guide for Users and System Administrators

David A. Curry

ADDISON-WESLEY PUBLISHING COMPANY, INC.
Reading, Massachusetts   Menlo Park, California   New York   Don Mills, Ontario
Wokingham, England   Amsterdam   Bonn   Paris   Milan   Madrid   Sydney   Singapore   Tokyo
Seoul   Taipei   Mexico City   San Juan

The publisher offers discounts on this book when ordered in quantity for special sales.
For more information please contact:

        Corporate & Professional Publishing Group
        Addison-Wesley Publishing Company
        One Jacob Way
        Reading, Massachusetts 01867

Library of Congress Cataloging-in-Publication Data

Curry, David A. (David Allan), 1962–
    Unix system security : a guide for users and system administrators
  / David A. Curry
       p. cm. -- (Addison-Wesley professional computing series)
    Includes bibliographical references (p.) and index.
    ISBN 0-201-56327-4 (hardcover)
    1. Computer security. 2. UNIX (Computer file) I. Title.
  II. Series
  QA76.9.A25C87 1992   91-43652
  005.4'3--dc20   CIP

Cover design by Joyce Weston
Text design by Webster Design
Text set in 11 point Times

ISBN 0-201-56327-4
1 2 3 4 5 6 7 8 9-MU-95949392
First printing, May 1992

Addison-Wesley Professional Computing Series

Brian W. Kernighan, Consulting Editor

Many of the designations used by manufacturers and sellers to distinguish their products are claimed as trademarks. Where those designations appear in this book and Addison-Wesley was aware of a trademark claim, the designations have been printed in initial capital letters.

The programs and applications presented in this book have been included for their instructional value. They have been tested with care, but are not guaranteed for any particular purpose. The publisher does not offer any warranties or representations, nor does it accept any liabilities with respect to the programs or applications.

UNIX is a registered trademark of UNIX System Labs, Inc. VAX, VMS, VT, and ULTRIX are trademarks of Digital Equipment Corporation. HP-UX is a trademark of the Hewlett-Packard Company. Sun Microsystems and NFS are registered trademarks of Sun Microsystems, Inc. SunOS, NIS, Sun-3, Sun-4, SPARC, and SPARCstation are trademarks of Sun Microsystems, Inc. Ethernet is a trademark of the Xerox Corporation. TransScript is a registered trademark of Adobe Systems, Inc. Yellow Pages is a registered trademark in the United Kingdom of British Telecommunications, plc. X Window System is a trademark of the Massachusetts Institute of Technology.

The publisher offers discounts on this book when ordered in quantity for special sales.
For more information please contact:

Corporate & Professional Publishing Group
Addison-Wesley Publishing Company
One Jacob Way
Reading, Massachusetts 01867

Library of Congress Cataloging-in-Publication Data

Curry, David A. (David Allan), 1962–
    Unix system security : a guide for users and system administrators
/ David A. Curry
        p. cm. -- (Addison-Wesley professional computing series)
    Includes bibliographical references (p.) and index.
    ISBN 0-201-56327-4 (hardcover)
    1. Computer security. 2. UNIX (Computer file) I. Title.
    II. Series
    QA76.9.A25C87 1992   91-43652
    005.4'3--dc20   CIP

Cover design by Joyce Weston
Text design by Webster Design
Text set in 11 point Times

ISBN 0-201-56327-4
1 2 3 4 5 6 7 8 9-MU-95949392
First printing, May 1992

Contents

Preface

History

The UNIX operating system, although now in widespread use in environments concerned about security, was not really designed with security in mind (Ritchie, 1975). This does not mean that UNIX does not provide any security mechanisms; indeed, several very good ones are available. However, most "out of the box" installation procedures from companies such as Sun Microsystems, Digital Equipment Corporation, and AT&T still set up the system in much the same way as it was originally shipped 15 years ago: with little or no security enabled.

The reasons for this state of affairs are largely historical. UNIX was originally designed by programmers for use by other programmers. The environment in which it was used was one of open cooperation, not one of privacy. Programmers typically collaborated with each other on projects, and hence preferred to be able to share their files with each other without having to jump over security hurdles. Because the first sites outside of Bell Laboratories to install UNIX were university research laboratories, where a similar environment existed, no real need for greater security was seen until some time later.

In the early 1980s, many universities began to move their UNIX systems out of the laboratories and into the computer centers, allowing (or forcing) the user population as a whole to use this new and wonderful system. Many businesses and government sites began to install UNIX systems as well, particularly as desktop workstations became more powerful and affordable. Thus, the UNIX operating system is no longer being used only in environments where open collaboration is the primary goal. Universities require their students to use the system for class assignments, yet they do not want the students to be able to copy from each other. Businesses use their UNIX systems for confidential tasks such as bookkeeping and payroll. And the government uses UNIX for numerous unclassified yet sensitive purposes.

To complicate matters, new features have been added to UNIX over the years, making security even more difficult to control. Perhaps the most problematic features are those relating to networking: remote login, remote command execution, file transfer, network file systems, and electronic mail. All of these features have increased the utility and usability of UNIX by untold amounts. However, these same features, along with the widespread connection of UNIX systems to the Internet (Quarterman and Hoskins, 1986) and other networks, have opened up many new areas of vulnerability to unauthorized abuse of the system.

Purpose of the Book

Over the years, a great deal has been written about UNIX system security. Papers are presented at almost every USENIX and Uniforum conference as well as others, and the USENIX Association sponsors an annual workshop on UNIX security. Electronic mailing lists exist for the purposes of reporting security problems and receiving fixes for them. Freely available software exists to analyze UNIX systems for security problems and report or correct them. But, in spite of all the work being done in this area, the results of this work have never been collected in one place, and average users or system administrators of UNIX systems still do not have the information necessary to protect their data and their systems from unauthorized use.

This book provides the information necessary to protect a UNIX system from unauthorized access. The methods an attacker can use to gain access to a UNIX system are described, as well as how to defend against them. In describing the bugs and loopholes used by attackers, it is sometimes necessary to provide information on how they are used. However, we try to strike a midway point between providing enough information so that the reader can understand the problem, while not providing enough information for an attacker to use the text as a cookbook for breaking into systems.

The primary focus of the book is on the most recent versions of UNIX (4.2BSD and 4.3BSD from Berkeley) and their most recent vendor derivatives (SunOS 4.x, ULTRIX 4.x, etc.), and System V Release 4 from AT&T. However, most of the information presented can be applied, with minor changes, to any version of UNIX since Seventh Edition. An attempt has been made to make the shell scripts and C programs used in the examples as portable as possible by avoiding many of the "convenience" features added in some versions of the operating system. While this means that some of the examples are not as efficient or "clean" as they could be, it also means that they will work on more systems. Industrious readers may feel free to recode any of the examples to use whatever new features are desired.

By following the procedures described in the text, and making use of the programs and shell scripts provided as examples, it is possible to secure a UNIX system against most attackers, even if it is connected to wide-area networks such as the Internet.

Organization of the Book

The book is divided into five parts.

In Chapter 1, we begin our discussion by considering four well-known cases of UNIX security being broken. This serves to make the reader aware of some possible types of attack on UNIX systems, as well as to provide a framework for later discussion.

Most of the information required to protect a single UNIX system is presented in the next three chapters. Chapter 2 discusses account and password security. File system security is covered in Chapter 3. Chapter 4 describes network security.

The third part of the book discusses some topics in more detail. These topics pertain primarily to networks of UNIX systems and systems that provide remote access. Chapter 5 describes the Network Information Service (NIS) (formerly called Sun Yellow Pages, or YP), the Network File System (NFS), and the Remote File Sharing (RFS) service. Workstations and the particular security problems they present are covered in Chapter 6. Terminals, modems, and the UNIX-to-UNIX copy program (UUCP) are discussed in Chapter 7.

Chapter 8 describes methods for detecting and responding to break-ins, and serves to separate the discussion of specific UNIX security issues from the material in the last part of the book.

The last chapters of the book cover topics that are directly related to UNIX system security, but are not part of the UNIX system itself. Chapter 9 discusses encryption and authentication, and the software and hardware devices used to implement them. Security policies are discussed in Chapter 10. Chapters 11 and 12 discuss publicly available security-related software and how to obtain information about current threats to UNIX security.

Conventions

Throughout the book, several type styles are used. For the most part the conventions used should be obvious, but some of them are reviewed here for the sake of clarity.

- *Italics* are used in the text for the names of specific files, e.g. */etc/passwd*, the names of specific users, e.g. *root*, and to introduce new terms and concepts. Within examples, *italics* are used to represent items that you should fill in with specific text. For example, *filename* indicates that you should replace the word "filename" with the name of a file.

- **Bold** is used in the text to provide special emphasis.

- `Constant width` is used in the text for the names of specific UNIX commands. It is also used in examples to represent output from the computer.

- **`Constant width bold`** is used in examples to indicate input to the computer, i.e., text that you should type.

Within the examples, the shell prompt is shown before any commands that you should type. If the prompt is shown as a dollar sign ($), this means that the command may be run with or without super-user privileges. If the prompt is shown as a pound sign (#), this means that the command must be run as the super-user, *root*.

Unless referring to a specific person already identified, pronouns are used in alternating genders ("he" and "she"). This is done to avoid awkward combinations like "s/he," "his/her," and so on. No particular meaning should be attached to the specific gender of the pronouns used in these sentences.

Background

This book assumes that the reader is familiar with the UNIX system, its commands, and its terminology. Readers who are unfamiliar with UNIX should consult *A Practical Guide to the UNIX System, Second Edition* by Mark G. Sobell, published by Addison-Wesley. Readers who wish to learn more about UNIX system administration (which will be helpful, but not necessary, in understanding some parts of this book) should consult the *UNIX System Administration Handbook* by Evi Nemeth, Garth Snyder, and Scott Seebass, published by Prentice Hall. Readers who would like to learn more about the history and "culture" of UNIX may wish to consult *Life With UNIX* by Don Libes and Sandy Ressler, published by Prentice Hall.

Acknowledgements

First and foremost, I am grateful to my wife, Cathy, and our sons, Trevor and Sean. Their love, patience, and encouragement helped make this book a reality.

Many thanks to the people who reviewed the book and provided technical and editorial critiques: Ralph Droms (Bucknell University), Tom Duff (AT&T Bell Laboratories), Fred Grampp (AT&T Bell Laboratories), Dan Farmer (Sun Microsystems), Brian Kernighan (AT&T Bell Laboratories), Rich Kulawiec (Hospital of the University of Pennsylvania), Doug McIlroy (AT&T Bell Laboratories), Michael Merritt (AT&T Bell Laboratories), Jim Reeds (AT&T Bell Laboratories), Jeff Schwab (Purdue University), and Steve Simmons (Industrial Technology Institute). Thanks also to John Wait and Alan Apt, my editors at Addison-Wesley, for their support and assistance while writing the book.

A good portion of the information about UNIX security presented in this book has come from discussions with friends and colleagues, and from suggestions received from the readers of an earlier paper I wrote on UNIX security (Curry, 1990). Thanks to all of you, especially Matt Bishop, Dan Farmer, Phil Klimbal, Doug Moran, Donn Parker, Peter Neumann, and Jeff Schwab. Finally, special thanks go to Rich Lynn of Digital Equipment Corporation, who obtained a copy of the *ULTRIX Security Guide for Administrators* for me, to Ken van Wyk of the CERT/CC, who answered my several requests for information, and to John Wack of NIST, who provided a wealth of information about how to form a response team, and about the FIRST.

This book was produced using AT&T's Documenter's Workbench, Release 2.0 (eqn, tbl, troff) with the -ms macro package on a Sun Microsystems

SPARCstation 1 running SunOS 4.1.1. PostScript output was produced by the TransScript package from Adobe Systems. The index was generated using a set of `awk` and `sh` programs described in (Bentley and Kernighan, 1988).

The author would like to hear from any readers with comments, suggestions, or bug reports: `davy@ecn.purdue.edu`.

Chapter 1
UNIX Security Stories

In this chapter, we examine four well-known stories of UNIX security being broken. The purpose of this examination is twofold. First, the stories show that there are numerous ways to attack a UNIX system successfully, and they provide food for thought about just what it is we're trying to protect ourselves against with the procedures described in the rest of the book. Second, they provide us with a background to justify the procedures in the book. Throughout the following chapters, we will refer back to these stories in order to show how a specific procedure guards against an attacker using the methods described here.

1.1 The Internet Worm

On the evening of November 2, 1988, a self-replicating program, called a *worm*, was released on the Internet (Seely, 1988; Spafford, 1988; Eichin and Rochlis, 1989). Overnight, this program had copied itself from machine to machine, causing the machines it infected to labor under huge loads, thus effectively denying service to the users of those machines. Although the program successfully attacked only two types of computers, it spread quickly, as did the concern, confusion, and sometimes panic of system administrators whose systems were affected. While many system administrators were aware that something like this could theoretically happen—most of the security loopholes exploited by the worm were well known—the scope of the worm's break-ins came as a great surprise to most people.

What the Worm Did

The worm began by exploiting three security problems in Berkeley-derived versions of the UNIX operating system. Using one of these loopholes, the attacking machine sent a small *bootstrap* shell script to the machine under attack, and executed it. The bootstrap compiled and executed a small C program that connected back to the attacking machine via TCP and downloaded pre-compiled object code that implemented the worm itself. It then tried to link this object code on the target machine and execute it, at which point the machine under attack became a new attacker, and began to go after more machines. One of the keys to limiting the worm's spread was the pre-compiled object code—only objects for Sun Microsystems Sun-3 systems and Digital Equipment Corporation VAX systems were included in the worm's "distribution." Had the worm's author wished, objects for other systems running Berkeley-derived versions of UNIX (Sun SPARC, Sequent, Pyramid, Gould, Sony, etc.) could have been included as well. As it was, some sites were totally immune to the worm, since their machines that were targeted by the worm were not Sun-3 or VAX systems (Spafford, 1988). Other sites were immune to the worm as well, either because they had fixed the bugs it exploited, or because they had protected themselves in other ways (described later in the book).

One of the bugs exploited by the worm was the debug function of the sendmail program (Eichin and Rochlis, 1989). Among its many features, sendmail includes the ability to send mail to a program, such that the program is executed with the body of the mail message as input. This feature is normally permitted only when the program is specified in either the system-wide mail aliases file or a user's *forward* file, enabling the use of mail archivers, "vacation" programs, and the like. It is **not** normally allowed for incoming connections, except when debugging is enabled. Unfortunately, the sendmail program shipped with 4.3BSD and pre-4.1 versions of SunOS had debugging mode turned on. The worm utilized this by connecting to a machine's sendmail daemon, and sending a message to a "recipient" that was actually a command to strip off the mail headers and pass the remainder of the message to the shell. The remainder of the message was the bootstrap script, described earlier.

A second bug used by the worm was in the fingerd program (Eichin and Rochlis, 1989). This program exists on a machine to provide answers to remote hosts executing the finger utility to find out who is logged in, or obtain information about a user. The fingerd program reads a line of input from the remote system, and then looks up the information about the person or persons listed on that line. Unfortunately, the library routine used to read the line of input did not perform any range checking, allowing the buffer to overflow. Since the buffer was on the stack, the overflow allowed a new stack frame to be created, causing a small piece of code (provided by the worm) to be executed. This code caused a shell to be executed, and the shell's input was connected to the remote host. The bootstrap code was then sent to the shell, and the machine was infected. Because of the machine-dependent nature of this attack, it was only used on 4.3BSD VAXes, and failed on the Sun architecture.

The third problem the worm made use of was perhaps the most familiar to system administrators: the rsh program, and the related rexec library function (Seely, 1988). Both of these provide access to a shell on the remote system. rexec requires password authentication on the remote system, while rsh allows "trusted" access to specific hosts and/or user names via the use of system-wide *hosts.equiv* and per-user *.rhosts* files. The worm first tried to attack another system by using rsh, to test for a remote account with the same name as the user it was running as on the local machine. If this failed, the worm then tried to crack the passwords of every account on the local system. As soon as it found one, it would use `rexec` to connect to the remote machines listed in that user's *.forward* and *.rhosts* files, using the listed user names and the password it just discovered. If this too failed, the worm connected to the local machine with `rexec` and the just-discovered password, and proceeded to use `rsh` as that user, hoping for trusted access on one of the remote systems.

The worm began by trying the `rsh` and `rexec` attacks. If those failed, the `fingerd` attack was used, and finally, the `sendmail` attack (Seely, 1988). The worm also used numerous tricks in an attempt to cover its trail, including erasing its argument list, deleting its files as quickly as possible, hiding itself under the name `sh`, and re-invoking itself every few minutes such that all program runs were short (Eichin and Rochlis, 1989).

What the Worm Didn't Do

Although the worm spread rapidly and widely, infecting thousands of machines in the space of 48 hours, it did **not** do any lasting damage to any of the systems it infected. Its primary effect was one of denial of service: due to (presumably) a bug in the worm's code, a machine could end up running nothing but multiple copies of the worm a few hours after infection. Although it could have done any number of malicious things to the systems infected, the worm specifically **did not** (Seely, 1988)

- Delete any system files other than those it created during the bootstrap procedure.

- Modify any existing files on an infected system. The worm was not a virus—it propagated by copying and compiling itself on remote systems, not by modifying other programs to do its work.

- Install programs to be executed later by unsuspecting users. The worm's method of attack was strictly active; it did not wait for unsuspecting users to "help" it along.

- Record or transmit decrypted passwords. Although the worm did attempt to crack passwords, it did this locally on each system and did not propagate the information obtained to other systems or to a home base.

- Try to capture super-user privileges. The worm had no preference for which accounts it tried to break into first, and if it did happen to obtain special privileges, it did not make use of them.

- Propagate via UUCP, X.25, BITNET, or DECNET. The worm specifically required TCP/IP.

- Infect System V UNIX systems, unless those systems were modified to use Berkeley network programs such as `sendmail`, `fingerd`, and `rexec`.

The Worm's Aftermath

The Internet worm was perhaps the most widely described computer security problem ever, certainly in the popular media. It was covered in many newspapers and magazines around the country, including the *New York Times*, the *Wall Street Journal*, *Time*, *Newsweek*, and most computer-oriented technical publications, as well as on all three major television networks, the Cable News Network, and National Public Radio. Additionally, discussion continued for weeks afterward in several USENET newsgroups and Internet mailing lists.

On May 4, 1990, Federal District Judge Howard G. Munson sentenced Robert Tappan Morris, the 25-year-old Cornell University graduate student who authored the worm, to a $10,000 fine, 400 hours of community service, and three years' probation. Morris was the first person to be convicted by a jury under the 1986 Computer Fraud and Abuse Act, for breaking into a government network and preventing authorized use of the system. Under this law, he faced a maximum sentence of five years in prison and a $250,000 fine (Ould, 1990). The conviction was upheld by a unanimous decision in the U.S. Court of Appeals for the Second Circuit in March 1991. In June 1991, Morris' attorneys filed an appeal to the U.S. Supreme Court, arguing that Morris never intended to cause harm (UNIX Today!, 1991a). The Supreme Court let the decision stand in October 1991, declining without comment to hear the appeal (UNIX Today!, 1991b).

1.2 The Wily Hacker

In August 1986, Clifford Stoll (1988, 1989, 1990a), an astronomer by profession, was working at the computer facility of the Lawrence Berkeley Laboratory (LBL), an unclassified research laboratory at the University of California, Berkeley. At the time, Stoll was working to find the cause of a seventy-five-cent discrepancy in the lab's computer accounting system, which was used to bill users for their computer resource usage. As it turned out, the discrepancy was due to an improperly installed account which had no billing address associated with it. Little did Stoll suspect that the discovery of this account was the start of a year-long effort in tracking down the intruders and seeing them apprehended.

Shortly after discovering the bogus account, Stoll deleted it, since nobody in the lab had any knowledge of its existence. A short time later, the National Computer Security Center called to complain that someone had tried to break into one of their computers, and that the source of the break-in was a computer at LBL. Realizing that there was an intruder in the system, and suspecting that the culprit was probably a student at the nearby university, Stoll and his colleagues decided to try to catch the intruder in the act (Stoll, 1988). They connected printers to the various incoming lines of the computer, and printed out every keystroke the intruder typed, as well as all the output he received. They watched the unknown assailant break into several other computer systems around the country. Thinking that this could be more serious than he originally suspected, Stoll began working with the companies providing the telephone connections to the lab's computers to track the intruder.

Tracking the Intruder

LBL's computers are connected to the outside world, among other ways, via Tymnet, a nationwide telephone-based data network. After several weeks of unsuccessful tracing efforts, Stoll and his friends came up with a way to keep the intruder on the line long enough to be traced. Having noticed that the intruder seemed to be interested in defense-related material, they made up a new project purporting to deal with the Strategic Defense Initiative. They typed in all sorts of fictitious information about the project, and left it for the intruder to find. Eventually, he took the bait, and tracing began in earnest. Finally, on June 21, 1987, ten months after he was first detected, the intruder's call was traced all the way from the Oakland, California, Tymnet office, through the national Tymnet network and the international network operated by ITT, into the West German Datex network, and finally to a line in Hannover, West Germany (Stoll, 1989).

After the line was located, the German police stationed a policeman outside the intruder's apartment in Hannover. The next time the intruder broke into Stoll's system, Stoll was to call Tymnet, they would make the trace, notify the German authorities, and the police would arrest the intruder. However, Stoll never had the chance to do this. Arrest warrants were issued by the Germans after they raided a company called Focus Computer GmbH in Hannover, apparently because of a separate investigation, and the LBL intruder was arrested on June 29, 1987 (Stoll, 1989).

Eventually, Stoll discovered the name of the intruder, Markus Hess. He then discovered more—Hess, through his friend, Hans Hübner, who operated under the name "Pengo," had been selling the information he found during his exploits to the Soviet KGB. Among the KGB's requests that Hess and his friends filled: printouts and passwords (for which the KGB paid 30,000 Deutschmarks—about $18,000), source code to the UNIX operating system, designs for high-speed gallium-arsenide integrated circuits, and computer programs to engineer memory chips. The Soviets also offered 250,000 Deutschmarks ($150,000) for a copy of the source code to Digital Equipment Corporation's VMS operating system. Also on the KGB wish list was information on the Strategic Defense Initiative—the same (made-up) information Stoll used to finally catch the intruder (Stoll, 1989).

Final Outcome

In March 1989, the German authorities charged five people with espionage. One of the men, Karl Koch, who operated under the name "Hagbard," was found burned to death two months later in an isolated forest outside Hannover. No suicide note was found, and his death remains a mystery. Markus Hess, Dirk Bresinsky, and Peter Carl were convicted of espionage in a German court in February 1990. They were sentenced to up to two years in prison, fines of approximately $12,000, and the loss of their rights to participate in elections (Neumann, 1990). Hans Hübner cooperated with the state prosecutor in exchange for not being brought to trial (Stoll, 1990b).

What started as a simple billing error, caused by someone using an unauthorized computer account, turned into a case of international espionage. By the time the intruders were apprehended, the case had involved the FBI, CIA, National Security Agency, U.S. Army Criminal Investigations Division, U.S. Air Force Intelligence, and the West German *Bundeskriminalamt*. Telephone tracing involved officials from Tymnet, Pacific Bell, AT&T, ITT, RCA, and the West German *Bundespost*. Over 400 computers around the world were attacked, with somewhere between 30 and 50 being successfully penetrated. These computers were located at universities, corporations, defense contractors, and U.S. military bases. Presumably, since classified computers are not connected to the Internet, no classified material was obtained by the intruders or the KGB.

1.3 A True UNIX Trojan Horse

During the Trojan War, the Greeks pretended to abandon the siege of Troy, and left behind a large, hollow wooden horse. The Trojans opened the city gates and took the horse into Troy, regarding it as a sacrifice to the gods. During the night, Greek soldiers who had been hiding inside the horse opened the gates and the Greek army conquered the city. In the computer field, a Trojan horse is a program that masquerades as something it is not, fooling the person executing the program into doing something he doesn't suspect. This is typified by programs that emulate `login`. They prompt for a login name and password, and then print the message "login incorrect," and exit to the real `login` program, making the user think that she made an error entering her password. Little does the user know that she typed her password correctly, and that the Trojan horse has filed this information away for later use by its author.

Background

In his 1983 Turing Award lecture, Ken Thompson (1984), one of the original creators of UNIX, described a more insidious version of the Trojan horse. He began by pointing out that the C compiler is a self-reproducing tool, in that because the compiler itself is written in C, it can interpret things in a completely portable way. This is typified by the code that expands the "\n" escape sequence into a newline character:

```
...
c = next();
if (c != '\\')
```

```
        return(c);          /* normal character   */
    c = next();
    if (c == '\\')
        return('\\');       /* backslash          */
    if (c == 'n')
        return('\n');       /* newline character */
    ...
```

Because the existing compiler "knows" in a completely portable sense what character is encoded as a newline character in any character set, the compiler is able to recompile itself.

Thompson goes on to point out that if we wanted to modify the compiler to know about the sequence "\v" to represent the vertical tab character, the obvious code

```
    ...
    if (c == 'v')
        return('\v');
    ...
```

would not work, since the existing compiler does not know about the "\v" escape. For the first version of the compiler, the code would have to be written to return decimal 11, which is the ASCII representation of a vertical tab:

```
    ...
    if (c == 'v')
        return(11);
    ...
```

After installing this version of the compiler, the version using the "\v" escape can be compiled and installed, and the knowledge of the new escape sequence will perpetuate itself from that point on.

The Trojan Horse

From the above, Thompson pointed out that other parts of the compiler can be modified to do other similar things. In his example, the compile subroutine, which compiles the next line of source, is modified to recognize when it is compiling the source code for the login program:

```
    compile(line)
    char *line;
    {
        if (match(line, "code from login")) {
            compile("bug");
            return;
        }
    }
```

In Thompson's version of the bug, the compiler would miscompile the `login` command so that it would accept either the intended encrypted password, or a particular known password. This would allow anyone who knew the special password to gain access to any system running the miscompiled `login`.

Of course, Thompson's modification to the compiler would be immediately obvious to anyone examing the compiler source code. However, in much the same way that an interim compiler was used to instill knowledge of the "`\v`" escape, a similar interim compiler can be used to instill knowledge of the Trojan horse:

```
compile(line)
char *line;
{
    if (match(line, "code from login")) {
        compile("login-bug");
        return;
    }
    if (match(line, "code from C compiler")) {
        compile("compiler-bug");
        return;
    }
}
```

Now this version of the compiler is installed, and the above code is removed from the compiler source. The source is recompiled with the interim compiler, and the new version will reinsert the bugs whenever it is compiled. And the `login` command will remain bugged with no trace in its source code anywhere.

Trojan horses like these are a serious threat. While programs that emulate `login` and the like are fairly easy to detect and defeat, something of the sort Thompson describes is much better concealed. Once the interim compilers have been replaced with the final binaries, no source code exists anywhere to indicate what has been done. Furthermore, even if it is determined that the compiler is the problem, recompiling the compiler is useless, since the compiler will simply reinsert the Trojan horse. The only recourse is to reload the compiler from a known good set of backup tapes, or from the operating system distribution tapes. Of course, if the original Trojan horse was inserted on a vendor's development system, even this may not be enough.

1.4 Attacking UNIX with Viruses

Many people believe that UNIX is essentially immune to the threat of viruses in the traditional sense, since system files are typically not owned by the everyday users of the system, and hence cannot be modified with the ease that those on a personal computer (whose operating system typically has no protections) can. However, Tom Duff

(1989), a researcher at AT&T Bell Laboratories, has presented a simple scheme by which viruses can be used to attack UNIX systems.

What the Virus Does

Most modern UNIX systems use some form of demand paging, allowing the text and data segments of a program to be loaded on demand from the executable file. This requires that the size of the text segment (the executable code) be some multiple of the system's page size, typically 1024 bytes. However, programs' text segments are rarely exactly a multiple of 1024 bytes long, and so they are padded with nulls. UNIX programs also have an *entry point* recorded in them, which indicates the address in the text segment at which execution is to begin. This file layout is shown in Figure 1.1.

Duff's virus, when executed, examines each file in the current directory. Whenever it finds an executable file on which it has write permission, it examines that file to see if there are enough nulls at the end of the program's text segment. If so, the virus copies itself there, patches the copy's last instruction to jump to the binary's first instruction, and patches the binary's entry point address to point to the inserted code. Once a system is seeded with a few copies of the virus, sooner or later someone will execute one of the infected programs, and the infection will spread further, to all writable programs in the directory the infected program is called from. As different users execute the infected programs, the virus gains new permissions, enabling it to modify more and more files.

Effects of the Virus

Duff's initial attempt at spreading the virus involved planting it in the file *a.out* in users' private *bin* directories (which are often writable), and hoping that someone

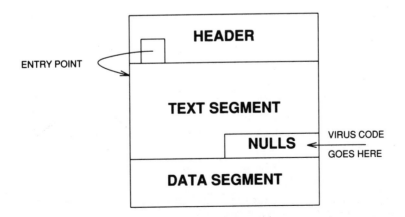

Figure 1.1 Executable File Layout

would execute *a.out* when no such file existed in his working directory. However, this attempt proved fruitless. Duff's next attempt installed 48 copies of the virus in the various directories searched by users in which he had write permission (the list is easily obtained by examining everyone's *.profile* and/or *.cshrc*). In eight days, with the assistance of an automated software distribution system that spread copies of an infected program, the virus had spread to 466 files on 46 different systems.

Duff's virus is fairly benign, in that its only purpose in life is to reproduce itself. Other than a slight performance degradation while the virus searches for writable files, it is not really noticeable. However, Duff points out that it is fairly easy to modify the virus to execute any other program, for example, a shell. If the infected program is set-user-id *root*, this will give the attacker a super-user shell.

A Variation of the Virus

In addition to the more familiar type of virus in which machine-language programs are modified, it is also possible under UNIX to attack a system with viruses based on shell scripts. Duff mentions this attack in his paper, and Doug McIlroy (1989) of AT&T Bell Laboratories has expanded on the idea. He proposes a simple shell script that, when executed, searches for other shell scripts in some list of directories (e.g., the current directory) and, upon finding one, appends itself to the new script. This script can be written in a surprisingly small amount of code:

```
#!/bin/sh


for i in *                    #virus#
do   case "`sed 1q $i`" in
     "#!/bin/sh")
          grep '#virus#' $i >/dev/null || sed -n '/#virus#/,$p' $0 >>$i
     esac
done 2>/dev/null
```

The `for` loop runs through each file in the current directory, setting the shell variable *i* to the name of the file. The `case` statement extracts the first line of the file using `sed`, and then compares it with the value *#!/bin/sh*. If this matches (a shell script has been found), the virus checks with `grep` to see if the script has already been infected, and if not, infects it by copying itself using `sed` onto the end of the file. The output redirection to */dev/null* covers up any evidence should one of the commands fail.

Shell viruses are perhaps even more worrisome than machine-language viruses, since they are both more portable and unlimited in size. This allows them to be made arbitrarily large and complex. Because a large number of programs on a typical UNIX system are indeed shell scripts, including many programs run by the super-user, an infection of one of these programs can be catastrophic.

The commonly-held belief that UNIX is immune to viruses is obviously misguided. It is also untrue that multilevel secure systems that follow the Orange Book (see

Chapter 11) are immune to this type of threat, since the virus infects only programs that the user executing it has already been given permission to modify. Duff proved this in his experiments, by inadvertently infecting a multilevel secure system under development at his laboratory. (Note that this infection did not violate the multilevel security policy of the system; it just did "plain old damage" as it would to any other UNIX system.)

1.5 Summary

Lest these stories depress you to the point of giving up, it is important to note that all of the attacks described in this chapter can be effectively defended against using standard UNIX features. Neither the Internet worm nor Stoll's intruder would have been nearly as successful if the systems they attacked had followed simple security procedures. A system can be defended from virus attacks like Duff's by careful use of UNIX file permissions. And Trojan horses can be defended against by making it difficult for an attacker to gain the proper access to your system needed to install the Trojan horse in the first place. In the following chapters, procedures are described that can guard against all of these attacks, as well as others.

Chapter 2
Account Security

One of the easiest ways for an attacker to gain access to a system is by breaking into someone's account. This is usually easy to do, since many systems have old accounts whose users have left the organization, accounts with easily guessed passwords (or no password at all), or accounts with world-writable files that allow an attacker to modify them. This chapter describes the methods that can be used to protect UNIX accounts from attackers, as well as ways to detect unauthorized account activity.

2.1 Passwords

The password is the most vital part of UNIX account security. If an attacker can discover a user's password, he can then log in to the system and operate with all the capabilities of that user. If the password obtained is that of the super-user, the problem is more serious: the attacker will have free reign over the system, with read and write access to every file stored there. For this reason, choosing a secure password is extremely important.

The typical UNIX `passwd` program places few restrictions on what may be used as a password. Generally, it requires that passwords contain five or more lowercase letters, or four characters if nonalphabetic or uppercase letters are included. However, if the user "insists" that a shorter password be used (by entering it three times), the program will allow it. Newer versions on some systems require six and five characters, respectively, and have disabled the "insist" feature. In System V Release 4 (AT&T, 1990a, 1990b), `passwd` has been modified to be somewhat more secure. Passwords must be at least six characters long, with at least two letters and one digit or punctuation character. They may not be the login name or any shifted version of the login name, and the new password must differ from the old password by at least three characters. ULTRIX 4.x (Digital Equipment Corp., 1990) also has a more secure version of `passwd`. Although these are better than most versions of `passwd`, they still do not go far enough (as will be seen below). Most versions of `passwd` do not perform any checks for obviously insecure passwords, and thus it is incumbent on the system administrator to ensure that the passwords in use on the system are secure.

Morris and Thompson (1978) describe experiments to determine typical users' habits in the choice of passwords. In a collection of 3,289 passwords, 16% of them contained three characters or less, and an astonishing 86% were what could generally be described as insecure. Additional experiments performed by Grampp and Morris (1984) showed that by trying three simple guesses on each account—the login name, the login name in reverse, and the two concatenated together—an attacker can expect to obtain access to between 8 and 30% of the accounts on a typical system. A second experiment showed that by trying the 20 most common female first names, followed by a single digit (a total of 200 passwords), at least one password was valid on each of several dozen machines surveyed. Further experimentation by the author has found that by trying variations on the login name, user's first and last names, and a list of 1,800 common first names, somewhere between 10 and 20% of the passwords on a typical system can usually be determined.

Klein (1990) has performed a great deal of research into cracking passwords, and has tried numerous methods against a database of nearly 15,000 accounts. His experiments successfully guessed just over 24% of these passwords. Klein tried several tests, including

- up to 130 different variations on the login name, first and last name, and other personal data about the user (contained in the password file),

- various dictionary attacks including proper names, names of famous people, names and locations of films, sports, the King James Bible, common vulgar phrases, foreign language dictionaries, etc.,

- various permutations on the words including turning letters into control characters, capitalization of one or more letters in the word, reversing words, and so on,

- repeated letters ("a," "aa," "aaa," etc.) and mnemonic phrases (e.g., "roygbiv" for the colors in the rainbow), and

- word pairs, created by combining two short (3 or 4 characters) words together.

The results of this testing are summarized in Table 2.1. The number of matches reported for a category is the total number of matches regardless of the permutations required to get the match. The search size indicates the number of words actually tried from each category; Klein eliminated inter- and intra-dictionary duplicates in order to reduce the search time required. The cost/benefit ratio is the number of matches divided by the search size. The more words that needed to be tried to obtain a match, the lower the cost/benefit ratio. It is important to note that every UNIX system comes equipped with an approximately 25,000-word dictionary suitable for use in cracking passwords. This dictionary is used by spelling checkers, and resides in */usr/dict/words*. Some systems have other on-line dictionaries as well. In general, all of these files are available to anyone who wants to use them.

Table 2.1

Passwords Cracked From a Sample Set of 13,797 Accounts

Type of Password	Size of Dictionary	Duplicates Eliminated	Search Size	Number of Matches	Percent of Total	Cost/Benefit Ratio
User/account name	130	–	130	368	2.7%	2.830
Character sequences	866	0	866	22	0.2%	0.025
Numbers	450	23	427	9	0.1%	0.021
Chinese	398	6	392	56	0.4%	0.143
Place names	665	37	628	82	0.6%	0.131
Common names	2268	29	2239	548	4.0%	0.245
Female names	4955	675	4280	161	1.2%	0.038
Male names	3901	1035	2866	140	1.0%	0.049
Uncommon names	5559	604	4955	130	0.9%	0.026
Myths & Legends	1357	111	1246	66	0.5%	0.053
Shakespearean	650	177	473	11	0.1%	0.023
Sports terms	247	9	238	32	0.2%	0.134
Science fiction	772	81	691	59	0.4%	0.085
Movies and actors	118	19	99	12	0.1%	0.121
Cartoons	133	41	92	9	0.1%	0.098
Famous people	509	219	290	55	0.4%	0.190
Phrases and patterns	998	65	933	253	1.8%	0.271
Surnames	160	127	33	9	0.1%	0.273
Biology	59	1	58	1	0.0%	0.017
/usr/dict/words	24474	4791	19683	1027	7.4%	0.052
Machine names	12983	3965	9018	132	1.0%	0.015
Mnemonics	14	0	14	2	0.0%	0.143
King James Bible	13062	5537	7525	83	0.6%	0.011
Miscellaneous words	8146	4934	3212	54	0.4%	0.017
Yiddish words	69	13	56	0	0.0%	0.000
Asteroids	3459	1052	2407	19	0.1%	0.007
Total	86280	23553	62727	**334**	**24.2%**	0.053

Source: Klein, 1990.

Password Length

The National Computer Security Center (1985a) defines the probability of guessing a particular password as

$$P = \frac{L \times R}{S} \tag{2.1}$$

L is the password's lifetime, the maximum amount of time it can be used before it must be changed. R is the guess rate, the number of guesses per unit time that it is possible to make. S is the password space, the total number of unique passwords that can be used. S is defined in turn as $S = A^M$, where A is the number of characters in the alphabet (the set of characters that may be used in a password) and M is the password length.

If we assume that most people restrict their passwords to upper- and lowercase letters, numbers, and punctuation, A takes a value of about 92. Assuming password lifetimes of up to one year, and assuming that passwords can be tried at a rate of 1,000 per second (a reasonable value on many of today's architectures), we can compute the probabilities of guessing passwords of various lengths:

Table 2.2

Password Lifetime	Password Length	Probability of Guessing
1 month	6	1 in 250
	7	1 in 21,500
	8	1 in 1,980,000
3 months	6	1 in 78
	7	1 in 7,200
	8	1 in 660,000
6 months	6	1 in 39
	7	1 in 3,600
	8	1 in 330,000
12 months	6	1 in 19
	7	1 in 1,800
	8	1 in 165,000

Of course, as we lower our estimate of A (for example, it would probably be more realistic to assume only letters and numbers, for a value of 62) or increase our estimate of R (to account for faster processors), these probabilities only get worse.

Manipulating equation 2.1 also gives us a procedure for determining the minimum acceptable password length for a given system:

1. Establish an acceptable password lifetime, L, which is the maximum amount of time a password may be used before it must be changed. A typical value might be one month.

2. Establish an acceptable probability, P, that a password will be guessed during its lifetime. For example, the probability might be no more than 1 in 1,000,000.

3. Solve for the size of the password space, S, using the equation derived from equation 2.1:

$$S = \frac{L \times R}{P} \qquad (2.2)$$

4. Determine the length of the password, M, from the equation

$$M = \frac{\log S}{\log A} \qquad (2.3)$$

M will generally be a real number that must be rounded up to the nearest whole number.

Using this procedure with L equal to 1 month, R equal to 1,000 guesses per second, A equal to 92, and P equal to 1 in 1,000,000, we end up with M equal to 7.85, which rounds up to 8. Thus, the minimum acceptable password length to insure no better than a 1 in 1,000,000 chance of guessing the password is eight characters.

The above discussion pertains to an attacker making random guesses at randomly chosen passwords. But as mentioned previously, "educated guesses" can be made as well by using dictionary attacks and the like. These attacks can decrease an attacker's search time tremendously. While the above analysis is useful for understanding just how easily passwords can be determined, the results are only useful as upper bounds on password guessing time (that is, they represent worst-case times from the attacker's point of view).

Selecting Passwords

The object when choosing a password is to make it as difficult as possible for an attacker to make educated guesses about what you've chosen. This leaves her no alternative but a brute-force search, trying every possible combination of letters, numbers, and punctuation. A search of this sort, even conducted on a machine that could try one million passwords per second (most of today's workstation-class machines can try around one thousand per second or less), would require, on the average, over one hundred years to complete. With this as our goal, and by using the information in the preceding sections, a set of guidelines for password selection can be constructed:

- **DON'T** use your login name in any form (as-is, reversed, capitalized, doubled, etc.).

- **DON'T** use your first, middle, or last name in any form. Don't use any nicknames you may have.

- **DON'T** use your spouse's, girlfriend's, boyfriend's, or child's name.

- **DON'T** use a word contained in English or foreign language dictionaries, spelling lists, or other lists of words.

- **DON'T** use other information easily obtained about you. This includes license plate numbers, telephone numbers, social security numbers, the brand of your automobile, the name of the street you live on, etc.

- **DON'T** use a password of all digits, or all the same letter.

- **DON'T** use a password shorter than seven characters.

- **DO** use a password with mixed-case letters. Not just a capitalized word, but throw some uppercase letters in the middle somewhere.

- **DO** use a password with nonalphabetic characters, e.g., digits or punctuation.

- **DO** use a password that is easy to remember, so that you don't have to write it down.

- **DO** use a password that you can type quickly, without having to look at the keyboard. This makes it harder for someone to steal your password by looking over your shoulder.

Although this list may seem to restrict passwords to an extreme, there are several methods for choosing secure, easily remembered passwords that obey the above rules. Some examples of these methods are

- Choose a line or two from a song or poem, and use the first letter or each word. For example, "In Xanadu did Kubla Kahn a stately pleasure dome decree" becomes "IXdKKaspdd." (Since this is longer than eight characters, the last two letters could be dropped.)

- Use the relationships between numbers and words: "One for the money" becomes "14money," "Two for the show" becomes "24show," "To be or not to be" becomes "2bnot2b," and so on (De Alvaré, 1990). One problem with this method is that it often produces passwords that are too short.

- Alternate between one consonant and one or two vowels, up to seven or eight characters. This provides nonsense words that are usually pronounceable, and thus easily remembered. Mix some uppercase letters in as well. Examples include "RoboWega" and "QuaDpoP."

- Choose two short words and concatenate them together with a punctuation character between them. Again, mix in some uppercase letters and/or digits.

For example, "Dog;raiN," "bOOk.mug3," "KID?goat." For added security, reverse one of the words.

The importance of obeying these password selection rules cannot be overemphasized. The Internet worm, as part of its strategy for breaking into new machines, attempted to crack user passwords. First, the worm tried simple choices such as the login name, user's first and last names, and so on. Next, the worm tried each word in an internal dictionary of 432 words (presumably Morris had reason to believe these words were likely passwords). If all else failed, the worm tried using the system spelling dictionary, */usr/dict/words*, trying each word (Spafford, 1988). The password selection rules above produce passwords immune to all three of these attacks. However, now that the above examples have appeared in print, they are most likely part of many attackers' lists of things to try. Don't use the above examples verbatim; provide your own variations on the ideas.

Password Generators

Many organizations, including the National Computer Security Center (1985a), advocate the use of *password generators* as opposed to allowing users to select their own passwords. A password generator will typically generate a few random strings of characters (often by following the consonant-vowel-consonant algorithm), and ask the user to choose one of these strings as his password. Some generators provide a method for the user to request another set of choices, in case none in the first set are to his liking.

The advantage of a password generator is clear: the passwords that the program generates, because they are random strings, are not listed in any dictionary or word list (provided the program checks and does not give out those words that are listed). This means that the only avenue available to an attacker in cracking this password is a brute-force search, which as mentioned previously is too time-consuming. Unfortunately, poorly written password generators also have a disadvantage. Random strings, even pronounceable words, that do not make sense are not remembered as well as those that have meaning. De Alvaré (1990) reports that an "elaboration" process is needed to make a word easy to remember. This elaboration process involves associating the word to a meaning or a picture, and then repeating this association as often as necessary to memorize the word. Since memorizing meaningful words involves this elaboration process, the words are easier to remember. Conversely, users tend to write down or store on-line generated passwords that have no meaning. Both of these practices essentially defeat whatever security was supposed to be provided by the password in the first place.

Password generators do have their place, and well-written ones actually can generate passwords that are both easy to remember as well as secure. The version of `passwd` provided with ULTRIX 4.*x* (Digital Equipment Corp., 1990) can be asked to generate passwords using the −a option, or the system administrator can force individual users to select their passwords from a list of machine-generated ones instead of entering their own. Most versions of UNIX however, do not come with a password generator, but installing one in place of the standard `passwd` program is not difficult. Should you decide to write one, or obtain one from other sources, the National Computer Security Center (1985a) has provided a wealth of information on selecting good generation algorithms, pitfalls to avoid, and so on.

Password Aging

Password aging is a system by which each password has a maximum lifetime, after which it expires and must be changed. Usually the user is prompted to change her expired password the next time she logs in. Many systems also implement a minimum password lifetime, which prevents users from changing their password when it expires, and then immediately changing it back to the old value. Several newer versions of UNIX have implemented password aging in some form or another, with some being better than others.

Although password aging is generally a good idea, and does increase the security of a system, it does have one drawback. Considering the rules for password selection presented earlier, it can take a bit of thought to choose a good, secure password. If a user is surprised by a password aging system, requiring him to choose a new password "on the spot," many times he will choose a poor password. Some password aging systems try to counter this drawback by warning the user ahead of time with messages such as, "your password will expire in three days."

System V Release 4

In the System V Release 4 version of password aging (AT&T, 1990a), passwords have both a minimum and maximum lifetime associated with them. The maximum value specifies the maximum number of days a password may be used before it must be changed. The minimum value specifies the number of days that must pass before the password can be changed again. There is also a third number, which specifies the number of days before password expiration that the user should be given a warning of the upcoming expiration.

The values for the minimum and maximum password lifetimes are set to null by default under System V Release 4 (disabling password aging). They can be set to any value desired by editing the MINWEEKS and MAXWEEKS values in the file */etc/default/passwd*. Using the `passwd` command, the super-user can set the minimum and maximum lifetimes to different values for individual users. A user can be forced to change his password (by simply marking it expired), or prevented from changing it at all (by setting the minimum lifetime to infinity).

On System V Release 4, the command

> # **passwd -x** *maxdays* **-n** *mindays login*

is used to set the password lifetime for *login* to *maxdays* days, and set the minimum change time to *mindays* days. If *mindays* is greater than *maxdays*, the user is prevented from ever changing his password. If *maxdays* is set to −1, password aging is disabled for that user. The command

> # **passwd −f** *login*

is used to mark *login*'s password as expired, forcing the user to change his password the next time he logs in. The command

> # **passwd −w** *numdays login*

sets the number of days before password expiration to start warning the user. The minimum and maximum password times, as well as the number of warnings and the last time the password was changed can be displayed for a user using the command

> # **passwd −s huey**
> huey   PS 06/23/90   14   84   7

The −a option to passwd, used in conjunction with the −s option, can be used to display this information for all users.

System V Release 3.x

System V Release 3.*x* (AT&T, 1986) and systems based on it such as HP-UX 7.*x* (Hewlett-Packard, 1989a), also support password aging, although in a more rudimentary form. The password aging information is appended to the encrypted password in */etc/passwd* as a comma followed by up to four characters in the format:

> ,   Mmww

where the meanings of these characters are

,   The delimiter between the password and the aging information.

M   The maximum password lifetime, in weeks (see below).

m   The minimum password lifetime, in weeks (see below).

ww   The week (counting from January 1, 1970) when the password was last changed. This field is maintained automatically by the system.

All times are specified in weeks using a 64-character alphabet as shown in Table 2.3:

Table 2.3

Character	Number of Weeks
. (period)	0 (zero)
/ (slash)	1
0 through 9	2 through 11
A through Z	12 through 37
a through z	38 through 63

For example, a typical password file entry looks like:

```
huey:4A8VDJoAtRn46:123:1:Huey Duck:/usr/huey:
```

To modify this password file entry so that *huey* must change his password every six months (18 weeks) and may not change it more often than every two weeks, the line would be changed to read:

```
huey:4A8VDJoAtRn46,G0:123:1:Huey Duck:/usr/huey:
```

After this change, *huey* will have to change his password the next time he logs in, and then every six months thereafter. The first time he changes his password, the system will append a two-letter code indicating the week (counting from January 1, 1970) in which the password was changed.

There are two special cases in this password aging implementation:

- If M and m are both zero (i.e., ".."), the user is forced to change her password at the next login. No further password aging is applied to this login.

- If m is greater than M (e.g., "./"), then only the super-user can change the password for that login.

SunOS 4.1

SunOS 4.1 (Sun Microsystems, 1990) also supports password aging, although in an unfortunately inconvenient way. The minimum and maximum times must be set by the super-user for each account individually; there are no default values. This means that password aging is implemented on a *per-user* basis, rather than on a *per-system* basis as it can be with System V Release 4. Furthermore, the networked password file supplied by NIS (see Chapter 5) does not support password aging, so it must be implemented individually on each system a user can log in to. On a network of a hundred workstations, this is a daunting task. However, the mechanism is there if it's needed. (Of course, on systems that do not support NIS the same is true. But since one of the purposes of NIS is to centralize password file administration, it is unfortunate that password aging cannot be centralized as well.)

On SunOS 4.1, the command

passwd -x *maxdays* **-n** *mindays* *login*

is used to set the password lifetime for user *login* to *maxdays* days, and the minimum change time to *mindays* days. The command

passwd -e *login*

causes *login*'s password to be marked as expired, forcing the user to change it the next time she logs in. The minimum and maximum password lifetimes, as well as the last time the password was changed, can be displayed for a user using the command

```
# passwd -d louie
louie   11-17-90   14     60
```

The −a option to passwd, using in conjunction with the −d option, prints this information for all users.

ULTRIX 4.x

Password aging under ULTRIX 4.x (Digital Equipment Corp., 1990) is controlled by the edauth command. When invoked with a login name as argument, edauth allows the super-user to edit the minimum and maximum lifetimes of the user's password. The system administrator can also control whether the user is allowed to enter his own password or must choose from a machine-generated list, and whether or not the user is allowed to change his password at all. The minimum and maximum lifetimes of a user's password, as well as the last time the password was changed, can be examined using the command

```
# shexp -q login
```

4.3BSD-Reno

Password aging under 4.3BSD-Reno (CSRG, 1990) is implemented with only a single value, the date the password expires. This value can be set by the system administrator using the chpasswd program. Unfortunately, when the user changes his password, the time is reset to zero, effectively disabling password aging on the account. The system administrator must check for these zero values and reset them by hand. (This is expected to be fixed in the next Berkeley release.)

Other Systems

Other UNIX vendors are beginning to ship password aging systems as well. Check your system's documentation or consult with your vendor to determine if your particular UNIX variant supports password aging.

Shadow Password Files

The standard UNIX password file contains the encrypted password of each and every user. Moreover, this file must be world-readable in order for several nonprivileged commands (such as ls) to work. Unfortunately, this means that if an intruder has gained access to your system, she can copy the password file to her machine, and then attempt to crack the passwords at her leisure. What starts out as a single broken-into account can quickly become several. Because only a few commands (login, passwd, su) ever need to look at the encrypted password, and all of these commands are privileged, nonprivileged users should not be allowed to obtain the encrypted passwords for other users.

Some newer UNIX systems, such as 4.3BSD-Reno, System V Release 4, SunOS 4.x, ULTRIX 4.x, and HP-UX 7.x, have solved this problem with a mechanism called a *shadow password file.* The standard password file is modified so that the encrypted password field is no longer stored there. This eliminates the need to modify or grant extra privileges to programs such as `ls`, which need the password file but not the encrypted password value. A second file, the shadow, is created to store the encrypted passwords of all users. This file is protected so that it may only be read or modified by privileged programs. In this way, if an attacker copies the standard password file, he does not receive the encrypted passwords, and thus cannot attempt to crack accounts on a remote machine. The shadow password file is often used to store password aging parameters as well.

System V Release 4

On System V Release 4 (AT&T, 1990a), the shadow password file is stored in the file */etc/shadow*, while the normal password file is stored in the usual place, */etc/passwd*. No special action must be taken to enable shadow passwords; they are enabled by default.

System V Release 3.x

Standard System V Release 3.*x* (AT&T, 1986) does not provide shadow password files. However, some systems based on it, such as HP-UX 7.*x* (Hewlett-Packard, 1989b), do provide this facility. On HP-UX, the shadow password file is stored in */.secure/etc/passwd*, and the normal password file, */etc/passwd*, has asterisks (*) placed in the password field of each line. The shadow password facility on HP-UX must be enabled by converting your system to a trusted system. This is done by using the System Administration Manager utility, `sam`. From `sam`'s main menu, select the *Auditing and Security (Trusted System)* item, and then select *Convert to Trusted System*. There are several things that must be done before doing this however; consult your documentation before executing `sam`.

SunOS 4.x

Under SunOS 4.*x* (Sun Microsystems, 1990), both a shadow password file and a shadow group file are used. These are stored in */etc/security/passwd.adjunct* and */etc/security/group.adjunct*, respectively. In the normal password file, */etc/passwd*, the encrypted password field is replaced with ##*name*, where *name* is the login name. In the normal group file, */etc/group*, the encrypted password field is replaced with #$*name*. Shadow passwords are enabled as part of the Sun C2 security package. Unfortunately, to enable the shadow password facility, system auditing must also be enabled (as another part of the C2 package). This may not be desirable in some cases.

ULTRIX 4.x

On ULTRIX 4.*x* (Digital Equipment Corp., 1990), the shadow password is stored in the authorization database, along with numerous other pieces of information. If the system is running at the UPGRADE or ENHANCED security levels, the password field in the normal password file, */etc/passwd*, is ignored and the shadow password is used instead. The system security level is set using the `secsetup` command.

4.3BSD-Reno

Under 4.3BSD-Reno, (CSRG, 1990) shadow passwords are stored in the file */etc/master.passwd*, and the password field in the normal password file, */etc/passwd*, contains an asterisk (*). This shadow password system is enabled by default, and no special actions must be taken to enable it.

Most vendors' shadow password facilities are not enabled by default. Consult your system documentation for information about whether your vendor provides this capability, and how to enable it.

Password Policies

Although asking users to select secure passwords will help improve security, by itself this is not enough. One of the unfortunate truisms of password security is that, "left to their own ways, some people will still use cute doggie names as passwords" (Grampp and Morris, 1984). For this reason, it is important to form a set of password policies that all users must obey.

First and foremost, it is important to impress on users the need to keep their passwords secret. Passwords should never be written down on desk blotters, calendars, and so on. Further, storing passwords on-line must be prohibited. This is especially troublesome, since many communications programs on personal computers encourage the storage of passwords to implement automated login procedures. In either case, by writing the password down or storing it on-line, the security of the password becomes dependent on the security of the piece of paper or the computer file, which is usually less than the security offered by the password encryption software.

A second important policy is that users must never give out their passwords to others. Many times, a user feels that it is easier to give someone else her password in order to copy a file, rather than to set up the permissions on the file so that it can be copied without a password. Unfortunately, by giving out her password to another person, the user is placing her trust in the other person not to distribute the password further, write it down, and so on. She is also placing her trust in that person to only copy the one file, rather than perusing all the other files in her account.

Finally, it is important to establish a policy that users must change their passwords from time to time, usually once or twice a year. This is easy to do if your system has a password aging facility as described earlier, and difficult to do if it does not. There are ways to implement this policy without password expiration software, such as saving a copy of the password file and then comparing the encrypted passwords in it to the encrypted passwords in the current file, but this method can be circumvented. You will be able to tell if a user has executed `passwd`, but not whether he actually chose a different password. (System V Release 4 `passwd`, as mentioned earlier, forces the user to use a different password.)

This set of policies should be printed and distributed to all current users of the system. It should also be given to all new users when they receive their accounts. In order to give the policy as much weight as possible, you should try to get it signed by the most "impressive" person in your organization (e.g., the president of the company). For more information on security policies, see Chapter 10.

Checking Password Security

The procedures and policies described in the previous sections, when properly implemented, will greatly reduce the chances of an attacker breaking into your system via a stolen account. However, as with all security measures, the system administrator is responsible for verifying that the policies and procedures are being adhered to.

The best way to check the security of the passwords in use on a system is to use a password cracking program much like a real attacker would use. If any passwords are cracked, they should be changed immediately. There are a few freely available password cracking programs distributed via various source archive sites (see Chapter 11). The "core" of a simple cracking program is shown in Example 2.1. The complete program is given in Appendix A. The code in Example 2.1 runs through a list a words, making several guesses with each word against the account password. Each guess is tried twice—once "forward" and once reversed. The first guess is the word itself with all capitalization preserved. This is followed by guesses with the word in all lowercase, all uppercase, and with the first letter capitalized.

One of the most important things to note about this type of password cracking program is that it is **slow**. The standard UNIX library `crypt` routine used for encrypting passwords is **designed** to be slow, in order to prevent attackers from using it to crack passwords. Running the program in Appendix A on a 25 MIPS system with a password file of 250 accounts and using *lusr/dict/words* as the wordlist would take over three weeks to complete. This is because on a 25 MIPS system, `crypt` can only encrypt about 26 passwords per second, and the program makes a total of about 1.9 million guesses. However, we shouldn't let these figures lull us into a false sense of security. Several versions of `crypt` have been written that are designed to be fast. The fastest one the author has used operates at about 1,000 passwords per second on a 25 MIPS system, which reduces the time to complete our cracking from three weeks to just 16 hours. Versions optimized for a specific processor can go even faster. With times like these, and the easy availability of both fast versions of `crypt` and very fast processors, it is more important than ever that secure password selection rules be followed.

Proactive Password Checkers

As an alternative to attempting to crack passwords to find insecure ones, several security experts (Klein, 1990; Bishop, 1990) are recommending *proactive* password check-

Example 2.1 The core of a cracking program

```
for (i = 0; i < ndictwords; i++) {
    if (!strcmp(pw->pw_passwd, crypt(wordlist[i], pw->pw_passwd)))
        return(wordlist[i]);

    reverse(wordlist[i], buf);
    if (!strcmp(pw->pw_passwd, crypt(buf, pw->pw_passwd)))
        return(buf);

    lower(wordlist[i], buf);
    if (!strcmp(pw->pw_passwd, crypt(buf, pw->pw_passwd)))
        return(buf);

    reverse(buf, buf);
    if (!strcmp(pw->pw_passwd, crypt(buf, pw->pw_passwd)))
        return(buf);

    upper(wordlist[i], buf);
    if (!strcmp(pw->pw_passwd, crypt(buf, pw->pw_passwd)))
        return(buf);

    reverse(buf, buf);
    if (!strcmp(pw->pw_passwd, crypt(buf, pw->pw_passwd)))
        return(buf);

    capital(wordlist[i], buf);
    if (!strcmp(pw->pw_passwd, crypt(buf, pw->pw_passwd)))
        return(buf);

    reverse(buf, buf);
    if (!strcmp(pw->pw_passwd, crypt(buf, pw->pw_passwd)))
        return(buf);
}
```

ers. These programs replace the standard password changing program (or are "wrapped around" it), and check the user's password selection for security before allowing it to be used. This is done by checking the password against the user's login name, first and last name, looking for the password in dictionaries and wordlists, and so on. By preventing the user from selecting an insecure password in the first place, the need for trying to crack passwords is eliminated. Since the user is still allowed to select his own password, the pitfalls of generated passwords are avoided.

Most proactive passwords checkers currently available (see Chapter 11) are configurable. The system administrator is allowed to define rules for what constitutes a good password at her site, thus determining the level of security passwords provide. Some programs will also explain to the user why a password is not acceptable ("you may not use your first name" as opposed to "password unacceptable"). Although this is generally a nice feature, since it keeps users from complaining that it's "impossible" to find an acceptable password, Klein (1990) points out that if an attacker can gain access to the rules of what is and is not acceptable, he can use this information to more precisely target his password guessing activities.

2.2 Expiration Dates

Many sites, particularly those with a large number of users, typically have several old accounts lying around whose owners have since left the organization. These accounts present a major security problem: not only can they be broken into if the password is insecure, but because nobody is using the account anymore, it is unlikely that the break-in will be noticed. This was one of the means the wily hacker used to break into LBL: he made use of an account still in place for a researcher who was away on sabbatical. Since the account was "legal," nobody would have noticed had Stoll not already been alerted because of the bogus account that caused the accounting error (Stoll, 1989).

The simplest way to prevent unused accounts from accumulating is to place an expiration date on every account. The expiration date should be near enough in the future that old accounts will be deleted in a timely manner, yet far enough in the future that the users will not become annoyed every time their account expires. A good figure is usually one year from the month the account was installed, or six months on systems with a high turnover, such as university systems for undergraduates. By basing the expiration date on the account creation date, expirations are spread out over the year rather than clustering them all at the beginning or end, reducing the work for the system administrator. The expiration date can be stored in the password file in the GECOS (full name) field, separated from the user's name by a comma. A simple shell script such as that shown in Example 2.2 can be run on the first day of each month to check for expired accounts.

On the first day of each month, any user whose account has expired should be contacted to be sure he is still employed by the organization, and that he is actively using the account. Any user who cannot be contacted, or who has not used her account recently, should be deleted from the system. If a user is unavailable for some reason (e.g., on vacation or sabbatical) and cannot be contacted, his account should be disabled by replacing the encrypted password in the password file entry with an asterisk (*). This makes it impossible to log into the account, yet leaves the account available to be re-enabled on the user's return.

One note about using this script—the `chfn` program, which allows users to change the information in the GECOS field of their account, must either be modified to not allow users to change their expiration dates, or it must be protected so that only the super-user may execute it. Some versions of the `passwd` program accept a `-f` option that does the same thing; this may be harder to disable. If you cannot disable these programs, you may wish to modify the script to keep the expiration information in another file, rather than in the GECOS field.

Example 2.2 checkexpire.sh

```
#!/bin/sh
#
# checkexpire - search the password file for expired accounts
#
# We assume a format in the GECOS field of
#
#        :fname lname, mm/yy:
#
# Where mm and yy are the numeric month and year.
#

(echo DATE `date`; cat /etc/passwd) | awk '
BEGIN   {
    #
    # To translate month names to numbers.
    #
    months["Jan"] =  1; months["Feb"] =  2; months["Mar"] =  3;
    months["Apr"] =  4; months["May"] =  5; months["Jun"] =  6;
    months["Jul"] =  7; months["Aug"] =  8; months["Sep"] =  9;
    months["Oct"] = 10; months["Nov"] = 11; months["Dec"] = 12;
}

/^DATE/ {
    #
    # Save current month and year, obtained from the DATE
    # line in our input.
    #
    curmonth = months[$3];
    curyear  = $7 - 1900;
    next;
}

{
    #
    # Split the password file line into fields, and save the
    # GECOS and login fields.
    #
    split($0, pwfields, ":");
    gecos = pwfields[5];
    login = pwfields[1];

    #
    # Split the GECOS field at the comma.  If there is
    # no comma, then there is no expiration date.
    #
```

```
    if (split(gecos, tmp, ",") != 2) {
        print login " has no expiration date.";
        next;
    }

    #
    # Save the expiration date, and split it up into
    # month and year.
    #
    expdate = tmp[2];
    split(expdate, date, "/");
    month = date[1];
    year = date[2];

    #
    # If it expired in a previous year, print a note.
    #
    if (curyear > year) {
        print login " has expired - expiration " expdate;
        next;
    }

    #
    # If it expired in a previous month of this year,
    # print a note.
    #
    if (curyear == year && curmonth > month) {
        print login " has expired - expiration " expdate;
        next;
    }
}'
exit 0
```

2.3 Guest Accounts

Guest accounts, by their nature, are rarely used, and are always used by people who should only have access to the system for the short period of time they are guests. The most secure way to handle guest accounts is to install them on an as-needed basis, and delete them as soon as the people using them leave. Guest accounts should never be given simple passwords such as "guest" or "visitor," and should never be allowed to remain in the password file when they are not being used.

Restricted Shells

Many versions of UNIX, particularly those based on System V, provide a *restricted* shell, called rsh (it can also be invoked as sh -r). This shell is useful for guest accounts, since it prohibits the user from accessing parts of the system she shouldn't. Specifically, `rsh` prohibits the following actions:

- Changing the working directory (`cd`)

- Setting the value of `$PATH`

- Specifying command or path names containing "/"

- Redirecting output (">" and ">>")

These restrictions are enforced after the interpretation of the *.profile* file. Their purpose is to prevent the user from examining the contents of any other directories (using `cd` or path names containing "/"), executing any programs not "approved" by the system administrator (by changing `$PATH` or using path names containing "/"), or changing the contents of files (using output redirection).

Typically, to set up a guest account to use the restricted shell, the account is set up to invoke */bin/rsh* in the password file. The *.profile* is used to set up `$PATH` and so on, and then change directories into a subdirectory of the guest account's home directory. Many times, `$PATH` will use a special *bin* directory that contains only commands known to be secure instead of the typical search path. These restrictions are usually enough to protect most guest accounts. However, it should be pointed out that restricted shells are not a complete solution—there are ways to break through them, although they are complicated and not very well known.

Under System V Release 4, the Korn shell (`ksh`) also supports a restricted mode when invoked as `rksh` or `ksh -r`.

2.4 Well-Known Accounts

Most system attackers are aware that many systems have a set of well-known accounts on them that are usually easy to attack. These accounts often have no password or a "standard" password that is widely known. In order to prevent this sort of attack, well-known accounts should be carefully protected.

Vendor Accounts

Most vendors' installation procedures install several default accounts in the password file. These include accounts such as *daemon*, *sys*, *bin*, *uucp*, *news*, and *ingres*, as well as others. These accounts are often never logged into, but are instead merely place holders for software ownership, etc. Proper vendor installation procedures will install these accounts with an asterisk in the password field, preventing anyone from logging into them. However, several vendors' installation procedures install these accounts with **no** password, making it possible for anyone to log into them.

Whenever a new release of the operating system is installed, the vendor-installed password file should be carefully checked to see that the vendor accounts contained there cannot be logged into, or if they must be logged into, that they are protected with secure passwords.

The command shown below can be used to check the password file for accounts that have no password:

```
% awk -F: '$2 == ""' /etc/passwd
```

Accounts that have no password should either be given a password if you expect to use the account, or disabled or deleted if you do not expect to use the account. An account can be disabled (logins prevented) by placing an asterisk (or some other character) in the encrypted password field in the password file. For example:

```
diag:*:12:1:Diagnostics:/tmp:
```

Since the asterisk is an impossible value for an encrypted password, there is no way for this account to be logged into directly. This does not make it entirely secure, however, as will be explained in section 4.1.

Service Accounts

Service accounts are accounts that are set up with special programs listed as their login shell. These accounts typically have no password, and are used, for example, to allow people to log in as *who* to obtain a list of who is on the system, to log in as *lpq* to check the printer queue, and so on. In and of themselves, these accounts do not present much of a security problem, since they only execute a single command and then log the user back off the system. However, the programs these accounts execute should be carefully examined to insure that there is no way for an attacker to obtain a shell or execute commands through them. The home directories of these accounts should be carefully protected so that an intruder cannot create a *.rhosts* or *.profile* file in them, allowing him to log in or execute commands in that way.

2.5 Group Accounts vs. Groups

Group accounts have become popular at many sites, but can actually be a major security problem. A group account is a single account shared by several people, e.g., by all the collaborators on a project. As mentioned in the section on password policies, users should not share passwords—the group account concept directly violates this policy. The proper way to allow users to share information, rather than giving them a group account to use, is to place these users into a group. This is done by editing the group file, */etc/group*, and creating a new group with the users who wish to collaborate as members.

A line in the group file looks like

```
groupname:password:groupid:user1,user2,user3,...
```

The *groupname* is the name assigned to the group, much like a login name. It may be the same as someone's login name, or different. The maximum length of a group name is eight characters. The *password* field is unused in Berkeley-derived versions of UNIX (versions without the `newgrp` command), and should contain an asterisk (*) in this case. The *groupid* is a number from 0 to 65535 inclusive. Generally numbers below 10 or 100 are reserved for special purposes, but you may choose any unused number. The last field is a comma-separated (no spaces) list of the login names of the users in the group. If no login names are listed, then the group has no members (this is commonly done when the group is used primarily for file ownership purposes). To create a group called *workers* with *huey*, *duey*, and *louie* as members, you would add a line such as this to the group file:

```
workers:*:123:huey,duey,louie
```

After the group has been created, the files and directories the members wish to share can be changed so that they are owned by this group, and the group permission bits on the files and directories can be set to allow sharing. Each user retains his own account, with his own password, thus protecting the security of the system.

For example, to change *huey*'s *programs* directory to be owned by the new group and properly set up the permissions so that all members of the group may access it, the `chgrp` and `chmod` commands would be used as follows:

```
# chgrp -R workers ~huey/programs
# chmod -R g+rw ~huey/programs
```

2.6 Protecting an Account

Even if an account is protected by a strong password, there are ways for an attacker to gain access to the account or otherwise wreak havoc. It is important to protect your account from these attacks; this can be done by observing several simple rules.

The Search Path

The shell uses a *search path* to determine which directories to search for commands when they are executed. In the Bourne (`sh`) and Korn (`ksh`) shells, the search path is set using commands such as

```
PATH=$HOME/bin:/usr/local/bin:/usr/bin:/bin
export PATH
```

Directories are listed in the order they are to be searched, separated by colons (:). Two colons together (::) indicate the current directory. In the C shell (`csh`), the search path is set using the command

```
set path = ( ~/bin /usr/local/bin /usr/bin /bin )
```

Most users place the current directory, ".", somewhere in their path as well, usually at the front. This allows them to develop their own programs and execute them easily, even if they have the same name as a system command. Unfortunately, it also allows an attacker to easily create Trojan horses. For example, consider a program called `ls` that does something insidious that the attacker wants to do. If she places this program in some directory where her victim is likely to be working, and the victim has "." at the front of his search path, the first time he types `ls` the attacker's program will be executed rather than the system program of the same name.

To defend yourself against this type of attack, you should only place the current directory (".") at the **end** of your search path. In this way, when you execute what you believe to be a system command, you will always get the system version of the command before any version in the current directory. Of course, you are still vulnerable to commands not in the system directories—for example, an attacker might make a Trojan horse called `mb` (a common misspelling of `mv`), and you could still get caught. To defend against this attack as well, the safest thing to do is not to put the current directory anywhere in your search path. The only inconvenience this will cause you is that you will have to type `./command` instead of `command` to execute commands in the current directory. This is a small price to pay for the added protection.

Startup Files

Many programs, such as shells, editors, mail readers, and so on have startup files associated with them. These files typically reside in a user's home directory, and contain commands that are to be executed whenever the program is invoked. Some common startup files include *.profile*, *.cshrc*, *.login*, *.mailrc*, *.exrc*, and *.emacs*. These files are easy prey for an attacker, since once they have been set up they are rarely if ever looked at again. If an attacker can edit one of these files and add commands to them, he can easily take over an account, modify its files, etc. To protect against this, make sure that all your startup files are writable only by you (see the next section).

The `ex` and `vi` editors have a particular problem with regard to startup files. Not only are commands in the *.exrc* file in the home directory executed, but if there is a *.exrc* file in the current directory, the commands in that file are executed as well. Thus, an attacker need only leave a *.exrc* file in some directory where her victim commonly works, and she can have full access to the victim's account. Most modern versions of `ex` and `vi` guard against this problem by ignoring any *.exrc* file not owned by the user invoking them. However, early versions of these editors did not check the ownership of the file. To determine if your version of the editor protects you, enter the editor and type

```
:se all
```

If you see a variable listed named `nosourceany`, (or `sourceany`, if it is set), then you are safe, provided the variable is not set. If you don't see this variable, then you are at risk. You should protect yourself by running `ls -a` in a directory before invoking the editor. If you see a *.exrc* file, determine that its contents are safe before entering the editor.

File and Directory Modes

UNIX provides file protection modes to enable users to control who has access to their files and directories. These permissions are described in detail in Chapter 3, but we will mention them briefly here. Simply put, the only person who should be able to write the files or directories in your account is you (with the possible exception of other members of your group, if you are sharing files). If others are allowed write access to your files, they can add, change, or delete information in those files. This can be particularly dangerous if any of your startup files can be changed. If others are allowed write access to your directories, they can create or delete files in those directories. This can be dangerous if your search path specifies one of these directories, since an attacker can add or replace commands in these directories with Trojan horses. Duff's virus attack made use of people's writable directories with great success (Duff, 1989).

The simplest way to make sure that none of your files or directories are writable by others is to execute the commands

```
$ cd
$ chmod -R go-w .
```

or, if your version of chmod does not understand the -R option,

```
$ cd
$ find . -exec chmod go-w {} \;
```

This command will recursively descend through your entire home directory, turning off write permission for anyone other than yourself.

2.7 Super-User

The super-user, *root*, is the most powerful user on the system. This account has the power to shut down the system, terminate any process, create new accounts, change any account's password, and can read write, or delete any file on the entire system regardless of its permissions. This means that this account must be protected even more stringently than other accounts on the system. One-time access to the super-user account by an intruder can lead to permanent consequences unless the operating system is reloaded from the distribution tapes, since it may not be possible to determine every change made by the attacker.

Operating as Root

Aside from the procedures in the preceding sections for setting the search path and keeping startup files protected, there are several common sense rules to be used when operating as the super-user:

- Never place the current directory (".") in *root*'s search path. Programs in the current directory can be executed using the form `./command`. Similarly, never place private users' *bin* directories in *root*'s search path.

- When using the `su` command to become super-user, always execute `/bin/su` instead of just `su`, in order to avoid Trojan horse `su` programs which could steal the *root* password.

- Never run another user's program as *root*; it could be a Trojan horse.

- Never leave a super-user shell on your terminal or workstation unattended, not even for "just a minute."

- Change the *root* password often, and be very careful about password selection. See section 2.1 on selecting a good password.

- Never give the *root* password to anyone you don't trust to have access to your entire system. And never give it to anyone, whether you trust him or not, unless there is a demonstrated need for him to have it.

- Don't let anyone run as super-user, even for just a few minutes, even if you're watching over his shoulder.

- Rather than logging in as *root*, log in as yourself and then execute `su`. This provides logging on the console or in the system log file as to who is running as *root* and when.

It is a good idea to codify these rules, and any others you feel apply to your site, into a policy that is given to all people who have access to the *root* password. See Chapter 10 for more information on security policies.

2.8 Monitoring Account Security

The system administrator should periodically monitor account security in order to check for two things: users logged in when they "shouldn't" be (e.g., late at night, when they're on vacation, etc.) and users executing commands that they wouldn't normally be expected to use (secretaries compiling programs, etc.). Both of these items, if detected, can indicate that system security has been compromised.

The Last Login Time

Most modern UNIX systems record the last time each user logged in, usually in the file *usr/adm/lastlog*. This time is printed as part of the login process, and usually looks like one of the two lines below:

```
Last login: Wed Jan  1 08:03:37 on ttyh4
Last login: Mon Dec 24 19:31:04 from foo.bar.com
```

Users should be trained to carefully examine this line each time they log in, and to report unusual login times or logins from unknown remote hosts to the system administrator. This is an easy way to detect accounts that have been compromised, since each user should remember the last time she logged into the system.

The *utmp* and *wtmp* Files

The file */etc/utmp* is used to record who is currently logged into the system. This file can be displayed using the who command (as well as others):

```
$ who
root          console    May 15 14:21
huey          ttyh1      May 15 07:48
duey          ttyp0      May 15 13:27    (foo.bar.com)
```

For each user, the login name, terminal being used, and login time are displayed. If the user is logged in remotely over the network, the name of the remote host he is coming from is displayed as well.

On some systems, */etc/utmp* is installed as a world-writable file to allow window systems and the like to write in it without having super-user permissions. This can be a security problem in several ways. First, it allows an attacker to delete the entry showing him logged in; this allows him to "hide." A more serious problem is that an attacker can change the names of terminal devices in the file, so that the next time a program such as wall or comsat is executed, it will write to some other file. This may allow the attacker to create accounts or cause other damage. If at all possible, the */etc/utmp* file should not be world-writable. Unfortunately, some window systems (in particular suntools) require that it be writable by everyone.

The file */usr/adm/wtmp* (*/etc/wtmp* on some systems) records each login and logout time for every user. This file has the same format as */etc/utmp*, and can also be displayed with the who command:

```
$ who /usr/adm/wtmp
louie         ttyh0      May 12 07:48
              ttyh0      May 12 17:03
duey          ttyp3      May 13 13:27    (foo.bar.com)
              ttyp3      May 13 21:17
root          console    May 15 14:21
              console    May 15 15:04
```

A line that contains a login name indicates the time the user logged in, a line with no login name indicates the time the terminal was logged off. Unfortunately, the output from this command is rarely as orderly as in the example above; if several users log in before others log out, the login and logout times are all mixed together and must be matched up by hand (or with the aid of programs like awk and sort) using the terminal name.

The `last` Command

The `last` command sorts out the entries in the *wtmp* file, matching up login and logout times. With no arguments, `last` displays the entire file; with a user name or terminal name as an argument, the output can be restricted to the user or terminal in question. `last` always displays its output in reverse order, from most recent login to least recent.

```
$ last
reboot     ~                        Wed Aug 28 03:03
shutdown ~                          Wed Aug 28 03:03
huey       ttyh2                    Tue Aug 27 10:16 - 10:33 (00:16)
duey       ttyp5   foo.bar.com      Tue Aug 27 09:49 - 10:00 (00:10)
ftp        ftp     big.school.edu   Mon Aug 26 21:07 - 21:26 (00:19)
louie      ttyh0                    Sun Aug 25 09:44 - 09:54 (00:09)
root       console                  Sat Aug 24 09:15 - 10:10 (00:54)

wtmp begins Sat Aug 24 09:00
```

For each login session, the login name, terminal used, remote host (if the user logged in via the network), login and logout times, and session duration are shown. Additionally, the times of all system shutdowns and reboots (generated by the `shutdown` and `reboot` commands) are recorded. Unfortunately, system crashes are not recorded. In newer versions of UNIX, pseudo-logins such as those via the `ftp` command are also recorded; an example of this is shown on the fifth line of output in the above example.

The *acct* File

The file */usr/adm/acct* (or */usr/adm/pacct* on some systems) records each execution of a command on the system, who executed it, when, and how long it took. Provided accounting is enabled on your system (many systems have it disabled by default, consult your vendor's documentation), this information is logged each time a command completes.

The `lastcomm` Command

On Berkeley-based systems, the *acct* file can be displayed using the `lastcomm` command. With no arguments, all the information in the file is displayed. However, by giving a command name, login name, or terminal name as an argument, the output can be restricted. Sample output from `lastcomm` is shown below.

```
$ lastcomm
head             huey     ttyp3     0.16 secs Fri Dec 28 17:57
cat              huey     ttyp3     0.16 secs Fri Dec 28 17:57
tset             huey     ttyp3     0.50 secs Fri Dec 28 17:57
```

stty		huey	ttyp3	0.05 secs Fri Dec 28 17:57
sed		huey	ttyp3	0.25 secs Fri Dec 28 17:57
hostname		huey	ttyp3	0.02 secs Fri Dec 28 17:57
sh	S	root	—	0.53 secs Fri Dec 28 17:55
atrun		root	—	0.09 secs Fri Dec 28 17:55
cat		louie	ttyh4	0.02 secs Fri Dec 28 17:53
stty		louie	ttyh4	0.05 secs Fri Dec 28 17:53
stty		louie	ttyh4	0.08 secs Fri Dec 28 17:53
date		louie	ttyh4	0.05 secs Fri Dec 28 17:53
awk		louie	ttyh4	18.42 secs Fri Dec 28 17:45
tee	X	louie	ttyh4	7.27 secs Fri Dec 28 17:45
cat	X	louie	ttyh4	18.48 secs Fri Dec 28 17:45
lpd	F	root	—	1.47 secs Fri Dec 28 17:53
rcp		root	—	0.22 secs Fri Dec 28 17:53
csh	S	root	—	1.50 secs Fri Dec 28 17:53

The first column indicates the name of the command. The second column displays certain flags indicating special things about the command: an "F" indicates the program spawned a child process, "S" means the program ran with the set-user-id bit (see Chapter 3) set, "D" means the process exited with a core dump, and "X" means the process was killed before it exited. The remaining columns show the name of the user who ran the command, the terminal she ran it from (if applicable), the amount of CPU time used by the command, and the date and time the process started.

The `acctcom` Command

Under System V Release 4, the `lastcomm` command also exists, but the `acctcom` command can be used as well. This command accepts several options; a few of the more useful are `-l` *line* to restrict information to commands run on the given terminal line, `-u` *user* to restrict the output to commands run by *user*, and `-g` *group* to restrict the output to commands run by members of *group*. Options can be given to control the data displayed, such as I/O counts, system and user CPU time, process exit status, and so on. Sample output from `acctcom` is shown below.

```
% acctcom
```

COMMAND NAME	USER	TTYNAME	START TIME	END TIME	REAL (SECS)	CPU (SECS)	MEAN SIZE(K)
ls	root	console	09:51:31	09:51:31	0.41	0.41	0.14
acctcom	root	console	09:51:33	09:51:33	0.82	0.80	0.09
#csh	root	?	09:20:26	09:51:44	1878.40	2.73	0.05
pwd	huey	pts/0	09:51:52	09:51:52	0.09	0.02	1.25
who	huey	pts/0	09:51:53	09:51:53	0.20	0.04	1.12
nroff	huey	pts/0	09:52:00	09:52:06	6.15	4.49	0.03
sh	huey	pts/0	09:52:00	09:52:06	6.20	0.04	1.44
mv	huey	pts/0	09:52:07	09:52:07	0.46	0.11	0.32

```
sh        huey   pts/0   09:52:07 09:52:07     0.51    0.04     1.56
more      huey   pts/0   09:52:07 09:52:12     5.55    3.67     0.02
sh        huey   pts/0   09:52:07 09:52:12     5.63    0.05     1.30
man       huey   pts/0   09:52:00 09:52:12    12.46    0.04     1.12
ftp       huey   pts/0   09:52:16 09:52:28    12.57    1.22     0.15
vi        huey   pts/0   09:52:32 09:52:35     3.68    0.68     0.24
vi        huey   pts/0   09:52:44 09:54:58   134.88    2.58     0.07
#csh      huey   ?       09:51:45 09:55:07   202.64    1.38     0.09
uname     louie  pts/2   09:55:12 09:55:12     0.03    0.03     0.83
hostname  louie  pts/2   09:55:12 09:55:12     0.17    0.06     1.12
sed       louie  pts/2   09:55:12 09:55:12     0.21    0.07     0.89
stty      louie  pts/2   09:55:12 09:55:12     0.02    0.03     0.83
vi        louie  pts/2   09:55:15 09:55:24     9.28    0.81     0.22
#csh      louie  ?       09:55:07 09:55:24    17.91    1.19     0.12
```

The first column shows the name of the command. If it is preceded by a "#", this indicates that it was executed with super-user privileges. The second column shows the login name of the user executing the command. The third column displays the name of the terminal the command was executed from, or a "?" if the command was not associated with a terminal. The fourth and fifth columns show the starting and ending times of the command. The next two columns show the amount of real time and CPU time, in seconds, used by the command. The last column shows the average amount of memory, in kilobytes, used by the command.

The sa Command

The sa command is used to summarize the accounting files for purposes such as billing. It can also be used to some extent to search for users using excessive amounts of CPU time, or for long-running jobs such as password cracking programs. Called with no arguments, sa produces a summary for each command on the system providing the number of times the command was executed, the total amount of time (in minutes) the command was executed, the total amount of CPU time (also in minutes) used by the command, the average number of input-output operations per execution, and the average amount of memory (in kilobytes) used by the command.

```
% sa
        3    60017.94re    1981.40cp     594avio     20k   snoop
   216747   450773.39re    1877.76cp       8avio     35k   rcp
     4086     6193.15re    1785.86cp    1038avio     42k   find
    24338   834519.98re    1462.08cp      75avio     60k   uucico
    13208    69188.39re    1341.26cp      35avio    146k   vi
    .....
     3272    13688.58re    1336.57cp      24avio    127k   dump
     5613     3609.15re    1060.79cp      11avio     79k   na
```

```
   3720     1393.11re      976.01cp      22avio      304k    ccom
   2996     1747.86re      971.82cp      32avio      372k    troff
    121    70493.36re      843.58cp     627avio       39k    mlock
```

In the above example, the snoop program might be suspect, not only because of its name, but because of the exorbitant amount of CPU time it has used in only three invocations.

With the −m option, sa will produce for each user a list of the total number of programs executed, the total amount of CPU time (in minutes) used, the total number of input-output operations performed, and the total amount of time (in seconds) used. This list can sometimes be useful for finding users using more time than expected (for example, a secretary using excessive CPU time might be an indication that an attacker is also using the account).

```
% sa -m
   root     1205337    47182.90cpu    25271922tio    1083500157k*sec
   daemon    334149     2232.88cpu     1589030tio      8521485k*sec
   huey          93        2.73cpu        2198tio        16323k*sec
   duey          91        2.19cpu        1711tio         8408k*sec
   .....
   louie      16796     1433.61cpu      881322tio     12145355k*sec
   uucp       56262     1488.37cpu     2130844tio      5637202k*sec
```

It should be noted that output from sa should be taken with a few grains of salt. There are all sorts of logical explanations for the output you may see that have nothing to do with password cracking, stolen accounts, or other security-related concerns.

The ps Command

The ps command displays a list of processes running on the system. The options differ from system to system, especially between Berkeley-derived and System V-derived versions, and you should consult your system documentation for specifics. However, for general monitoring purposes, the option string −axlww is most useful on Berkeley-based systems, while the option string −el is most useful on System V. These options tell ps to display as much information as possible about every process running. Some of the more useful fields in the output are

UID	The numeric user id of the user executing the process.
PID	The process id of the process. PPID is the parent process id.
TTY	The terminal the process was started from. If the process was not started from a terminal, a "?" is displayed.
TIME	The amount of CPU time, in minutes and seconds, the process has consumed.

"S or STAT"   The status of the process. "R" indicates running, "S" and "I" indicate sleeping (waiting for something to happen), "W" indicates swapped out, "D" and "P" indicate waiting on disk activity, "T" indicates stopped (by a signal), and "Z" indicates a "zombie" process, one which has exited but has not been cleaned up after.

COMMAND   The name of the command and its arguments.

If you run `ps` periodically, you will soon become used to seeing what is "normal" for your system. If you run it whenever you have a free minute or two (say, when you're on the phone or waiting for a file to print), you may be able to spot unusual activity that may indicate that your system has been broken into.

2.9 Summary

Account security can be improved in several ways, as discussed in this chapter:

- Follow good password selection criteria.

- If desired and your system supports it, implement a password generator.

- If desired and your system supports it, implement password aging.

- If your system supports it, use a shadow password file.

- Establish a set of password guidelines and policies.

- Use a proactive password changing program, or if this is not possible, use a password cracker to detect insecure passwords.

- Put expiration dates on all accounts.

- Carefully control guest accounts.

- Password-protect well-known accounts.

- Eliminate group and shared accounts.

- Avoid placing the current directory (".") in your search path.

- Write-protect your startup files and home directory.

- Codify rules and policies for operating as the super-user.

- Monitor account security regularly.

By implementing these mechanisms, you can be sure that you have made it difficult for an attacker to access your system via a stolen account. However, since no protection is foolproof, you should remain alert for break-ins.

Chapter 3
File System Security

The final defense against intruders is the permissions offered by the file system. These permissions allow users to control who may access their files and directories for reading, writing, searching, and executing. The file permissions also allow certain programs to operate with extra permissions (e.g., those of the super-user). In newer UNIX systems, permission bits on directories may be used to prohibit users from removing files that they do not own, and to control group ownership of files created in the directories.

3.1 File Permissions

Each file or directory has three sets of permissions associated with it: one set for the user who owns the file, one set for the users in the group with which the file is associated, and one set for all other users (the "world" permissions). Each set of permissions contains three identical permission bits, that control the following:

read   If set, the file or directory may be read. In the case of a directory, read access allows a user to see the contents of the directory (the names of the files contained therein), but not to access them.

write   If set, the file or directory may be written (modified). In the case of a directory, write permission implies the ability to create, delete, and rename files. Note that the ability to remove a file is **not** controlled by the file's permission bits, but rather the permission bits on the directory containing the file.

execute   If set, the file or directory may be executed (searched). In the case of a file, execute permission implies the ability to run the program contained in that file. Executing compiled (binary) programs requires only execute permission on the file, while executing shell scripts requires both read and execute permission, since the shell must be able to read commands from the file. In the case of a directory, execute permission implies permission to search the directory, that is, permission to access files contained therein. Note that access to files in a directory is **not** controlled by read permission on the directory (read permission controls whether the files are "visible," not "accessible").

In addition, there is a fourth set of three bits that indicate special features associated with the file:

set-user-id   If set, this bit controls the "set-user-id" status of a file. Set-user-id status means that when a program is executed, it executes with the permissions of the user who owns the program, in addition to the permissions of the user executing it. For example, ps, the process status program, is set-user-id *root*, because it needs to read from system memory, which normal users are not allowed to do. This bit is meaningless on non-executable files and directories.

set-group-id   If set, this bit controls the "set-group-id" status of a file. This behaves in exactly the same way as the set-user-id bit, except that the program operates with the permissions of the group associated with the file. This bit is meaningless on non-executable files, but on some systems it has a different meaning when set on a directory (see below).

sticky   If set, the "sticky" bit tells the operating system to do special things with the text image of an executable binary file. It is mostly a hold-over from older versions of UNIX, and has little if any use today. However, some newer systems give this bit a special meaning when set on a directory; this is described shortly. SunOS also uses the sticky bit on NFS swap files to inhibit some file system cache operations.

The ls Command

The ls command, when invoked with the −1 option, displays the permission bits associated with a file or directory in a symbolic form. Consider the output from ls −1 shown below:

```
$ ls -l
drwxr-xr-x  3 huey            512 Dec 27 15:58 dir1
-rwx------  1 huey          16384 Jun  1 13:45 progfile1
-rwsr-xr-x  1 huey          24576 Jan 23 16:35 progfile2
-rw-r-----  1 huey             40 Dec 29 11:42 textfile1
-rw-rw-rw-  1 huey           1024 Mar 23 08:19 textfile2
```

The first column shows the permissions on each file. The first character shows the type of file, "d" for a directory or "−" for a regular file. The next nine characters show the permission bits for the owner of the file (first three characters), the members of the group associated with the file (the middle three characters), and all other users (the last three characters). An "r" indicates read permission, a "w" indicates write permission, and an "x" indicates execute permission (search permission on a directory). An "s" in the owner's "x" position indicates set-user-id permission; in the group's "x" position it indicates set-group-id permission. A "t" in the others' "x" position indicates the sticky bit. When an "s" or "t" appears, the execute permission for that class of users is assumed to be enabled as well as the set-user-id, set-group-id, or sticky bit. If the underlying execute bit is not set, the "s" or "t" usually appears capitalized. A "−" in one of these slots indicates that the given permission is not granted.

The directory *dir1* has read, write, and search permission enabled for its owner, *huey*, and read and search permission enabled for *huey*'s group and all other users. This means that anyone may list the files in *dir1* or access them, but only *huey* may create, delete, or rename files there.

The program *progfile1* has read, write, and execute permission enabled for its owner, *huey*, and no permission enabled for anyone else. This means that only *huey* may read, modify, or execute this file. The program *progfile2* on the other hand, also has read and execute permissions enabled for *huey*'s group and all other users. Any user may copy this file (read it) or execute it, but only *huey* may modify it. Additionally, because *progfile2* has the set-user-id bit set, whenever anyone executes this program, it will operate with *huey*'s permissions to access files.

The file *textfile1* has read and write permission enabled for *huey*, its owner, and read permission enabled for *huey*'s group. This means that *huey* may read or modify the file, and members of his group may read it. Users who are not in *huey*'s group have no permissions enabled on this file, so they cannot read or modify it. The file *textfile2* has read and write permissions enabled for its owner, its group, and all other users. This means that **anyone** may read or modify this file. In general, this is a bad idea since a malicious user may decide to delete or change data in the file, and these permissions give him full access to do this.

One point which is not obvious from the above is that file permissions depend not only on the permission bits associated with the file itself, but also on the permissions bits associated with all the directories "above" the file in the directory hierarchy. For example, if a directory is searchable only by its owner, then the files in that directory cannot be read by others even if they are world-readable. This is because search permission on the directory is needed in order to access the files in the first place.

The chmod Command

The chmod command is used to change file and directory permissions. Two arguments are required by chmod: the first argument is the permissions to set on the files and directories, and the remaining arguments are the names of the files and directories whose permissions are to be changed. The permissions argument may be specified in one of two ways: *absolute* mode or *symbolic* mode.

Absolute Mode

Absolute mode involves specifying the permissions as a complete set of bits to enable on the named files. An absolute mode permission is specified as a single number, constructed by adding together the values shown in Table 3.1.

For example, to create the permissions argument that grants the owner read, write, and execute permission, the group read and execute permission, and no permissions for all others, the following numbers are added together:

```
mode = 400 + 200 + 100 + 40 + 10 + 0
mode = 700 + 50 + 0
mode = 750
```

$ **chmod 750** *files...*

Symbolic Mode

Symbolic modes are constructed of three parts:

[who] op permission

who is a combination of

u   User (owner) permissions.

g   Group permissions.

o   Others' permissions.

a   All, or ugo.

If *who* is omitted, a is assumed. The *op* part of the mode is one of

+   To add *permission*.

−   To remove *permission*.

=   To assign *permission* explicitly (all other permissions for that category are cleared).

permission is any combination of

r   Read.

w   Write.

x   Execute.

X   Give execute permission if the file is a directory or there is execute permission for one of the other user classes (not available on all versions).

s   Set-user-id or set-group-id, only useful with u or g.

t   Set the sticky bit.

Table 3.1

PERM	OWNER	GROUP	OTHERS	PERM	
read	400	40	4	set-user-id	4000
write	200	20	2	set-group-id	2000
execute	100	10	1	sticky	1000
none	0	0	0	none	0

The letters u, g, or o indicate that the initial permission is to be taken from the current mode for that user class, and then modified as indicated by *op* and *permission*. If *permission* is omitted (only useful with "="), all permissions for that user class are cleared.

For example, to add execute permission for the group and others to a file, the command

$ **chmod go+x** *filename*

would be used. To remove all write permission from a file, any of the commands shown below could be used.

$ **chmod ugo-w** *file*
$ **chmod a-w** *file*
$ **chmod -w** *file*

Table 3.2 shows several example usages of both absolute and symbolic modes:

Table 3.2

Permissions Before	Mode	Permissions After
any	777	rwxrwxrwx
any	755	rwxr-xr-x
any	750	rwxr-x---
any	700	rwx------
any	666	rw-rw-rw-
any	644	rw-r--r--
any	640	rw-r-----

Permissions Before	Mode	Permissions After
any	600	rw-------
any	444	r--r--r--
any	400	r--------
any	4755	rwsr-xr-x
rwxrwxrwx	go-wx	rwxr--r--
rwxrwxrwx	go-w	rwxr-xr-x
rwxrwxrwx	go=	rwx------
rwxr-xr-x	g+s	rwxr-sr-x
rwxr-xr-x	ugo=r	r--r--r--
rwxr-----	go+X	rwxr-x--x
rw-r--r--	+x	rwxr-xr-x
rw-r--r--	g+w	rw-rw-r--
rw-r-----	go+X	rw-r-----
r--r--r--	a+w	rw-rw-rw-
r--------	ug=rw	rw-rw----

Most newer versions of chmod offer a -R option, which tells it to recurse through a directory tree applying the permission to all files and directories it encounters. The "X" symbolic mode is particularly useful with this option; for example, to make all files in a directory readable and, if applicable, executable by everyone, the command

    $ **chmod -R ugo+rX** *directory*

would be used.

For systems which do not have the -R option, similar behavior can be obtained using the find command (described in section 3.8). The equivalent find version of the command above is

    $ **find** *directory* **-exec chmod ugo+rX {} \;**

The chown Command

The chown command is used to change the ownership of a file or directory. The first argument is the name of the user who should own the file, and the remaining arguments are the names of the files and directories whose ownership is to be changed. On

Berkeley-derived systems, chown is executable only by the super-user. On System V systems, any user may execute chown on her own files, giving them away to any other user. Under System V Release 4, if the system is configured with the _POSIX_RESTRICTED_CHOWN option, the Berkeley behavior is enabled.

On newer systems, chown has a -R option to recurse through directories. On some systems, chown will also accept an argument of the form *user.group*, allowing both user and group ownership to be changed with one command. Both of these options make applying changes to entire directory hierarchies easier.

The chgrp Command

Much like chown, the chgrp command is used for changing the group ownership of a file or directory. The first argument is the name of the group that should own the file, and the remaining arguments are the names of files and directories whose ownership is to be changed. On Berkeley-derived systems and System V Release 4, a user may change the group ownership of a file to any other group in which he is a member. On System V systems before Release 4, a user may change the group ownership of a file to any other group, regardless of whether or not he is a member.

Access Control Lists

Some systems, particularly those that have a National Computer Security Center "Orange Book" rating (see Chapter 11), have changed the familiar UNIX file protection modes to *access control lists* (ACLs). Generally, ACLs allow the access permissions for a file to be enumerated specifically, rather than divided into the three groups (owner, group, world) provided by the normal UNIX file system. An ACL is a list of specific *(user, permission)* or *(user, group, permission)* entries; most UNIX vendors implementing ACLs use the latter form (Kramer, 1988). For example, a single file could have an ACL like

```
(huey,  *,  rwx)
(duey,  *,  rw)
(louie,  staff,  rw)
(louie,  *,  r)
(*,  wheel,  rwx)
(*,  staff,  r)
(*,  *,  NONE)
```

When a file is accessed, the ACL is processed in order, applying each list entry to the user. When a match is found, those permissions are applied. For example, in the above ACL, *huey* has read, write, and execute access to the file regardless of what group he is in. *duey* has read and write access regardless of his group. User *louie* always has read access to the file, but only has write access if he is in group *staff*. Any member of group *wheel* has full access to the file, while members of group *staff* have read access (except for *louie*, who would also have write access). Finally, all other users are denied any access to the file.

ACLs are a relatively new concept in UNIX, although they have existed in other systems for years. Some implementations provide a wider set of permissions than just read, write, and execute—permissions to delete, rename, and search are common choices. As security becomes more important in the UNIX community, it is likely that ACLs will become a part of vendors' standard implementations, rather than being reserved for the secure versions of the product.

3.2 The *umask* Value

When a file is created by a program, say a text editor or a compiler, it is typically created with all applicable permissions enabled (i.e., the permissions will be `rw-rw-rw` or `rwxrwxrwx`). Since this is rarely desirable (you usually don't want other users to be able to write your files), the *umask* value is used to modify the permissions a file is created with. Simply put, while the `chmod` command is used to specify the permissions that should be turned **on**, the *umask* value is used to specify the permissions that should be turned **off**.

umask values are specified in somewhat the same way as absolute modes to the `chmod` command, described in section 3.1, although the meanings of the numbers are different between the two commands. On most systems, the default *umask* is 022, which indicates that write permission for the group (20) and others (2) should be turned off whenever a file is created. If you instead wanted to turn off write permission for the group but turn off all permissions for others, you would set your *umask* to 027. And to set the *umask* such that any file you create is readable, writable, and executable by only you, you would use the value 077. These modes may always be changed later with the `chmod` command.

The *umask* value is specified in the *.profile* or *.cshrc* file read by the shell using the `umask` command. The *root* account should have the command

umask 022

in its */.profile* or */.cshrc* file, in order to prevent the accidental creation of world-writable files owned by the super-user.

3.3 The `write` System Call

Some newer versions of UNIX have modified the `write` system call so that if the user making the call is not the super-user, any set-user-id bit on the file being written is cleared on write. This prevents an attacker from finding a writable set-user-id file owned by the super-user and modifying it. This modification exists on current systems from Sun, Solbourne, MIPS, NeXT, IBM, and most versions of System V. It is **not** present in HP-UX 7.0, although it does appear in HP-UX 8.0.

3.4 The Sticky Bit on Directories

Some newer versions of UNIX, such as 4.3BSD and its derivatives, and System V Release 4, have given a new meaning to the sticky bit when it is set on a directory. If a directory has its sticky bit set, users may not delete or rename files in this directory that are owned by other users. This is particularly useful for directories such as *tmp* and */usr/tmp*, that are normally world-writable, enabling any user to delete another user's files. By setting the sticky bit, users are protected from others' malicious actions.

To set the sticky bit on a directory, use the command

$ **chmod +t** *directory*

3.5 The Set-Group-Id Bit on Directories

In SunOS 4.*x* (Sun Microsystems, 1990), the set-group-id bit has been given a new meaning when set on a directory. Two rules can be used for assigning group owner-ship to files under SunOS:

1. The System V mechanism, which says that a user's primary group id (the one listed in the password file) is assigned to any file she creates.

2. The Berkeley mechanism, which says that the group id of a file is set to the group id of the directory in which it is created.

If the set-group-id bit is set on a directory, the Berkeley mechanism is enabled. If the set-group-id bit is not set on a directory, the System V mechanism is enabled. Nor-mally, the Berkeley mechanism is used; this mechanism must be used if creating direc-tories for use by more than one member of a group.

To set the set-group-id bit on a directory, the following command should be used:

$ **chmod g+s** *directory*

3.6 Set-User-Id and Set-Group-Id Shell Scripts

Using the set-user-id and/or set-group-id bits, it is possible to make shell scripts operate with the added permissions given by these bits. However, these scripts **cannot** be made secure, regardless of how many safeguards are taken when writing them.

Interrupts, job control, symbolic links, and other features of the UNIX system can be used to subvert these scripts and obtain illicit access. There are numerous software packages available that claim to make set-user-id or set-group-id shell scripts secure, but none of them solve all the problems associated with these scripts.

Set-user-id and set-group-id shell scripts should **never** be allowed on any UNIX system. If you have a need for one, it should be written as a C program instead.

3.7 Devices

The security of devices is an important issue in UNIX. Device files (usually residing in */dev*) are used by various system programs to access the data stored on disk drives or in memory. Improperly protected devices can leave your system vulnerable to an attacker. The entire list of devices is too long to detail here, since it varies from system to system and vendor to vendor. However, there are a few general guidelines that apply to all systems:

- The files */dev/kmem*, */dev/mem*, and */dev/drum* should never be readable by unprivileged users. If your system supports the notion of the *kmem* group (Berkeley-based systems and some System V systems) and utilities such as ps are set-group-id *kmem*, then these files should be owned by user *root* and group *kmem*, and should be mode 640. If your system does not support the notion of the *kmem* group and utilities such as ps are set-user-id *root*, then these files should be owned by user *root* and should be mode 600.

- The disk devices on your system should all be owned by user *root* and group *operator*, and should be mode 640. If your system does not have a group *operator*, and the dump and df programs are set-user-id *root*, then these devices should be mode 600. A useful way to display the names of disk devices in use on your system is to run the df command.

- With very few exceptions, all other devices should be owned by user *root* and should be either mode 600 or mode 640. One exception is terminal devices, which will be owned by the user currently logged into them, and changed back to *root* when the user logs out.

Device files are created with the mknod command. On most systems, this command is restricted to the super-user. However, in some environments where file systems are shared over a network, it is possible for an attacker to make a device as *root* on one machine in a networked file system, and then use that device on another machine, the one owning the file system. In order to guard against this, devices that are not in the */dev* directory (as all the standard UNIX devices will be) should be considered suspect. Later in this chapter, a command to find all devices of this type is described.

3.8 Backups

It is impossible to overemphasize the need for a good system backup strategy. File system backups not only protect you in the event of hardware failures and accidental deletions, but they also protect you against unauthorized file system changes made by an intruder. In some cases, if the intruder is very active or destructive, the backups may be your only way of restoring your system to a known state. Additionally, backups may be useful in providing evidence of an intruder's activities (by capturing files which he later deletes) in the event you should decide to prosecute. Backups were one of the methods used to prove that Robert T. Morris was the author of the Internet worm (Lynn et al., 1989).

Different UNIX systems provide different backup programs; some are better than others. A good backup and restore program will be able to copy an entire file system, and then restore it to its exact state as of the last backup. This includes deleting files that were removed between the full and incremental backups, handling permissions changes on files, and so on. For these reasons, programs such as `tar` and `cpio` are not very good backup programs—yes, they can copy everything to the backup media and make for easy restores, but in the event a file system must be reconstructed from scratch, these programs are not designed for this and do a poor job of it. Instead, programs such as `dump`, which are designed solely for backup purposes, should be used.

A good backup strategy will dump the entire file system (a "full" or "epoch" dump) at least once a month. Incremental (or "partial") dumps should be done at least twice a week, and ideally they should be done daily. Incremental dumps either copy everything modified since the last full dump or copy everything modified since the last incremental dump. The former, although it does make for redundant copies of some files, is usually preferable because it reduces the number of backups a single restore depends on. This means that if one of the incremental backups is lost or destroyed, most of the material that was on that backup will also be on the following incremental, so very little is lost.

When running backups, be sure not to destroy one backup set until you have the next one. For example, if you only use one set of tapes for full dumps, and a disk fails in the middle of the backup, your previous full dump has been destroyed. A good procedure to follow is to have at least two (and preferably more) full "dump sets" that include all the tapes for a full dump and all the incrementals. These sets are cycled through in a round-robin fashion. It is also a good idea to occasionally pull one of the sets out of the cycle (at least the full dump part of the set) and remove it to an off-site storage location where it can be used to recover the system in case of fire, flood, or other catastrophes.

A very simple (but effective) backup strategy is shown in Table 3.3. This strategy uses a 28-day cycle, with full dumps every two weeks. On the second and fourth weeks, a lower-level partial dump is used to cut down on the size of the following partial dumps. All file systems are dumped once a week, while user file systems (file

Table 3.3

Day	Level	File Systems	Tape Set	Day	Level	File Systems	Tape Set
1	0	all	A	15	0	all	B
2	7	user	A	16	7	user	B
3	7	user	A	17	7	user	B
4	7	user	A	18	7	user	B
5	7	user	A	19	7	user	B
6	7	user	A	20	7	user	B
7	7	user	A	21	7	user	B
8	4	all	A	22	4	all	B
9	7	user	A	23	7	user	B
10	7	user	A	24	7	user	B
11	7	user	A	25	7	user	B
12	7	user	A	26	7	user	B
13	7	user	A	27	7	user	B
14	7	user	A	28	7	user	B

systems with home directories on them) are dumped daily. Two complete sets of dump tapes are used, and are alternated every two weeks. This provides four weeks of coverage at any given time. Twice a year, one set of full dump tapes should be pulled out of the cycle and sent to an off-site archive in case of disaster. This is most easily done on the day a full dump is to be done by using a new set of tapes, and sending the set of tapes which would have been overwritten off-site.

The last backup-related issue that pertains to security is one of "live" backups, that is, performing backups while in multi-user mode. Most file system backup programs are designed to run in single-user mode, when the file system being backed up is not mounted. When these programs are run on "live" file systems that are changing as they are being backed up, the backup programs can become confused, and a dump can be created that cannot be restored from later, or that is missing files that were being changed while the backup was in progress. There are some ways to counter this (mostly by skipping files that change during the backup), and many products now claim to be able to back up live file systems. However, it should be pointed out that given the nature of the UNIX file system, it is **impossible** to create a perfect backup (one in which **every** file can be restored to a known state) of a file system if that file system is being modified while it is being backed up. It is important to consider the trade-off between "perfect" backups (which require taking the system down for several hours) and increased system availability (which may produce unusable backup tapes or backups with missing files). Even if you decide to accept the risks of performing "live" backups, it is a good idea to occasionally perform a single-user mode backup, for example when making the copy to be sent off-site.

3.9 Monitoring File System Security

Checking for security problems in the file system is an important part of making your system secure. Primarily, you need to check for files that can be modified by unauthorized users, files that can inadvertently grant users too many permissions, and files that can inadvertently grant access to intruders. It is also important to be able to detect unauthorized modifications to the file system, and to be able to recover from these changes when they are made.

The `find` Command

The `find` command is a general-purpose command for searching the file system. Using various arguments, complex matching patterns based on a file's name, type, permissions, owner, modification time, and other characteristics can be constructed. The names of files that are found using these patterns can then be printed out, or passed as arguments to other UNIX commands. The general format of a `find` command is

$ **find** *directories options*

where *directories* is a list of directory names to search and *options* contains the options to control what is being searched for. The `find` program will recursively search the named directories, so it is unnecessary to specify both a directory and its subdirectories.

The `find` command has numerous options, many of which are not all that useful except in special circumstances. The options we will be concerned with in this section are:

-name *pattern*   Specifies a pattern (as with shell wildcards) to match against a file's name. For example, `foo` will match any file named *foo*, while `foo*` will match *foo*, *foobar*, and so on. If the *pattern* argument contains shell wildcards, it must be enclosed in single quotes (″).

-perm *permission*   Specifies a set of permission bits to look for on the file. Normally, this will only match if the permission bits on the file are exactly those given in *permission*. However, if *permission* is preceded by a minus sign (−), then this option will match if the bits in *permission* are set on the file, regardless of what other bits may also be set. The "−" also allows matching on the set-user-id and set-group-id bits, which are ignored when the "−" is not specified.

−type *character*   Matches if the file is of the type specified by *character*. These types are: "f" for a regular file, "d" for a directory, "c" for a character-special device, "b" for a block-special device, and "l" for a symbolic link. Some systems also accept other characters for special file types they support.

−a   Specifies logical *and*, for joining multiple options.

−o   Specifies logical *or*, for joining multiple options.

\(...\)   The arguments \(and \) can be used for grouping multiple options together to insure proper evaluation of −a and −o.

−print   Print the full path name of any file that matches the specified options.

−exec *command*   For each file that matches the specified options, execute the named *command*. Within the arguments to *command*, the special string { } will be replaced with the file name. The last argument to this option must be a semicolon, specified to the shell as \;. For example, to find all files whose names start with *foo* and execute ls −l on them, the command

```
# find . -name 'foo*' -exec ls -l {} \;
```

would be used.

In this chapter, all examples that use find must be run as the super-user. Without super-user permission, the commands would not be able to search directories that are protected, enabling an intruder to easily hide files.

The sum Command

Recall from Chapter 1 that Duff's virus program modified binary executable files without changing their size. Thus, a command such as ls is not capable of detecting a change of this sort. One might argue that the virus would change the modification time of the file and this could be detected; unfortunately, this is not the case. It is possible to change the modification time of a file to any time in the past or future, and the virus could be written to reset the modification time of any file it infects. To detect changes made to a file by programs such as Duff's virus, it is necessary to compare the contents of the file in question to the contents of a known good copy of a file. However, this is usually prohibitive, since it requires that two copies of every file on the system be maintained (the "in use" copy and the known good copy). Fortunately, UNIX provides an alternative mechanism that is almost as good.

The sum command computes a 16-bit checksum for each file named on its command line and displays this value and the number of 1024-byte (Berkeley) or 512-byte

(System V) blocks in the file. A checksum is a number that is dependent on the data in the file, and thus if the contents of the file are changed, for example by a virus, the checksum's value will change. This makes modifications to files easy to detect. When the system is first installed, sum can be run over every file on the system (except those that are expected to change). Later, sum can be run again, and the results compared to the checksums of the known good versions.

The Berkeley and System V versions of sum use different algorithms to compute the checksum, thus the output of the two commands cannot be compared. On most systems, however, this should not be a problem. It is also important to note that the algorithm used by sum **can** be fooled. A clever attacker could change a file in such a way that its checksum does not change, although this is difficult. Sites that are nevertheless concerned about this possibility should obtain a program which computes a *message-digest* for a file. These functions cannot be fooled in the way that sum can.

Finding Set-User-Id and Set-Group-Id Files

It is important to check the system on a regular basis for unauthorized set-user-id and set-group-id programs. Because these programs grant special privileges to the user who is executing them, improperly written programs can also inadvertently open up the system to attack by an intruder. In particular, set-user-id *root* programs should be closely examined—a favorite trick of intruders is to break into the super-user account once, and then leave a set-user-id *root* program (e.g., a shell) hidden somewhere that will enable them to regain super-user status even if the original loophole they used to gain access is later closed.

The find command to search the entire system for set-user-id files is

```
# find / -type f -a -perm -4000 -print
```

and the analogous command to search for set-group-id files is

```
# find / -type f -a -perm -2000 -print
```

After executing these commands (depending on the size of your system, they can take anywhere from a few minutes to a few hours to run), you will have a complete list of files with the set-user-id or set-group-id bits set on them. You should then examine each of these files, and determine whether or not they should actually have these permissions. You should be especially suspicious of programs that are **not** in one of your system's standard program directories (or a subdirectory of them). On most systems, the list of standard program directories will be:

/bin
/etc
/usr/adm
/usr/bin
/usr/etc
/usr/lib

/usr/ucb
/usr/local/bin
/usr/local/etc
/usr/local/lib

Security Problems with `dump` and `restore`

One file distributed with SunOS (and other systems), */usr/etc/restore* (*/etc/restore* on some systems), is distributed with the set-user-id bit set on it, and should not be, due to a security loophole. You should be sure to remove the set-user-id bit from this program by executing the command

> **# chmod u-s /usr/etc/restore**

The `dump` command (*/etc/dump* or */usr/etc/dump*) can also be exploited by an intruder if it has the set-user-id or set-group-id bits set. It has these bits set in order to allow operators to run system backups without the need for super-user access. If your system's `dump` command has either the set-user-id or set-group-id bits set, then you should turn off world-execute permission on the program. This can be done using the command

> **# chmod o-rwx /usr/etc/dump**

The `rdump` and `rrestore` commands on some systems also have these problems.

Finding Device Files

Device files are used to access system devices such as system memory, disk drives, tape drives, and so on. These files allow the programmer to treat a device as a single stream of data, much like an ordinary file. This simplifies programming, since (almost) nothing special needs to be done when working with devices instead of ordinary files. For example, it is perfectly reasonable to use `cat` to look at the contents of a magnetic tape, by simply issuing the command

> **# cat /dev/rmt8**

On all standard UNIX systems, all device files reside in the */dev* directory. (Nothing in the system requires this, it is just a convention.) As described earlier, some devices must be protected with proper file permissions in order to prevent the system from being compromised. If an intruder can create her own device files, it is possible to circumvent these permissions and compromise the system. In order to guard against this, you should periodically search the system for illicit device files and delete them. Additionally, the permissions on the real device files should be checked to insure that they are secure.

The `find` command to search the entire system for device files is as follows:

> **# find / \(-type b -o -type c \) -print**

This will produce a list of every device file on the system.

Finding World-Writable Files

World-writable files, particularly system files and users' startup files, can present a security problem if an intruder can gain access to your system and modify them. World-writable directories, especially those directories in users' search paths, also present a security problem, since an intruder can install his own programs in them. The `find` command to locate all world-writable files and directories on the system is

```
# find / -perm -2 -print
```

In this case, we do not use the `-type` argument to restrict our search, since we are interested in directories and device files as well as ordinary files.

This list will be fairly long, and will include some files that **should** be world-writable. You should not be concerned that the file */dev/null* is world-writable; it is supposed to be. Likewise, terminal devices in */dev* may be world-writable. You should also not be too concerned if line printer log files and the like are world-writable, unless you are concerned about the integrity of the information they contain. The directories */tmp* and */usr/tmp* should be world-writable, although if your system supports sticky bits on directories, this mechanism should be used. Finally, if your system supports symbolic links, these may be world-writable—the permissions on a symbolic link, although they exist, are meaningless.

Finding Unowned Files

Finding files that are owned by nonexistent users can often be a clue that an intruder has gained access to your system. Even if this is not the case, searching for these files gives you the opportunity to clean up files that should have been deleted at the same time the user herself was removed from the system. The command to find unowned files is

```
# find / -nouser -print
```

The `-nouser` option matches files that are owned by a user id not contained in the */etc/passwd* database. A similar option, `-nogroup`, matches files owned by nonexistent groups. Unfortunately, some versions of UNIX, particularly those based on System V Release 3, do not have these options to the `find` command.

Finding *.rhosts* Files

As will be explained in Chapter 4, the *.rhosts* file in users' home directories can present certain security problems if not properly installed. Some sites make it a policy that users may not create these files. To search for these files, it is only necessary to search the file systems that hold users' home directories. An example `find` command to search for these files is

```
# find home-directories... -name .rhosts -print
```

If your site specifies that users may not create these files, you could modify the
`find` command to delete any of these files it finds:

```
# find home-directories... -name .rhosts -exec rm -f {} \;
```

Similar commands can be used to check for *.netrc* files, which also present security
problems as described in Chapter 4.

Checklists

Checklists can be a useful tool for discovering unauthorized changes made to system
directories. They aren't practical on file systems that contain users' home directories
since these change all the time. A checklist is a listing of all the files contained in a
group of directories: their sizes, owners, modification dates, permissions, and so on.
Periodically, this information is collected and compared with the information in the
master checklist. Files that do not match in all attributes can be suspected of having
been changed.

There are several utilities that implement checklists available from public software
archives (see Chapter 11). However, a simple utility can be constructed using only the
standard UNIX `ls` and `diff` commands.

First, use the `ls` command to generate a master checklist. This is best done
immediately after installing the operating system, but can be done at any time provided
you're confident about the correctness of the files on the disk. A sample command is
shown below:

```
# ls -aslgR /bin /etc /usr > MasterList
```

The file *MasterList* now contains a complete list of all files in these directories. You
will probably want to edit it and delete the lines for files you know will be changing
often (e.g., */etc/passwd*, */etc/utmp*, */dev/null*, and so on). The *MasterList* file should be
stored somewhere safe where an intruder is unlikely to find it (since she could otherwise just change the data it contains), either on a different computer system or off-line
on magnetic tape or floppy disk.

To search for changes in the file system, run the above `ls` command again, saving
the output in some other file, say *CurrentList*. Now use the `diff` command to compare the two files:

```
# diff MasterList CurrentList
```

Lines that are only in the master checklist will be printed preceded by a less-than sign
(<). Lines that are only in the current list will be printed preceded by a greater-than
sign (>). If there is one line for a file, preceded by a less-than sign, this indicates that
the file has been deleted since *MasterList* was created (it may also indicate a file that
was deleted from *MasterList*). If there is one line for a file, preceded by a greater-than
sign, this indicates that the file has been created since *MasterList* was created. If there

are two lines for a single file, one preceded by a less-than sign and the other by a greater-than sign, this indicates that some attribute of the file has been changed since *MasterList* was created.

As an example, consider the output below (the line numbers at the left are not part of the output, but will be used for reference in the following discussion):

```
# diff MasterList CurrentList
1,4c1,4
 1     < total 136
 2     <    1 drwxr-s--x  2 root    staff       512 Feb  7 1990 .
 3     <    1 drwxrwsrwt  4 bin     staff       512 Jan  1 1990 ..
 4     <    8 -rwxr-xr-x  1 root    staff      7456 Feb  7 1990 date
 5     ---
 6     > total 280
 7     >    1 drwxr-s--x  2 root    staff       512 Mar 10 13:34 .
 8     >    1 drwxrwsrwt  4 bin     staff       512 Jan  2 13:34 ..
 9     >  152 -rwxr-xr-x  1 root    staff    147456 Jun 27 1990 csh
10     6c6
11     <  112 -rwxr-xr-x  1 root    staff    106496 Feb  7 1990 sh
12     ---
13     >  112 -rwsr-xr-x  1 root    staff    106496 Feb  7 1990 sh
```

The lines beginning with "<" (lines 1, 2, 3, 4, and 11) are from the master checklist, while the lines beginning with ">" (lines 6, 7, 8, 9, and 13) represent the current system. The other lines (5, 10, and 12) are printed by diff but can be ignored. This output shows several things:

1. The directory has been modified (something has been added or deleted) since the master checklist was created. This is indicated by lines 1 and 6 showing the difference in total space consumed by the directory's contents, as well as lines 2 and 7, which show that the modification time for "." has changed. (Lines 3 and 8 show that the modification time of the parent directory has changed also; this is unimportant to us in this example.)

2. There is only one line for the date command (line 4). Because it is marked with a "<," we know that the command has been deleted since the master checklist was created.

3. There is only one line for the csh command (line 9). Because it is marked with a ">," we know that this command has been installed since the master checklist was created.

4. There are two lines for the sh command (lines 11 and 13). This indicates that something about the command has changed since the master checklist was created. Careful examination of the two lines shows that someone has changed the mode of the program, making it set-user-id *root*.

By carefully constructing the master checklist, and by remembering to update it periodically (you can replace it with a copy of *CurrentList*, once you're sure the differences between the lists are harmless), you can easily monitor your system for unauthorized changes. To make the checklist scheme even more robust, the `sum` command can be used to compute a checksum for each file in the master checklist, and these checksums can be recomputed whenever *CurrentList* is rebuilt. The lists of checksums can be compared using `diff` as well, enabling you to detect programs that have been modified but whose attributes as reported by `ls` were not changed. A simple example of a complete script to do this is given in Appendix B. The software packages available from the public software archives implement basically the same scheme as the one described here, but offer many more options for controlling what files are checked and reported on.

3.10 Summary

In this chapter several methods for protecting the file system were discussed:

- Set appropriate file permissions on all files.

- If supported by your system, use the sticky bit on world-writable directories such as */tmp*.

- Set your *umask* value to something appropriate such as 022, 027, or 077.

- Do not allow set-user-id or set-group-id shell scripts on the system.

- Check the modes of all device files.

- Implement and use a comprehensive backup strategy.

- Use the `find` command regularly to search for insecurities in the file system.

- Implement some form of checklist scheme to check the file system for unauthorized modifications.

By using these methods, you can be reasonably sure that your file system is immune to most forms of attack. However, as mentioned before, no protection is foolproof, and you should remain alert for break-ins.

Chapter 4
Network Security

As trends toward internetworking continue, most sites will, if they haven't already, connect themselves to one of the numerous regional networks springing up around the country and indeed, around the world. In the United States, most of these regional networks are connected to one of the national network backbones (NSFNet, ESNET, NSI, etc.), which are in turn connected to various international networks, forming the Internet (Quarterman and Hoskins, 1986). This means that the users of your systems can access other hosts and communicate with other users around the world. Unfortunately, it also means that other hosts and users from around the world can access your machines, and attempt to break into them.

Before internetworking became commonplace, protecting a system from unauthorized access simply meant locking the machine in a room by itself. Now that machines are connected by networks, however, security is much more complex. This chapter describes the tools and methods available to make your UNIX networks as secure as possible. Most vendors of UNIX have incorporated some form of the Berkeley TCP/IP networking software (Leffler et al., 1989) into their systems. In this chapter, we discuss networking as it relates to the Berkeley software. Telephone-based dial-up networking via UUCP is discussed in Chapter 7.

4.1 Trusted Hosts

One of the most convenient features of the Berkeley networking software is the concept of *trusted* hosts. The software allows the specification of other hosts (and possibly users) who are to be considered trusted—remote logins and remote command executions from these hosts will be permitted without requiring the user to enter a password. This is very convenient, because users do not have to type their password every time they use the network. Unfortunately, for the same reason, the concept of trusted hosts is also extremely insecure.

The Internet worm made extensive use of the trusted host concept to spread itself throughout the Internet (Seely, 1988). Many sites that had already disallowed trusted hosts fared rather well against the worm (few such machines were successfully entered) as compared to those sites that did allow trusted hosts. Even though it is a security problem, there are some valid uses for the trusted host concept. This section describes how to properly implement the trusted hosts facility while preserving as much security as possible.

The *hosts.equiv* File

The file */etc/hosts.equiv* can be used by the system administrator to indicate trusted hosts. The host name of each trusted host is listed in the file, one host per line. If a user attempts to log in (using `rlogin`) or execute a command (using `rsh`) remotely from one of the systems listed in *hosts.equiv*, and that user has an account on the local system with the same login name, access is permitted without requiring a password. (There is one exception to this—the *root* account always requires a password, unless there is a *.rhosts* file (described below) present for *root*.)

Provided adequate care is taken to allow only local hosts in the *hosts.equiv* file, a reasonable compromise between security and convenience can be achieved. Nonlocal hosts (including hosts at remote sites of the same organization) should never be trusted. Also, if there are any machines at your organization that are installed in "public" areas (e.g., terminal rooms) as opposed to private offices, you should not trust these hosts.

On some systems that come with the NIS (Yellow Pages) software from Sun Microsystems (see Chapter 5), *hosts.equiv* is controlled with NIS. As distributed, the default *hosts.equiv* file often contains only a single line:

```
+
```

This indicates that **every known host** (i.e., any host whose name can be determined through either the hosts file or the name server) should be considered a trusted host. This is obviously incorrect, and presents a major security problem, since hosts outside the local organization should never be trusted. A correctly configured *hosts.equiv* should never list any "wildcard" hosts (such as the "+"); only specific host names should be used. When installing a new system from distribution tapes, you should be sure to either replace the default *hosts.equiv* with a correctly configured one, or delete the file altogether.

The *.rhosts* File

The *.rhosts* file is similar in concept and format to the *hosts.equiv* file, but allows trusted access only to specific host-user combinations, rather than to hosts in general. (Actually, *hosts.equiv* may be used to specify host-user combinations as well, but this is rarely done.) Each user may create a *.rhosts* file in his home directory, and allow access to his account without a password. Most people use this mechanism to allow trusted access between accounts they have on systems owned by different organizations who do not trust each other's hosts in *hosts.equiv*. For example, if *huey*'s *.rhosts* file contained the following lines,

```
foo.bar.com huey
big.school.edu louie
```

then *huey* could log in (or execute remote commands) on the local machine from his account on *foo.bar.com*. Further, *louie* could do the same (logging in or executing commands as *huey*) from the host *big.school.edu*.

As should be obvious, this file presents a major security problem. While *hosts.equiv* is under the system administrator's control and can be managed effectively, any user may create a *.rhosts* file granting access to whomever she chooses, without the system administrator's knowledge.

The only secure way to manage *.rhosts* files is to completely disallow them on the system. The system administrator should check the system often for violations of this policy (see Chapter 3). Unfortunately, this is sometimes too restrictive, and users will complain. As an alternative, *.rhosts* files can be allowed, provided only local hosts are listed in them. Adherence to this rule can also be checked automatically. One possible exception to this rule is the *root* account; a *.rhosts* file may be necessary to allow network backups and the like to be completed. If you should decide to allow *.rhosts* files, under no circumstances should they be made writable by anyone other than their owner.

One additional note on *.rhosts* files: In section 2.4, we stated that to disable an account so that nobody can log into it, an asterisk (*) should be placed in the encrypted password field of the password file. Although this does prevent a user from logging in when a password is required, it does not prevent him from logging in if he has a *.rhosts* file, since the password check is bypassed. If your system allows the use of *.rhosts* files, be sure to delete this file from the home directory of any accounts you disable.

The *.netrc* File

The *.netrc* file is used by the `ftp` command to allow automatic login to remote hosts without specifying passwords. (The file was also used by the old Berknet software distributed with 4.1BSD.) The *.netrc* file resides in a user's home directory and contains a list of host names, login names, and **unencrypted** passwords. Any intruder who can gain access to this file immediately gains access to all the remote systems listed there. In Chapter 2, we said that unencrypted passwords should **never** be stored on-line. This file directly violates that policy.

The only secure way to manage *.netrc* files is to completely disallow them on the system. The system administrator should check the system often for violations of this policy (see Chapter 3).

4.2 The `inetd` Program

Most versions of UNIX that support the Berkeley networking utilities have a program called `inetd`, which is used to start many of the daemons that provide network services. The idea behind `inetd` is that it waits for network connections on a number of ports, and when a connection on a specific port arrives, it invokes the server that should handle that request. This is preferable from a memory-use standpoint to having numerous (over a dozen) individual daemons running, waiting for connections.

The file */etc/inetd.conf* is used to specify which ports `inetd` is to wait for connections on, and which programs to start when connections arrive. (This file is called */etc/servers* on pre–4.0 versions of SunOS and some versions of System V.) With most newer versions of `inetd` (those based on the 4.3BSD version), */etc/inetd.conf* typically looks something like

```
# Internet services syntax:
#  <service> <skttype> <proto> <wait> <user> <path> <args>
#
ftp      stream tcp nowait root    /etc/ftpd    ftpd
telnet   stream tcp nowait root    /etc/telnetd telnetd
shell    stream tcp nowait root    /etc/rshd    rshd
login    stream tcp nowait root    /etc/rlogind rlogind
exec     stream tcp nowait root    /etc/rexecd  rexecd
finger   stream tcp nowait nobody  /etc/fingerd fingerd
tftp     dgram  udp wait    nobody /etc/tftpd   tftpd -s /tftpboot
comsat   dgram  udp wait    root   /etc/comsat  comsat
talk     dgram  udp wait    root   /etc/talkd   talkd
ntalk    dgram  udp wait    root   /etc/ntalkd  ntalkd
echo     stream tcp nowait root    internal
echo     dgram  udp nowait  root   internal
discard  stream tcp nowait root    internal
discard  dgram  udp nowait  root   internal
chargen  stream tcp nowait root    internal
chargen  dgram  udp nowait  root   internal
daytime  stream tcp nowait root    internal
daytime  dgram  udp nowait  root   internal
time     stream tcp nowait root    internal
time     dgram  udp nowait  root   internal
```

On each line, the following parameters are specified:

service   The name of the service as listed in the file */etc/services*. On systems using Sun Microsystems' Remote Procedure Call (RPC) software (as they do if they run NFS or NIS), this name may be followed by a slash (/) and an RPC version number.

socket_type	The type of connection the service expects to use: either a stream (`stream`) or datagrams (`dgram`).
proto	The protocol the service expects to use: either `tcp` for stream connections, or `udp` for datagram connections. On systems that use Sun RPC, `rpc/udp` is also a legal value.
wait	Specifies whether the server waits for a connection to die based on a timeout (`wait`) or terminates the connection based on information contained in the protocol (`nowait`). Most services should use the `nowait` option.
user	The user id that should run the server. This allows servers to be run with access privileges other than those of the super-user.
pathname	The path name to the server program that handles requests on this port. If this has the special value `internal`, the service is handled internally to `inetd`. This is used for some "trivial" network services such as the character sink and the character generator.
args	Arguments given to the server program when it is invoked. The first argument should be the name of the program.

The */etc/inetd.conf* file may be used to solve security problems in two ways. First, those services that you do not want to provide can simply be commented out of the file. When remote hosts attempt to connect to your system on that port, they will receive a "connection refused" error, or in the case of UDP services, the service will simply time out. Second, those services that may present a security problem if compromised but are still necessary to provide can at least be made to run as some non-privileged user, rather than as the super-user.

When deleting services from *inetd.conf*, it is important to consider what functionality will be lost if this service is disabled. Some likely candidates for deletion from *inetd.conf* include: `finger`, which allows remote users to find out about a local user; `tftp`, which allows file transfers to be made without providing a login or password; and `talk` and `ntalk`, which allow users to communicate interactively with each other using the `talk` program.

4.3 The File Transfer Protocol (FTP)

The File Transfer Protocol (FTP) (Postel and Reynolds, 1985), implemented by the `ftp` and `ftpd` programs, allows users to connect to remote systems and transfer files back and forth. Unfortunately, older versions of these programs also had several bugs in them that allowed intruders to break into a system. These bugs have been fixed by

Berkeley, and new versions are available. If your `ftpd` is a version prior to Berkeley's version 4.163 of November 8, 1988, when these bugs were fixed, you should get a newer version (see Chapter 11) if at all possible. Most versions of `ftpd` print their version number and/or date of compilation when connected to. You can try to determine the date on your version by executing the command shown below:

```
$ ftp -n localhost
Connected to host.my.domain
220 myhost FTP server (V5.30 Tue Mar 28 18:11:37 PST 1989) ready.
ftp> bye
221 Goodbye.
```

Unfortunately, some vendors change the version numbering from that used by Berkeley, so this may or may not provide useful information. If you're not sure, contact your vendor for more details.

Setting up Anonymous FTP

One of the more useful features of FTP is the *anonymous* login. This special login allows users who do not have an account on your machine to have restricted access in order to transfer files from a specific directory. This is useful if you wish to distribute software to the public at large without giving each person who wants the software an account on your machine. In order to securely set up anonymous FTP, you should follow the specific instructions below:

1. Create an account called *ftp*. Disable the account by placing an asterisk (*) in the password field. Give the account a special home directory, such as */usr/ftp* or */usr/spool/ftp*. This directory should be in a file system with plenty of free disk space.

2. Make the home directory owned by *ftp* and unwritable by anyone:

    ```
    # chown ftp ~ftp
    # chmod 555 ~ftp
    ```

3a. Make the directory *˜ftp/bin*, owned by the super-user and unwritable by anyone. Place a copy of the `ls` program in this directory:

    ```
    # mkdir ~ftp/bin
    # chown root ~ftp/bin
    # chmod 555 ~ftp/bin
    # cp -p /bin/ls ~ftp/bin
    # chmod 111 ~ftp/bin/ls
    ```

3b. If your system uses shared libraries, as SunOS 4.*x* does, you may also need to set up shared libraries in *ftp*'s area. The following instructions apply to SunOS

4.*x* only; other vendors' systems will vary. Consult the documentation on `ftpd` for specific information on your system.

```
# mkdir ~ftp/dev
# chmod 555 ~ftp/dev
# mknod ~ftp/dev/zero c 3 12
# chmod 644 ~ftp/dev/zero
# mkdir ~ftp/usr ~ftp/usr/lib
# chmod 555 ~ftp/usr ~ftp/usr/lib
# cp -p /usr/lib/libc.s[ao]* ~ftp/usr/lib
    you only need to copy the latest library version
# chmod 444 ~ftp/usr/lib/*
```

4. Make the directory *ftp/etc*, owned by the super-user and unwritable by any-one. Place copies of the password and group files in this directory, with all the password fields changed to asterisks (*). For added security, you should delete all but the *ftp* account from the password file, and all local groups from the group file. The only account that must be present is *ftp* (and some newer ver-sions of `ftp` don't even require that). This prevents attackers from gaining a list of account names on your system by transferring this file.

```
# mkdir ~ftp/etc
# chown root ~ftp/etc
# chmod 555 ~ftp/etc
# cp -p /etc/passwd /etc/group ~ftp/etc
    edit passwd, group and delete non-essential lines
# chmod 444 ~ftp/etc/passwd ~ftp/etc/group
```

5. Make the directory *ftp/pub*, owned by *ftp* and world-writable. Users may then place files that are to be accessible via anonymous FTP in this directory:

```
# mkdir ~ftp/pub
# chown ftp ~ftp/pub
# chmod 777 ~ftp/pub
```

Note that by making this directory world-writable you are allowing people you do not know to place files on your system. This can be dangerous, since in addition to depositing their own files, these unknown users can replace your distribution files with modified versions containing Trojan horses or other problems. An alternative method is to make the *pub* directory unwritable by the *ftp* account, which is used by anonymous users:

```
# chmod 577 ~ftp/pub
```

Then create a second directory, *incoming*, which is writable. In this way, files can still be left by anonymous users, but the material in the *pub* directory can be "trusted" since they cannot modify it.

Because the anonymous FTP feature allows anyone to access your system (albeit in a very limited way), it should not be made available on every host on the network. Instead, you should choose one machine (preferably a server or stand-alone host) on which to allow this service. This makes monitoring for security violations much easier. If you allow people to transfer files to your machine (using the world-writable *pub* directory, described above), you should check often the contents of the directories into which they are allowed to write. Any suspicious files you find should be deleted.

The *ftpusers* File

The file */etc/ftpusers* can be used on some systems to deny FTP access to individual users. Users listed in this file, one login name per line, may not log in to the system via FTP. If the file is not present, the list is assumed to be empty, and any user may use FTP to access the system (provided he can supply the proper password, etc.).

As a minimum, the super-user, *root*, and any other accounts with user id 0, should always be listed in this file. System accounts that do not normally have a human associated with them, such as *bin*, *daemon*, *news*, *sync*, *sys*, and *uucp*, should usually be listed as well.

The *shells* File

The file */etc/shells* can be used on some systems to deny FTP access to users whose login shell (listed in the password file) is not one of the shells contained in this file. Shells are listed in the file one per line. This prevents accounts that have special shells (e.g., service accounts, disabled accounts, etc.) from being used for FTP. A minimal */etc/shells* file will contain only /bin/sh and /bin/csh. Some sites may wish to add /bin/ksh and /bin/tcsh if those shells are installed on the system.

Trivial FTP

The Trivial File Transfer Protocol (TFTP) (Sollins, 1981; Finlayson, 1984), is used by some workstation vendors (e.g., Sun) to allow diskless hosts to boot from the network. Basically, TFTP is a stripped-down version of FTP—there is no user authentication, and the connection is based on the User Datagram Protocol instead of the Transmission Control Protocol. Because they are so stripped-down, many implementations of TFTP have security problems. You should check your hosts by executing the command sequence shown below:

```
$ tftp
tftp> connect yourhost
tftp> get /etc/motd tmp
Error code 1: File not found
tftp> quit
```

If your version does not respond with "*File not found*," but instead responds as follows

```
$ tftp
tftp> connect yourhost
tftp> get /etc/motd tmp
Received nn bytes in nn seconds
tftp> quit
```

your version of `tftpd` is insecure. In particular, versions of SunOS prior to release 4.0 are known to have this problem.

Most newer versions of `tftpd` implement a `-s` or `-r` option which, followed by a directory name, will restrict all file transfers to that directory. If your `tftpd` responded as in the second example above, you should check your */etc/inetd.conf* file (see section 4.2) and be sure that `tftpd` is being invoked with this option in effect.

4.4 Electronic Mail

Electronic mail is one of the main reasons for connecting to outside networks. It allows users to exchange messages and files in seconds, without the problems of the telephone (busy signals, not in the office, etc.). Unfortunately, some electronic mail software can open your system to abuse by an attacker.

The `sendmail` Command

On most versions of Berkeley-derived UNIX systems, the `sendmail` program is used to enable the receipt and delivery of mail. As with the FTP software, older versions of `sendmail` have several bugs that allow security violations. One of these bugs was used with great success by the Internet worm (Seely, 1988; Spafford, 1988). The current version of `sendmail` from Berkeley is version 5.65, of June 1990. Many vendors, however, still ship older versions. Any version of `sendmail` prior to version 5.61 is known to have security problems and should be replaced with a newer version. Chapter 11 details how to obtain the current release of `sendmail`.

To determine which version of `sendmail` you are running, usually all you need to do is connect to your `sendmail` server:

```
$ telnet localhost 25
Trying 127.0.0.1 ...
Connected to localhost.my.domain.
Escape character is '^]'.
220 myhost Sendmail 5.65/1.3 ready at Tue, 1 Jan 91 11:33:43 -0800
quit
221 host.my.domain closing connection
Connection closed by foreign host.
```

The first number displayed after the word "Sendmail" is the version number. Unfortunately, some vendors change the version number, and the results of this test are not as meaningful. If your version of this test does not give you a version number like 5.*xx* where *xx* is at least 50, your vendor has probably changed the version numbering. You will have to contact your vendor to determine which version of sendmail your system is running.

Generally, with the exception of the security problems alluded to above, sendmail is reasonably secure when installed by most vendors' installation procedures. There are, however, a few precautions that should be taken to ensure secure operation:

1. Remove the *decode* and *uudecode* aliases from the aliases file (*/usr/lib/aliases* or */etc/aliases*). Then run the newaliases command (or /usr/lib/ sendmail -bi if you don't have newaliases).

2. If you create aliases that allow messages to be sent to programs, be absolutely sure that there is no way to obtain a shell or send commands to a shell from these programs.

3. Make sure the *wizard* password is disabled in the configuration file, *sendmail.cf.* (Unless you modify the distributed configuration files, this shouldn't be a problem.) This means that there should be a line in */usr/lib/ sendmail.cf* (or */etc/sendmail.cf*) which looks like

    ```
    OW*
    ```

Most recent versions of sendmail do not even support the wiz command anymore. You can verify that yours does not by executing the following commands:

```
$ telnet localhost 25
220 myhost Sendmail 5.65 ready at Tue, 1 Jan 91 11:33:43 -0800
wiz
500 Command unrecognized
quit
221 host.my.domain closing connection
Connection closed by foreign host.
```

If your sendmail does not respond with "*500 Command unrecognized,*" but instead responds with

```
$ telnet localhost 25
220 myhost Sendmail 5.65 ready at Tue, 1 Jan 91 11:33:43 -0800
wiz
You wascal wabbit!  Wandering wizards won't win!
quit
221 host.my.domain closing connection
Connection closed by foreign host.
```

then your version has the `wiz` command, but it is not enabled. If your version responds with

```
$ telnet localhost 25
220 myhost Sendmail 5.65 ready at Tue, 1 Jan 91 11:33:43 -0800
wiz
Please pass, oh mighty wizard.
quit
221 host.my.domain closing connection
Connection closed by foreign host.
```

then your version has the `wiz` command, and you should be sure to disable the password as described above, since this presents a major security problem.

4. Make sure your `senamail` does not support the `debug` command. This can be done with the following commands:

```
$ telnet localhost 25
220 myhost Sendmail 5.65 ready at Tue, 1 Jan 91 11:33:43 -0800
debug
500 Command unrecognized
quit
221 host.my.domain closing connection
Connection closed by foreign host.
```

If your `sendmail` does not respond with "*500 Command unrecognized,*" but instead responds as follows

```
$ telnet localhost 25
220 myhost Sendmail 5.65 ready at Tue, 1 Jan 91 11:33:43 -0800
debug
200 Debug set
quit
221 host.my.domain closing connection
Connection closed by foreign host.
```

then you are vulnerable to attack and should replace your `sendmail` with a newer version if at all possible.

By following the procedures above, you can be sure that your mail system is reasonably secure, at least from past security problems.

The `binmail` Command

On most Berkeley-based systems, there are actually two versions of the `mail` command—one in */usr/ucb/mail*, and one in */bin/mail*. The version in */usr/ucb* (also called `Mail`, or `mailx` on System V systems) is usually used by users to send and receive mail. The version in */bin*, usually called `binmail` to avoid confusion, is used by `sendmail` to deliver mail to local mailboxes.

There is a bug in most Berkeley versions (and hence vendors' versions based on the Berkeley versions) of `binmail` that can allow an attacker to obtain access to a super-user shell. If your version of */bin/mail* is older than February 20, 1991, when this bug was fixed, it should be replaced with a newer version.

The version of */usr/bin/mail* shipped with all versions of ULTRIX prior to version 4.2 contains a bug which can allow unprivileged users to obtain super-user permissions. If you are running version 4.1 of ULTRIX, and cannot upgrade to version 4.2 for some reason, you can install the version 4.2 */usr/bin/mail* program on your version 4.1 system. If you are running a version of ULTRIX prior to version 4.1, you must upgrade to version 4.2 to obtain the fixed version of */usr/bin/mail*.

The `rmail` Command

The `rmail` program is similar to */bin/mail*, except that it is used by the UUCP software (described in Chapter 7) to deliver mail. Older versions of this program also had a bug that allowed an attacker to execute commands as the super-user.

4.5 Finger

The finger service (Zimmerman, 1990), provided by the `finger` and `fingerd` programs, allows you to obtain information about a user such as her full name, home directory, last login time, and in some cases when she last received mail and/or read her mail. The `fingerd` program allows users on remote hosts to obtain this information.

A bug in `fingerd` was also exercised with success by the Internet worm (Seely, 1988; Spafford, 1988). If your version of `fingerd` is older than November 5, 1988, it most likely contains the bug used by the worm, and should be replaced with a newer version, or the service should be disabled by commenting it out of */etc/inetd.conf* as described previously. New versions are available from several of the sources described in Chapter 11. The date of your version can usually be determined by running the command

```
# strings /etc/fingerd
```

and searching for the version number and modification date. (Some versions of UNIX, notably Sun's, have moved */etc/fingerd* to */usr/etc/in.fingerd*.)

The `finger` service opens up a privacy issue that has recently been debated by several organizations. Depending on what version of `finger` your system runs, it may be the case that the information provided is "sensitive," and you don't want this information given out to unknown users at remote sites. Should you determine that `finger` presents an unacceptable situation with regard to privacy, the service can be disabled by commenting it out of *etc/inetd.conf*, or a special version can be written to provide less information to users at remote sites.

4.6 Forgery and Spoofing

Many of the Internet services such as SMTP and NNTP (Network News Transfer Protocol) are implemented by clients and servers that speak a simple ASCII protocol. It is possible for an attacker to connect to one of these servers using the `telnet` command, giving it a third argument, as shown in the examples in section 4.4. The attacker can then type commands to the server as if he were a client program, and generate forged mail or network news. If an attacker is aware of some vulnerability in the server, he can also use this method to attempt to break in to your system.

In the case of SMTP, the `sendmail` program places headers on each mail message that are generated using data other than that provided by the client however, and so it is usually possible to detect forged mail. Network news however, does not perform much authentication, and forged news is often difficult to detect. There isn't too much that can be done about these problems, since authentication software is generally expensive (either in time or money) to implement. However, privacy-enhanced mail, described in Chapter 9, can be used to authenticate electronic mail.

4.7 Network Configuration

In recent years networking software and hardware has advanced to the point where it can be used to control access to a network. By configuring your network in specific ways, it is possible to prevent outside hosts from connecting to your systems except through certain secure points.

Firewall Machines

One of the newer ideas in network security is that of a *firewall*. Basically, a firewall is a special host that sits between your outside-world network connection(s) and your internal network(s), as shown in Figure 4.1. This host does not send out routing information about your internal network, and thus the internal network is "invisible" from the outside. In order to configure a firewall machine, the following considerations need to be taken:

1. The firewall does not advertise routes, that is, it does not send information out to other network entities about how to get to the networks "behind" it. This is done by running `routed` (or `in.routed`) with the `-q` option. This means

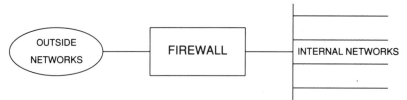

Figure 4.1 Firewall Configuration

that users on the internal network must log in to the firewall in order to access hosts on remote networks. Likewise, in order to log in to a host on the internal network from the outside, a user must first log in to the firewall machine. This is inconvenient, but more secure.

2. All electronic mail sent by your users must be forwarded to the firewall machine if it is to be delivered outside your internal network. The firewall must receive all incoming electronic mail, and then redistribute it. This can be done either with aliases for each user or by using name server MX records.

3. The firewall machine should not mount any file systems via NFS or RFS, or make any of its file systems available to be mounted (see Chapter 5).

4. The firewall machine should not run NIS, or if it must, it should be in a different domain than the rest of the hosts on the network (see Chapter 5).

5. Password security on the firewall must be rigidly enforced. Only users who require access to outside networks and users who must log in to your systems from remote hosts should have accounts on the firewall.

6. The firewall host should not trust any other hosts via *hosts.equiv* or *.rhosts*, regardless of where they are. Furthermore, the firewall should not be trusted by any other host on your local networks.

7. Anonymous FTP and other similar services should only be provided by the firewall host, if they are provided at all. The */etc/ftpusers* and */etc/shells* files should be used to restrict access as much as possible.

8. Services that are not needed should be disabled in */etc/inetd.conf*. Only the minimum services required for system operation should be allowed.

9. If possible, `syslog` on the firewall machine should be configured to log all information to a remote host (see section 4.8). This will prevent an intruder from deleting information from the log files.

10. If not needed, compilers and loaders should be deleted from the firewall machine. This will prevent attackers from compiling programs there (this would have been sufficient to stop the Internet worm).

11. Change the modes of */bin*, */usr/bin*, */usr/ucb*, */lib*, */usr/lib*, and */etc* and their subdirectories to 711 or 511. This ensures that read and write permissions are disabled where possible.

12. If your system logs all information into /var instead of /usr (as newer Sun and Berkeley systems, and System V Release 4 do), mount /usr and other file systems read-only if possible. Note that the root file system (/) cannot be mounted read-only in most configurations.

Carlin (1990) provides a more complete list that can be used when the firewall system is to be a Sun workstation.

The purpose of the firewall is to prevent attackers from accessing other hosts on your network. This means, in general, that you must maintain strict and rigidly enforced security on the firewall, but the other hosts are less vulnerable, and hence security may be somewhat lax. But it is important to remember that the firewall is not a complete defense against intruders—if an attacker can break into the firewall machine, he can then try to break into any other host on your network.

Gateways and Routers

The Internet Protocol (IP) (Postel, 1981a), Transmission Control Protocol (TCP) (Postel, 1981b), and User Datagram Protocol (UDP) (Postel, 1980) all carry certain control information that can be used to restrict access to certain hosts or networks within an organization. The IP packet header contains the network addresses of both the sender and the recipient of the packet. Further, the TCP and UDP protocols provide the notion of a *port*, which identifies the endpoint of a communications path (usually a network server). In some instances, it is desirable to deny access to a specific TCP or UDP port (e.g., if the network server for that port is insecure), or even to certain hosts and networks altogether.

Routing Tables

One of the simplest approaches to preventing unwanted network connections is to simply remove certain networks from a gateway's routing tables. This makes it impossible (or nearly impossible) for a host to send packets to these networks. (Most protocols require bidirectional packet flow even for unidirectional data flow; thus breaking one side of the route is usually sufficient.)

This approach is commonly taken in firewall systems, by preventing the firewall from advertising local routes to the outside world. The approach is deficient in that it often prevents too much—e.g., in order to prevent access to one system on the network, access to all systems on the network is disabled.

Packet Filtering

Many commercially available gateway systems (more correctly called routers) provide the ability to filter packets based not only on sources or destinations but also on source-destination combinations. This mechanism can be used to deny access to a specific host, network, or subnet from any other host, network, or subnet.

Gateway systems from cisco Systems support an even more complex scheme, allowing finer control over source and destination addresses. Via the use of address masks, one can deny access to all but one host on a particular network. The cisco systems also allow packet screening based on IP protocol type and TCP or UDP port numbers.

There has recently been some attempt to make UNIX systems used as gateways capable of performing packet filtering. Mogul (1989) describes a mechanism by which the networking code in the operating system asks a user-level process to pass judgement about every packet that is to be forwarded. The user-level process is controlled by a configuration file that allows packets to be accepted or rejected based on source and destination addresses, source and destination port numbers, and protocol type. Cheswick (1990) describes a firewall-like implementation with some special "pass-through" versions of `ftp` and `telnet` that allow users on the "interior" side of the firewall to access the outside world without having accounts on the firewall system. Unfortunately, the work described in these papers is not freely or commercially available at this time, although Sun Microsystems offers an alternative version of pass-through `ftp` and `telnet` as a "consulting special," which can be used on Sun systems when a Sun system is being used as a firewall.

4.8 Sophisticated Network Attacks

There are several more sophisticated methods of attacking a TCP/IP network than those described up to this point. Most of these involve a great deal of programming effort, as well as the ability to construct one's own network packets. Although this is by no means impossible, it is usually beyond the abilities of most attackers.

Sequence Number Prediction

One method, described by Robert T. Morris (1985) (the author of the Internet worm) involves predicting the *sequence numbers* used by TCP in order to masquerade as a trusted host on the local network. During connection establishment, the two sides of a TCP connection, C and S, negotiate the sequence numbers to be used by each host. These sequence numbers increment with each packet sent, allowing the protocol to detect dropped and duplicate packets. Morris' scheme supposes that there is a way for an attacker to *predict* the sequence number that S will use, and then use a third host, X, to masquerade as host C.

Routing Attacks

Bellovin (1989) describes two types of attack based on packet routing. The first involves the use of *source routes*, which are a mechanism for a host to specify a specific network path to follow when sending a packet. If an attacker can modify his packets and change the source route before sending them to host H_1, he can cause the responses to these packets to be sent to host H_2 instead of his host. If H_2 trusts H_1, this can be devastating.

The second routing attack involves the Routing Information Protocol (RIP) (Hedrick, 1988). This protocol is used by gateways and routers to determine the appropriate paths through the network to remote hosts. If an attacker can send bogus routing information to a host—e.g., claiming to be the route to an individual workstation or even an entire network—she can then receive all packets destined for that host or network. This sort of attack is fairly easy to mount, since many implementations of RIP do very little checking on the sources of the information they receive. Most commercial gateway systems can be configured to ignore routing information received from untrusted sources; this practice is typically called *policy-based routing*. The gated software available for UNIX systems (see Chapter 11) also allows untrusted routing updates to be ignored. Unfortunately, the standard routed program that comes with most versions of UNIX will believe routing information from anyone who sends it.

Domain Name System (DNS) Attacks

Bellovin (1989) also points out that the Domain Name System (DNS) (Mockapetris, 1987a, 1987b) is vulnerable to attack. If the intruder can implement a routing attack as described above and intercept all packets destined for a domain name server, he can use his own name server to supply bogus addresses of subverted machines for any host name lookup. Early versions of the Berkeley Internet Name Domain (BIND) server did not check to see that answers to queries came from the host that was asked; this enabled an attacker to simply respond to a query with bogus information before the "real" response was received. This has been fixed in recent versions of BIND.

Another possible problem with the DNS is one of privacy. By using the *zone transfer* (AXFR) command in the protocol, it is possible for a user on a remote system to obtain a list of every host name and address in a given domain. The DNS also permits the (optional) storage of host and operating system information for each listed host. An attacker who is aware of a specific vulnerability on some brand of host or operating system could thus use the DNS zone transfer information to search the network for hosts that are susceptible to this vulnerability.

The Simple Network Management Protocol (SNMP)

Lastly, Bellovin (1989) brings up the subject of the Simple Network Management Protocol (SNMP) (Case et al., 1990). This protocol is designed to allow network managers to obtain information from gateways, routers, and other network objects. It also allows these objects to be reconfigured dynamically. Obviously, any network component that runs SNMP should be heavily protected using whatever authentication schemes are provided by the vendor in order to guard against unauthorized reconfiguration.

4.9 Monitoring Network Security

Monitoring network security is more difficult than other monitoring tasks, because there are so many ways for an attacker to attempt to break in. However, there are some programs available to aid you in this task. Unfortunately, some of these monitoring programs can also be used by attackers to steal information from the network.

The `syslog` Facility

The `syslog` facility, provided with most Berkeley-derived versions of UNIX, is a mechanism that enables any command to log error messages and informational messages to the system console, as well as to a log file. Typically, error messages are logged in the file *usr/adm/messages* along with the date, time, name of the program sending the message, and (usually) the process id of the program. A sample segment of the *messages* file is shown below:

```
$ tail /usr/adm/messages
Mar 12 14:53:37 mysys login: ROOT LOGIN ttyp3 FROM sys1.my.domain
Mar 12 15:18:08 mysys login: ROOT LOGIN ttyp3 FROM sys2.my.domain
Mar 12 16:50:25 mysys login: ROOT LOGIN ttyp4 FROM sys3.my.domain
Mar 12 16:52:20 mysys vmunix: sd2c:  read failed, no retries
Mar 13 06:01:18 mysys vmunix: /: file system full
Mar 13 08:02:03 mysys login: ROOT LOGIN ttyp4 FROM sys1.my.domain
Mar 13 08:28:52 mysys su: huey on /dev/ttyp3
Mar 13 08:38:03 mysys login: ROOT LOGIN ttyp4 FROM sys1.my.domain
Mar 13 10:56:54 mysys automount[154]: host sys4 not responding
Mar 13 11:30:42 mysys login: REPEATED LOGIN FAILURES ON ttyp3
                FROM foo.bar.com
```

Of particular interest in this example are the messages from the `login` and `su` programs. Whenever someone logs in as *root*, `login` records this information. Generally, logging in as *root* directly, rather than using the `su` command, should be discouraged, as it is hard to track which person is actually using the account. Once this ability has been disabled, as described in Chapter 7, detecting a security violation of this type becomes a simple matter of searching the *messages* file for lines of this type.

`login` also logs any case of someone repeatedly trying to log in to an account and failing. After three attempts, `login` will refuse to let the person try anymore. Searching for these messages in the *messages* file can alert you to an attacker attempting to guess someone's password.

Finally, when someone uses the `su` command, either to become *root* or someone else, `su` logs the success or failure of this operation (this is often logged to the file *usr/adm/sulog* as well). These messages can be used to check for users sharing their passwords, as well as for a cracker who has penetrated one account and is trying to penetrate others.

The output from `syslog` is controlled via the file */etc/syslog.conf*. This file specifies where messages of various priorities are written. Each message has two components: a *facility*, such as *kern* for kernel messages, *auth* for the authorization system, *mail* for the mail system, etc., and a *priority*, such as *emerg* for emergency, *alert* for alerts, *err* for errors, *notice* for notification of non-critical events, and so on. The complete list is described in the manual page for *syslog.conf*.

An example *syslog.conf* file from the current (4.3BSD) version of `syslog` might look like

```
#
# Log all errors, authorization notices, and kernel debugging
# information to the console.
#
*.err;kern.debug;auth.notice;user.none          /dev/console

#
# Log all errors, all daemon messages, authorization notices, and
# critical mail messages to /usr/adm/messages.
#
*.err;kern.debug;daemon,auth.notice;mail.crit   /usr/adm/messages

#
# Send all alerts, kernel and daemon error messages to any terminal
# logged in as "operator".
#
*.alert;kern.err;daemon.err;user.none           operator

#
# Send all alerts to any terminal logged in as "root".
#
*.alert;user.none                               root

#
# Send emergency notices to everyone logged in.
#
*.emerg;user.none                               *

#
# Send authorization notices to the syslogd running on remotehost.
# for additional logging.
#
auth.notice                                     @remotehost
```

This shows several things that can be done with messages: they can be sent to a file, sent to anyone logged in as a specific user id, or sent to another `syslog` running on a remote system. This last is particularly useful, since individual workstations can be configured to send all "important" messages to a central system for logging, so that the system administrator can see them collected in a single place.

The `netstat` Command

The `netstat` command is used to examine various network tables stored by the operating system. This command can be executed periodically to check for suspicious activity.

Listing Active Connections

When given the `-a` option, `netstat` will display a list of all current network connections:

```
$ netstat -a
Active Internet connections (including servers)
Proto Recv-Q Send-Q  Local Address     Foreign Address     (state)
udp       0      0   *.chargen         *.*
udp       0      0   *.daytime         *.*
udp       0      0   *.discard         *.*
udp       0      0   *.echo            *.*
udp       0      0   *.time            *.*
udp       0      0   *.talk            *.*
udp       0      0   *.biff            *.*
.....
tcp       0      0   myhost.1020       host1.login         ESTABLISHED
tcp       0      0   myhost.1014       host2.login         ESTABLISHED
tcp       0      0   myhost.1018       host3.login         ESTABLISHED
tcp       0      0   myhost.1022       host2.login         ESTABLISHED
tcp       0      0   myhost.1009       host1.login         ESTABLISHED
tcp       0      0   myhost.1004       host1.login         ESTABLISHED
tcp       0      0   myhost.1007       host3.login         ESTABLISHED
tcp       0      0   myhost.1008       host4.shell         ESTABLISHED
tcp       0      0   myhost.1017       host2.shell         ESTABLISHED
tcp       0      0   myhost.1001       host5.shell         ESTABLISHED
tcp       0      0   *.chargen         *.*                 LISTEN
tcp       0      0   *.daytime         *.*                 LISTEN
tcp       0      0   *.discard         *.*                 LISTEN
tcp       0      0   *.echo            *.*                 LISTEN
tcp       0      0   *.time            *.*                 LISTEN
tcp       0      0   *.finger          *.*                 LISTEN
tcp       0      0   *.nntp            *.*                 LISTEN
tcp       0      0   *.uucp            *.*                 LISTEN
tcp       0      0   *.exec            *.*                 LISTEN
tcp       0      0   *.login           *.*                 LISTEN
tcp       0      0   *.shell           *.*                 LISTEN
tcp       0      0   *.printer         *.*                 LISTEN
```

```
tcp        0      0   *.telnet        *.*              LISTEN
tcp        0      0   *.ftp           *.*              LISTEN
.....
```

The "Local Address" part of the table shows the port number in use on the local machine. If the port number is listed in the file */etc/services*, its name is displayed in place of its number. The "Remote Address" column shows what systems and port numbers, if any, are connected to this port. The "(state)" column shows the state of TCP connections. ESTABLISHED means that a connection exists between the two ports. LISTEN means that the server on the local machine is waiting for connections on that port. In the UDP protocol there is no concept of a connection, so this column will be blank. Further, there is no way to determine with `netstat` what hosts are sending UDP packets to your host.

Displaying the Routing Table

When given the `-r` option, `netstat` displays a list of all known network routes:

```
$ netstat -r
Routing tables
Destination       Gateway      Flags   Refcnt  Use        Interface
localhost         localhost    UH      3       48411      lo0
default           gw           UG      3       67752      le0
some-remote-net   foo.bar.com  UG      2       26797      le0
my-local-net      myhost       U       40      19897805   le0
.....
```

In this output, each line shows the gateway used to get to a given destination. In the "Flags" column, a "U" indicates the gateway is up, a "D" indicates the route was obtained dynamically, a "G" indicates a gateway (i.e., a route to a network), and an "H" indicates a route to a host. The special destination *default* indicates where all traffic for which there is no other route will be sent. The names for networks in the "Destination" column are obtained from the file */etc/networks*. By maintaining this file carefully and listing all networks you might have a route to, and not listing any other networks, it becomes easy to use `netstat -r` to detect bogus routes—rather than displaying a network name, `netstat` will display the network number for any unknown network.

Logging FTP Connections

Most newer versions of `ftpd` can be given a `-l` option, telling it to log incoming connections via `syslog`. To implement this, the line for `ftpd` in */etc/inetd.conf* should be changed to read

```
ftp      stream tcp  nowait  root  /etc/ftpd      ftpd -l
```

and a line should be added to *letc/syslog.conf* that reads something like

```
daemon.info                            name-of-ftp-logfile
```

Monitoring Network Traffic

Several companies manufacture products to monitor network traffic at the packet level, such as the Sniffer™ from Network General and the Lanalyzer™ from Excelan. These systems are typically based on a personal computer of some sort, and plug directly into the Ethernet or other local area network. These systems watch every packet that is placed on the network, and decode the packets by source and destination address, source and destination port, protocol type, and so on.

Some UNIX vendors provide this capability as well, via packages such as the Network Interface Tap under SunOS, the Packetfilter under ULTRIX 4.*x*, and the Berkeley Packet Filter under 4.3.BSD-Reno These interfaces allow for programs such as `etherfind`, a SunOS program, and `tcpdump`, a freely available program. These programs monitor all packets on an Ethernet, subject to assorted restrictions such as source and destination hosts, source and destination ports, packet lengths, protocol types, and so on.

These hardware and software packages can be very useful in debugging a broken or overloaded network. They are marginally useful in a monitoring sense, in that while they are capable of detecting packets from unknown sources, the amount of spurious data produced while looking for these packets is so high as to make finding them difficult. These systems also present a security problem: if an attacker can either gain access to your network to plug in a packet monitor, or can gain access to a workstation and run `etherfind` or `tcpdump`, then he can easily watch all traffic on the network. This includes file transfers, passwords, and everything else. This is discussed further in Chapter 6.

4.10 Summary

This chapter has discussed the procedures for making your system more secure when it is connected to a TCP/IP network:

*   Check the *letc/hosts.equiv* file to ensure it only contains the names of local hosts.

*   Do not allow *.rhosts* files on the system, with the possible exception of *root*.

*   Do not allow *.netrc* files on the system.

*   Remove unnecessary services from the *letc/inetd.conf* file, and run the remaining services with as few privileges as possible. For example, `finger` can be run as *nobody* (or some other "regular" user) rather than as *root*.

- Check your version of FTP to be sure that it is secure.

- If you allow anonymous FTP, be sure it is set up properly.

- Check your version of TFTP to be sure that it is secure.

- Check your version of `sendmail` to be sure that it is secure.

- Check your versions of */bin/mail* and */bin/rmail* to be sure that they are secure.

- Check your version of `finger` to be sure that it is secure.

- Consider the use of a firewall system to protect your internal network from the outside world.

- Chapter 11 describes how to find out about newer versions of many of the programs described in this chapter, and where to obtain them. These sources should be consulted regularly so that you can obtain any fixes for security problems discovered in these programs.

Performing these tasks will make your system fairly secure from attacks over the network. However, as we have said repeatedly, no protection is foolproof, and you should be alert for any break-ins.

Chapter 5
NIS, NFS, and RFS

Most versions of UNIX today, especially those offered by workstation manufacturers, provide the ability to share files over a network via a network file system. Several vendors also offer a method to centrally maintain password files, host files, and other administrative databases. These software packages, while making the task of system administration much simpler, can also present several security problems if not configured correctly. In this chapter, we discuss the most common distributed name service, NIS, and the two most common network file systems, NFS and RFS.

5.1 The Network Information Service (NIS)

The Network Information Service (NIS) (Sun Microsystems, 1990) is a distributed name service that allows information to be stored on a single system and accessed from any host on the network. The information is stored in special files called *maps*. The contents of the maps are usually derived from files residing in the */etc* directory, for example, */etc/passwd*, */etc/group*, */etc/hosts*, and so on. An NIS *domain* shares a common set of maps. On a network running NIS, there is at least one server per domain that keeps a set of NIS maps for other hosts to access. Each domain has a name, and each host belongs to one domain. Those hosts that belong to the same domain share the same set of maps.

Prior to 1990, NIS was called Yellow Pages (YP) by Sun, and is still called by this name in many references (this is also why all the command names start with "yp"). The name was changed because Yellow Pages is a trademark in the United Kingdom.

There are two types of NIS servers. The *master* server maintains the master copy of the maps, and reconstructs them when information changes. There may only be one master server in each NIS domain, although a single host may be the master for more than one domain. A *slave* server obtains copies of the maps from the master server whenever their contents change. Typically there are two or three slave servers for each domain, so that service will not be interrupted when the master server machine is down. Each NIS server, master or slave, runs a process called `ypserv` that looks up information in the maps in response to network queries and returns the data.

NIS clients run processes that request data from the maps on the servers. A client does not care whether it obtains the data from the master or a slave server, since the data is the same on all servers. A client program obtains information from a server through the *binding process*, that does the following:

• The program running on the client asks a local process called `ypbind` for the name of an NIS server.

• The function of `ypbind` is to remember the network address of the `ypserv` processes running on the servers, and to keep track of their availability. It searches for a server that is responding, and returns this information to the client program.

• The client program sends its request directly to the NIS server.

• The `ypserv` process on the server takes the request, looks up the data in the maps, and returns the information to the client.

The purpose of all this is to allow a large number of hosts to access the same data without having to maintain the data files on each host. For example, to install an account on a hundred workstations without NIS would require editing the password file on each host. With NIS, the password file only needs to be edited on the NIS master server, and then every host can obtain the information through NIS.

The Password File

When configured to run under NIS, the password file, */etc/passwd*, contains a special line that tells programs to contact an NIS server for the information. This line looks like one of the following:

```
+::0:0:::
+:
```

For the purposes of this section, we will refer to this line as the *NIS password line*. When a program reads the password file to look up an account, it begins with the first line in the file and reads sequentially. If the program finds the information it is looking for before encountering the NIS password line, it will use the information it finds. Otherwise, if the NIS password line is encountered, all future reads from the file will actually be turned into NIS requests. Anything in the password file following the NIS password line will never be accessed. Therefore, the NIS password line should always be the last line in the file.

This procedure allows the system administrator to grant "network wide" accounts as well as "local" accounts. To give a user an account on all hosts in the NIS domain, a password file line for that user is placed in the password file on the NIS master host for that domain, where it can be accessed by all NIS clients in that domain. To give a user an account on only a single host, a password file line for that user is placed in the password file on the local host, before the NIS password line. When the local host attempts to look up the user, it will find his password file line in */etc/passwd*, and will use that data rather than contacting the NIS server. Any other host (where the user does not have an account) will not be able to find the line in the local password file, and will ask the NIS server for the data. Since the NIS server does not have the information, the lookup will fail.

Perhaps the biggest problem with an NIS-controlled password file is the format of the NIS password line itself. If the leading "+" is deleted from the line through careless editing, then the line becomes

```
::0:0:::
```

This is actually a valid password file line for an account with a null login name, no password, and user id zero (*root*). An attacker can simply log in with a null login name, and she will have super-user access to the system. For this reason, you should always use the second form of the NIS password line, shown below:

```
+:
```

If the "+" is accidentally deleted from this line, it does not become a valid password file line. Unfortunately, on most systems equipped with NIS, the `vipw` utility for editing the password file will rewrite this line in the older, unsafe format.

The Group File

Under NIS, the group file, */etc/group*, is maintained in much the same way as the password file. There may be some number of "local" lines in the file, followed by the *NIS group line*,

```
+:
```

Any line in the file following the NIS group line will never be accessed.

Since the NIS group line does not look like a "normal" group file line if the "+" is accidentally deleted, the precautions described above for the password file do not apply.

Other Files

The password and group files are special cases in NIS. These are the only two files that require a special line to turn control over to NIS. These two files and the mail aliases file (*/etc/aliases* or */usr/lib/aliases*) are the only files in which local information may be stored and accessed before NIS lookups take place.

There are several other files that are normally managed by NIS. These files are never accessed directly on an NIS client; they are accessed only through NIS. This means that changes made to these files on any host other than the NIS master will have no effect. Although the list may vary somewhat from vendor to vendor and version to version, the following files are the ones usually maintained by NIS (this list is for SunOS 4.1):

- */etc/aliases* (*/usr/lib/aliases*)
- */etc/bootparams*
- */etc/ethers*
- */etc/group*
- */etc/hosts*
- */etc/hosts.equiv*
- */etc/netgroup*
- */etc/networks*
- */etc/passwd*
- */etc/protocols*
- */etc/services*

Other NIS maps can be created by the system administrator and may contain whatever information is desired.

Netgroups

A *netgroup* is a group of users or hosts that can be used in several files controlled by NIS to grant or deny access to the users or hosts in the netgroup. Netgroups are defined in the file */etc/netgroup*, which is maintained as an NIS map.

Consider the following sample *netgroup* file:

```
ahosts          (hosta1,,) (hosta2,,) (hosta3,,)

bhosts          (hostb1,,) (hostb2,,) (hostb3,,)

staff           (,huey,) (,duey,) (,louie,)

allhosts        ahosts bhosts
```

This file defines four netgroups, called *ahosts*, *bhosts*, *staff*, and *allhosts*. The *allhosts* netgroup is actually a "super group" containing all the members of the *ahosts* and *bhosts* netgroups.

Each member of a netgroup is defined as a triple: (*host, user, domain*). Typically, the *domain* field is not used, and is simply left blank. If either the *host* or *user* field is left blank, then any host or user is considered a match. Thus the triple (*host,,*) matches any user on the named host, and the triple (*,user,*) matches the named user on any host.

Netgroups in the Password File

Netgroups can be used in the password file to grant or deny access to a given set of users. For example, if the password file contains the line

```
+@staff:
```

then *huey*, *duey*, and *louie* may log in to the host. This mechanism can be used in place of the NIS password line to grant access to only a subset of users rather than all users in the NIS password file map.

Alternatively, netgroups can also be used to deny access to a given set of users. If the password file contains the lines

```
-@staff:
+:
```

then all users in the NIS password file map **except** *huey*, *duey*, and *louie* may log in to the host.

It should be noted that in many NIS implementations, the "+@" and "-@" constructs do not work correctly; you should verify their behavior on your system before using them.

Netgroups in *hosts.equiv*

As described in Chapter 4, the file */etc/hosts.equiv* contains a list of host names (and optionally user names) that may have remote access to a host without a password. This file can also be controlled using netgroups.

If the */etc/hosts.equiv* file contains lines such as

```
+@ahosts
-@bhosts
```

then users from *hosta1*, *hosta2*, and *hosta3* will be allowed to access the local host without passwords, while users from *hostb1*, *hostb2*, and *hostb3* will be denied access without a password (but they may still log in after providing a password).

In a more complicated example, the lines

```
+@ahosts +@staff
+@bhosts -@staff
```

can be used. The first line specifies that *huey*, *duey*, and *louie* may access the local host without a password if they are coming from *hosta1*, *hosta2*, or *hosta3*. The second line says that all users from *hostb1*, *hostb2*, and *hostb3* **except** *huey*, *duey*, and *louie* may access the local host without a password. Other combinations are possible as well; they are described in detail in the *hosts.equiv* manual page on your system. (It should be noted that the "+@" and "-@" syntax is broken in many versions of NIS; be sure to verify the behavior of your system before trusting this mechanism.)

There is one major security problem with NIS control of the *hosts.equiv* file that was mentioned in Chapter 4 and deserves to be mentioned again here. If the file contains the line

    +

then users from **any** host anywhere on the network (including hosts outside your organization if you are connected to a wide-area network) may access the local host without a password. This means that if the local host has a user named *joe*, any user named *joe* on any host that can reach yours over the network may log in as *joe* on the local host without a password. Except in very special cases, such as when the local network is not connected to any other networks and all other systems on the local net are trusted, the line shown above should **never** be used in *hosts.equiv*. Unfortunately, some vendors' installation procedures, including Sun's, install a *hosts.equiv* file with just such a line.

The ypset Command

The ypset command can be used to tell ypbind (the process that returns the location of the NIS server) which host should be used as the server for a given NIS domain. The command

    # **ypset -d** *domainname hostname*

tells the local ypbind process that any requests for information in the NIS domain *domainname* should be sent to the host *hostname*. The command

    # **ypset -h** *host1* **-d** *domainname host2*

can be used to tell the remote ypbind process on *host1* that requests for domain *domainname* should be sent to *host2*.

The primary purposes of ypset are to allow hosts that are not on a network with an NIS server to use NIS, and to allow debugging. However, ypset also presents a security problem, since it can be used to substitute a "bogus" NIS server for an "official" one. The remedy for this problem is described in the next section.

Known Security Problems

There are several known security problems with NIS, most of which are easily remedied. This section describes the known security problems and how to eliminate them.

As mentioned previously, many systems that run NIS have a */etc/hosts.equiv* file installed that contains a single line:

    +

This line should be deleted, as it grants "trusted" access to all hosts on the network.

Also mentioned previously, the NIS password line that looks like

```
+::0:0:::
```

can be dangerous if the "+" is accidentally deleted. This line should be replaced with one that looks like

```
+:
```

which will not become a valid password file line if the "+" is deleted.

Some versions of the NIS map-building procedure on the NIS server leave the maps world-writable. This means that anyone can change the contents of the maps to return whatever information he desires (for example, the password for *root* could be changed). The file *Makefile* in (usually) */usr/etc/yp* or */var/spool/yp* should be checked and, if necessary, modified to use the chmod command to make these maps read-only (mode 444).

As mentioned above, the ypset command can be used to tell ypbind what host to obtain information from for a specific NIS domain. This is valuable for debugging purposes, but can be a security problem if an attacker can tell ypbind to obtain the information from a server of her choosing (where she can modify the maps). Most newer versions of ypbind will not listen to a locally-issued ypset command unless the -ypset option is given on the command line when they are started. They will not listen to a remotely-issued ypset command (one with the -h option) unless the -ypsetme option is given on the command line when they are started. You should check your system startup files to ensure that ypbind is **not** started with these options.

5.2 The Network File System (NFS)

The Network File System (NFS) (Sun Microsystems, 1990) is designed to allow hosts to share files over the network. One of the most common uses of NFS is to allow disk-less workstations to be installed in offices, while keeping all disk storage in a central location. File systems are mounted across the network, making them appear as if they are on a local disk when in fact they are stored on a different host. As distributed by most vendors, NFS has no security features enabled. This means that any host on the network may access your files via NFS, regardless of whether you trust them or not.

Fortunately, there are several easy ways to make NFS more secure. The more commonly used methods are described in this section, and these can be used to make your files quite secure from unauthorized access via NFS. Secure NFS, introduced in SunOS 4.0, takes security a step further, by using public- and private-key encryption techniques to ensure authorized access. Unfortunately, secure NFS has not solved the key management problem (storing keys where they cannot be accessed illicitly) very well, meaning that it is only secure if each and every user is very careful with his key.

The *exports* File

The file */etc/exports* is perhaps the most important part of NFS configuration. This file lists which file systems are *exported* (made available for mounting via NFS) to other systems. This section describes the usual *exports* file format as used by most vendors' implementations, including Sun versions prior to SunOS 4.0. The formats used by SunOS 4.*x* and System V Release 4 are described afterward.

A line in the *exports* file contains the name of a file system to be exported and a list of hosts that may mount it. If no hosts are listed, then any host may mount the file system. Because it may be tedious to list each host individually, netgroups (described earlier) may be used instead of individual host names. For example, consider the *exports* file below:

```
/
/usr            hosta1 hosta2 hosta3
/usr/local      bhosts hostc1
```

This file indicates the the root file system (/) may be mounted by any host on the network, since no hosts are listed on the line. The */usr* file system may be mounted by *hosta1*, *hosta2*, and *hosta3*, but access will be denied for any other host. The */usr/local* file system may be mounted by any host in the *bhosts* netgroup (see the sample *netgroup* file above) and by *hostc1*.

Because the default behavior when no hosts are listed is to make a file system available to any host, NFS is very insecure when not configured properly. Most vendor installation procedures will create this file with no hosts or netgroups listed, making all file systems available to all hosts. You should always specify exactly which hosts are allowed to mount a given file system; if nothing else, simply create a single netgroup with all local hosts in it and use the name of the netgroup on each file system listed in the *exports* file.

The SunOS 4.x *exports* File

The format of */etc/exports* was changed in SunOS 4.0 to allow file system access to be more finely controlled. Instead of simply listing hosts and netgroups on each line with a file system, a series of options may be specified using the format

> *filesystem*   −*option*, *option*, . . .

As with the older format, if no options are specified, the file system is exported read-write to all hosts on the network. The options are

> ro Export this file system read-only. Hosts may mount it and read files, but may not modify them.

> rw=*host*:*host*: . . . Export the file system read-mostly. The file system will be exported read-only to most hosts, but the hosts listed will have read-write access. If no hosts are listed, all hosts will have read-write access (the default).

access=*host*:*host*: ... Only give access to the named hosts. This is the equivalent of specifying host names on the line in the older file format. Because listing all hosts may be tedious, netgroups may also be used.

Consider the following sample *exports* file:

```
/
/usr            -ro,access=ahosts
/usr/local      -access=bhosts:hostc1
```

This specifies that the root file system (/) may be mounted by any host. The */usr* file system may be mounted by hosts in the *ahosts* netgroup, but with read-only permission. The */usr/local* file system may be mounted read-write (the default) by any host in the *bhosts* netgroup, as well as by *hostc1*.

As mentioned above, because the default behavior when no -access option is given is to make a file system available to any host, NFS is very insecure when not configured properly. The Sun installation procedure will create this file with no hosts or netgroups listed, making the entire system available to all hosts. You should always specify exactly which hosts are allowed to mount a given file system; if nothing else, simply create a single netgroup with all local hosts in it and use the name of the netgroup with a -access option on every file system in the *exports* file.

Whenever you make changes to the *exports* file under SunOS 4.*x*, you should run the command

 # exportfs -a

to make these changes take effect.

The System V Release 4 *dfstab* File

The System V Release 4 version of NFS (AT&T, 1990b) has been modified to work in conjunction with RFS (see section 5.3). This modification entailed merging the commands and files used by the two packages into a single set of commands and configuration files.

Instead of using a */etc/exports* file, System V Release 4 uses a file called */etc/dfs/dfstab*. This file contains lines of the form

```
share -F nfs -o specific-options pathname
```

Where *pathname* is the name of the directory to be exported, and *specific-options* is a comma-separated list of options, as follows:

ro Export this file system read-only. Hosts may mount it and read files, but may not modify them.

rw=*host*:*host*: ... Export the file system read-mostly. The file system will be exported read-only to most hosts, but the hosts listed will have read-write access. If no hosts are listed, all hosts will have read-write access (the default).

access=*host*:*host*: . . . Only give access to the named hosts. Because System
V Release 4 does not use NIS, netgroups are not meaningful in this list.

After modifying the */etc/dfs/dfstab* file, the command

```
# shareall -F nfs
```

should be executed to make the changes take effect.

Restricting Super-User Access

Under most implementations of NFS, the super-user (user id 0) is not allowed to have
unrestricted access to file systems through NFS. This is implemented by transparently
changing the user id of any NFS request issued by *root* to the special user id *nobody*,
which is usually either −2 (older systems) or 65534 (newer systems). This means that
if an attacker is able to gain super-user permissions on a client workstation, he will not
be able to read any files mounted through NFS that he would not be able to read if he
were any other user. The only way to change this behavior such that the super-user can
access files is to patch a kernel variable using the debugger.

Unfortunately, while this behavior is generally a good thing from a security standpoint, there are occasions where allowing the super-user to access files through NFS is
desirable. In SunOS 4.0, NFS was modified to allow this. Two other options that can
be used in the exports file are

   root=*host*:*host*: . . .   Allow super-user access from the named hosts. Net-
      groups may not be used in this list, and a maximum of ten hosts may be
      specified.

   anon=*uid*   Treat accesses from unknown users as if they came from user id
      uid. By default, the NFS server considers super-user accesses to be
      unknown, and the default value for *uid* is −2 (65534) as described above.
      By setting *uid* to 0, super-user access can be allowed for all hosts permit-
      ted to mount the file system.

These options may also be specified to the share command under System V
Release 4.

For reasons that will be described in the next chapter, super-user access should in
general not be allowed through NFS. If you must grant super-user access, it is usually
preferable to do so on a host-by-host basis using the −root option, rather than by
doing so on a wholesale basis by using the −anon option.

Handling Set-User-Id and Set-Group-Id Programs

As described in Chapter 3, set-user-id and set-group-id programs can present a security
problem because they grant special privileges to the user executing them. Under
SunOS 4.*x* and System V Release 4, a special option has been added to the mount

command that allows you to modify the behavior of set-user-id and set-group-id programs.

The general form of the mount command is

```
# mount -o options filesystem mountpoint
```

where *options* is a comma-separated list of options. One of these options, nosuid, indicates that set-user-id and set-group-id bits on programs in this file system should be ignored. In other words, if a user executes a set-user-id or set-group-id program stored on this file system, it will *not* execute with any special permissions. This option may also be specified in the list of file systems to be mounted automatically at system startup time (*/etc/fstab* on SunOS, */etc/vfstab* on System V Release 4).

In order to protect your system from unauthorized set-user-id and set-group-id programs, it is recommended that you mount all file systems with the nosuid option, except those file systems that contain "approved" (and necessary) programs. Generally, this means that all file systems except */*, */usr*, and perhaps */usr/local* should be mounted with the nosuid option.

Monitoring NFS Security

Most vendors do not provide many commands to monitor NFS security. In general, security is left to the *exports* file, which specifies which hosts have access, and it is assumed that whatever those hosts do is "acceptable."

The showmount Command

The showmount command can be used on an NFS file server to display the names of all hosts that currently have something mounted from the server. With no options, the program simply displays a list of all the hosts. With the −a and −d options, the output is somewhat more useful. The first option, −a, causes showmount to list the hosts along with the directories they have mounted. For example,

```
$ showmount -a
hosta1:/usr
hosta1:/usr/local
hosta2:/usr
hosta3:/home
```

There will be one line of output for each directory mounted by a host. With the −d option, showmount will display a list of directories that are mounted by some host.

The output from showmount should be checked for two things. First, only machines local to your organization should appear there. If you have set up your *exports* file correctly, this should not be a problem. Second, only "normal" directories should be mounted. If you find unusual directories being mounted, you should find out who is mounting them and why—although it is probably innocent, it may indicate someone trying to subvert your security mechanisms.

The `showmount` command also has a `-e` option, which can be used to obtain a list of all file systems exported by the server. If the exports are restricted with netgroups or host names, this information is also displayed.

Under System V Release 4, `showmount` has been renamed `dfmounts`, and the output has been modified slightly. With no arguments (or with just the `-F nfs` argument), `dfmounts` will display a list similar to that shown by `showmount`. If an optional server name is specified, `dfmounts` will display a list for that server instead of the local host.

The `nfswatch` Command

The `nfswatch` command, available from the public source archive sites described in Chapter 11, can be used to monitor NFS traffic on a network. Although primarily intended for debugging, `nfswatch` is capable of displaying a list of file systems and which hosts are accessing them. This information can be useful for tracking an attacker attempting to access data through NFS.

Many commercially available packet monitoring systems are also capable of monitoring NFS traffic in much the same way that `nfswatch` does.

5.3 The Remote File Sharing Service (RFS)

The Remote File Sharing Service (RFS) (AT&T, 1990b) is an alternative to NFS first introduced in System V Release 3. It is typically found only on System V-based systems, although SunOS 4.1 also supports it. Unlike NFS, which provides a "generic" file system with most (but not all) of the properties of a UNIX file system, RFS provides an exact copy of a UNIX file system. Although this means that RFS is restricted to UNIX systems (unlike NFS, which can be implemented on almost any operating system), it also means that RFS can provide some things that NFS cannot, such as access to remote devices like tape drives, line printers, and named pipes.

RFS groups hosts into *domains* for the purposes of mounting file systems. These domains are similar to (but not the same as) NIS domains. Each domain will have a primary name server and zero or more secondary name servers. Note that these name servers have nothing to do with the Internet Domain Name Servers described in Chapter 4. Rather, these name servers maintain a list of servers and resources. When a client machine requests a resource to mount (e.g., a file system), one of the name servers responds to the client, telling it where to get that resource.

There are four levels of security that allow you to protect your RFS resources:

• Connect security

• Mount security

• User and group mapping

• Regular UNIX file permissions

These are described in the following sections. The commands described in the following sections pertain to the System V Release 4 version of RFS. This description also applies, with minor differences, to System V Release 3 systems. The differences between the System V version of RFS and the version supplied with SunOS 4.1 are described in the section "SunOS 4.1 RFS."

Connect Security

When a remote host tries to mount its first resource from your system via RFS, it tries to set up a connection to your host via the network. Once this connection has been set up, any resource you have made available for mounting can be mounted by that host. By default, any host is allowed to make this network connection. However, you can restrict access to a given set of machines by using the RFS verification procedure. This procedure requires each remote host to specify a password before being allowed to connect to your host.

To set up RFS verification, use the command

```
# rfadmin -a domainname.hostname
Enter password for hostname:
Re-enter password for hostname:
```

for each host *hostname* in the domain *domainname*. This command will prompt you for a password that the system administrator for *hostname* must provide each time his system makes an initial mount request to your system. If the password provided is incorrect, the connection request will be refused.

By default, RFS will check passwords on connection requests only for those hosts for which you have provided a password. If a password has not been provided for a given host, that host will be allowed to connect to your host with no password check. To change this, you should modify your system RFS startup script (invoked in init run-level 3) to issue the command

```
rfstart -v
```

This will tell RFS to deny connection requests from any host that has not been given a password, as well as from any host that specifies an incorrect password.

Mount Security

Once a connection has been established between your host and a remote host, the remote host may mount any file system that you have made available. This is done with the `share` command. The format of a `share` command is as follows:

```
share -F rfs -o specific-options -d description pathname
```

where *pathname* is the name of the directory to be exported, *description* is a short description of the resource (optional), and *specific-options* is a comma-separated list of options, as follows:

`ro` Export this file system read-only. Hosts may mount it and read files, but may not modify them.

`rw=`*host*`:`*host*`: . . .` Export the file system read-mostly. The file system will be exported read-only to most hosts, but the hosts listed will have read-write access. If no hosts are listed, all hosts will have read-write access (the default).

`access=`*host*`:`*host*`: . . .` Only give access to the named hosts. Hosts not in this list will not be permitted to mount this resource.

To automatically make file systems available at system startup time, `share` commands may be placed in the file */etc/dfs/dfstab*.

User and Group Mapping

Unlike NFS, in which user and group ids (except that of the super-user) are passed "straight through," RFS by default maps all users to a special guest user id. This provides the maximum level of security for your resources, since no user will have any special permissions. Unfortunately, it also tends to make the system rather unusable, since users may not even be able to access their own files. For this reason, RFS allows a sophisticated means of *mapping* remote user and group ids.

User and group id mappings are created by editing the files *uid.rules* and *gid.rules* in the directory */etc/rfs/auth.info*. Both of these files have the same format, and allow you to set up global rules (rules that apply to all users on all hosts that do not have host-specific mappings) as well as host-specific rules. The following procedures should be used to define a global mapping:

1. The global block must begin with the keyword `global` on a line by itself.

2. If you wish to specify a default mapping for all users, add a `default` line. This line may look like either

   ```
   default transparent
   ```

   or

   ```
   default local
   ```

   The `default transparent` line indicates that each remote user id will have the permissions of the same user id on the local system (as with NFS). In the `default` *local* line, *local* is replaced with a local user id or login name, and indicates that any remote users not otherwise mapped will have the permissions of the *local* user on your system.

3. Certain users may be excluded from the default mapping defined above by using a line of the form

   ```
   exclude range
   ```

where *range* is either a single user id (e.g., 0), or a range of user ids (e.g., 0-100). For example, to exclude the remote super-user from a `transparent` mapping (thus prohibiting remote super-user access), the line

```
exclude 0
```

would be used.

4.　Specific user ids and login names may be mapped to other user ids and login names by using the `map` command. This command may take one of two forms:

```
map remote:local
```

or

```
map remote
```

In the first form, the remote user id *remote* is mapped into the local user id *local*. For example, the line

```
map 0:nobody
```

could be used to emulate the super-user mapping performed by NFS. The second form of the command says that the remote user id *remote* should be mapped to the same user id on the local system.

Mappings for specific hosts are set up in much the same way, except that instead of a `global` line, a line of the form

```
host domainname.hostname
```

is used. The *gid.rules* file is constructed in a similar fashion, except that group ids are used instead of user ids. After editing either the *uid.rules* or *gid.rules* files, you should execute the `idload` command to make your changes take effect.

If you use login or group names (as opposed to numeric id numbers) in the *uid.rules* or *gid.rules* files, you must place copies of the */etc/passwd* and */etc/group* files from the remote systems into directories named */etc/rfs/auth.info/domainname/hostname* for each host. Because keeping these files up to date is difficult (you must update them each time they are changed), it is recommended that you use only numeric ids when constructing your mapping rules.

Monitoring RFS Security

Several commands can help you monitor the security of your RFS system.

The `idload` Command

When run with the `-k` option, the `idload` command displays the current user and group mappings in effect. The output from this command looks like:

```
# idload -k
TYPE   MACHINE        REM_ID    REM_NAME    LOC_ID        LOC_NAME

USR    GLOBAL         DEFAULT   n/a         1000          n/a
USR    GLOBAL         0         n/a         60001         guest_id
USR    mydom.hosta    DEFAULT   n/a         transparent   n/a
USR    mydom.hosta    0         n/a         60001         guest_id
USR    mydom.hostb    DEFAULT   n/a         60001         guest_id
USR    mydom.hostb    0         n/a         100           n/a

GRP    GLOBAL         DEFAULT   n/a         60001         guest_id
```

Note that only rules for systems that currently have remote resources mounted will be displayed.

The `dfshares` Command

The `dfshares` command can be used by any user, and will display a list of all resources in the domain that are available for mounting via RFS, the servers that are offering them, and the access mode (read-only, read-write) at which they are offered. The `dfshares` command does **not** indicate, however, whether the local host has permission to mount each resource.

The `dfmounts` Command

The `dfmounts` command displays a list of the remote hosts that have resources mounted from your system. For each resource, the path it is mounted on and the names of all clients that have it mounted are displayed.

SunOS 4.1 RFS

The version of RFS supplied with SunOS 4.1 (Sun Microsystems, 1990) is based on the version supplied with System V Release 3. It is maintained in a manner similar to that described above, with the following differences:

- The `nsquery` command is used to obtain a list of available resources, rather than the `dfshares` command.

- The `rmntstat` command is used to obtain a list of remote hosts that have resources mounted, rather than the `dfmounts` command.

- Instead of the `share` command, SunOS 4.1 uses the `adv` (advertise) command. The `-o` option for specifying options is not supported. Instead, client host names may be specified on the command line to restrict mounting to those clients, and the `-r` option may be used to specify read-only access. To advertise resources automatically at system startup time, `adv` commands are placed in the file *etc/rstab*.

- All files pertaining to RFS are stored in the */usr/nserve* directory instead of the */etc/rfs* directory.

- Instead of using the `rfstart -v` command to enable connect security, the command

      # **dorfs start -v**

  is used.

- The `-k` option to `idload` is not supported.

5.4 Summary

In this chapter we described the procedures used to make NIS, NFS, and RFS more secure:

- Use "`+:`" instead of "`+::0:0:::`" in the password file when running NIS.

- Be sure that the NIS map files are writable only by the super-user.

- Use the `-access` option on all file systems in the *exports* (or `dfstab`) file when running NFS.

- Wherever possible, use the `nosuid` option when mounting NFS file systems.

- When running RFS, use the `-access` option on all `share` commands.

- Implement user id and group id mappings when running RFS.

By using these procedures you can assure yourself that your system is more secure from attack over the network. However, you should as always remain alert for break-ins.

Chapter 6
Workstations

Back in the "olden days" of computing (say, the early 1980s), most users shared the same large computer, using some type of character-oriented terminal such as a VT-100. This was convenient, in that the system console (and the system itself) could be locked away in the computer room where only authorized personnel could access it. Nowadays, most users access the system through desktop workstations. This means that each user has her very own UNIX system—computer, console, and all—right on her desk. Each user can access her own system through its console, allowing her to reboot the system, turn it on and off, and so on.

There are several ways for an attacker to gain access to your system if he can obtain access to the system console. Because the console is no longer locked away in the computer room but instead resides on each user's desk, gaining access to the console is not very difficult. If the attacker can obtain privileged access to a single workstation, it is then a simple task to break into other workstations on the same network. This chapter discusses methods to protect workstations and the network from this type of abuse.

6.1 Single-User Mode

There are two modes of operation for most UNIX systems, called *single-user* and *multi-user*. In the usual mode of operation, multi-user, all system services (printing, remote login, mail, etc.) are running, and any user may access the system through a terminal, modem, or network connection. Single-user mode is for use by the system administrator when repairing the system after a crash, backing the system up to tape, or installing new hardware and software. When the system is in single-user mode, most system services are not operational, and the system may only be accessed from the system console. When a UNIX system is booted in single-user mode (or taken from multi-user to single-user), a shell is started on the system console. This shell has all the privileges associated with a super-user login. On many UNIX systems, the *root* password is not required before this shell is started, meaning that if an attacker has access to the system console and can place the system in single-user mode, he can gain super-user access to the system without providing a password.

Most workstations use the attached monitor and keyboard as the system console. They typically provide some special key sequence to allow the system to be stopped and rebooted. For example, on a Sun workstation, the special key sequence L1-A followed by one of the commands

> `> b -s`

or

> `ok boot -s`

is used to reboot the system in single-user mode. Workstations from other vendors, as well as many larger "computer room" systems, have similar sequences.

Fortunately, most vendors are aware of the security problems presented by this feature, and have modified UNIX to deal with the problem. The type of modification varies from vendor to vendor, but usually falls into one of three categories, summarized in the following paragraphs.

Use `su` instead of `sh`.   One of the simplest methods is to modify the `init` program, which is responsible for starting the system and running the /etc/rc files, to start up a copy of `su` instead of `sh` when coming into single-user mode. The `su` program then prompts for the *root* password, and if it is entered correctly, starts a shell. This approach is taken on most System V Release 3.*x* systems and their derivatives, such as HP-UX 7.*x*. It is also used in System V Release 4.

Modify the `init` process.   Some vendors have modified the `init` program directly, making it prompt for the super-user password before starting the shell. This tends to be a slightly cleaner approach in the sense that it does not rely on another program to perform the task (since the program may not exist on a badly damaged file system), although the difference is minimal. This approach is taken in SunOS 4.*x*.

Do nothing.   Still other systems, particularly those based on 4.*x* BSD, do not make any effort to prompt for a password when coming up in single-user mode. For sites running true Berkeley UNIX this is often not a major problem, since the source code is available and can be modified. But for vendor-supplied versions of the operating system, source is not usually available. There are still ways to get around the problem, however. One of the simplest ways is to use a debugger or binary file editor to patch the string "/bin/sh" in the `init` program to read "/bin/su". This can be dangerous however, since some versions of `su` do not do "the right thing" if the password file has been damaged or deleted when the system crashed. Another of the methods involves modifying the file /etc/rc (or one of its relations, such as /etc/rc.single) to execute either the `su` or `login` programs when coming up in single-user mode, which forces the user to enter the password before proceeding. This method is error-prone, since it is often possible to interrupt out of the boot sequence in such a way that this execution is bypassed.

6.2 Super-User Access

Super-user access to workstations can be problematic, since the super-user can modify any file on the system. If the workstation has its own disks, this means that an attacker who gains super-user access can modify any command on the disk, replacing it with a Trojan horse. If user files are also stored on local disks, the attacker can read, modify, and delete these files as well. To some extent though, this is an old problem—it exists on all UNIX systems, not just workstation systems.

The real workstation security problem lies with those systems that obtain their data via NFS or RFS. Although it is possible to configure both NFS and RFS to disallow *root* access to most file systems, a truly diskless workstation (one with no disks at all) will still require at least some *root* access, namely to its own root file system. Many sites also allow some workstations (usually those used by the system administrators) to have super-user access to network file systems. This means that an attacker who can gain super-user access to a desktop workstation that mounts file systems via the network with *root* access enabled (e.g., by booting it in single-user mode) can create a file on another machine (the server) without having super-user access to that machine.

Illicit Devices

One of the principal problems in this regard is that the super-user is allowed to create special device files. Recall from Chapter 3 that there is no requirement that device files reside in the /*dev* directory; they may reside anywhere in the file system. Most normal system devices are read- and write-protected so that only authorized users may access them. However, consider an attacker who has gained super-user access to a desktop workstation that has *root* access to some server's file system. The attacker can create her **own** device, using the mknod command, in the network file system mounted on this workstation. She can also make the permissions on this device anything she desires so that she can log into the server system (using any account she has broken into) and read that device without super-user permissions. Since device files are interpreted on the local system, this means that by creating the device file on a remote workstation, the attacker has gained access to the server system's device through this file, even though the "real" device file may still be read- and write-protected.

One of the simplest ways to prevent an attacker from doing this is to first protect all workstation consoles by making the system prompt for the *root* password whenever it enters single-user mode; this procedure is described in Chapter 7. Second, publicly accessible workstations should not be allowed to mount any file systems via NFS or RFS with *root* access enabled. Unfortunately, truly diskless workstations such as those supported by SunOS 4.*x* and System V Release 4 **must** have *root* access enabled on their root file systems. These directories are usually stored on the file server in the /*export*/*root* directory. In order to prevent an attacker from using these file systems as described above, any directory on the server that contains diskless workstation root partitions should be made accessible only to the super-user:

```
# chmod 700 /export/root
```

Although an attacker will still be able to create devices in this area, he will not be able to access them from the server.

Operating as Other Users

The biggest problem with super-user access though, is the fact that the super-user can become any other user (by using the su command) **without** providing a password. This means that in the case of workstations that mount file systems through NFS or RFS, even protecting the file systems by mounting them with *root* access disabled is not enough. If an attacker can obtain super-user access to a single system, she can issue the command

```
# su username
```

to become the user *username* and read, write, or delete *username*'s files. Unfortunately, other than carefully protecting the workstation from illicit *root* access, there is no way to defend against this.

6.3 Network Access

Most networks used in workstation environments send their data in the clear, that is, it is not encrypted. This means that any host connected to the network that has the ability to watch all network traffic (as opposed to only the traffic destined to itself) can be used to steal information from the network. Most workstations and personal computers are capable of watching all traffic on the network, and in fact a great deal of software exists for just such a purpose.

Stealing Information from the Network

The Network Interface Tap (NIT) on SunOS, the Packetfilter on ULTRIX, and the Berkeley Packet Filter (BPF) on 4.*x* BSD systems are all special programming interfaces that allow a program to intercept any or all network traffic. The etherfind program provided with SunOS and the similar tcpdump program available from several source archive sites are perfect examples of programs explicitly designed to take information off the network. Of course, the real purpose of these programs and interfaces is to allow a system administrator to monitor network performance and debug network problems. However, they can also be used by an attacker to intercept information such as passwords (sent at the start of login sessions) or the contents of files (as sent by NFS and RFS). As an example, consider the following example use of tcpdump:

```
# tcpdump -x -q dst host hostb and dst port login
18:59:03.273163 hosta.my.dom.1021 > hostb.my.dom.login: tcp 0
                4500 002c 1dec 0000 3c06 5844 8012 0427
                8012 0451 03fd 0201 359d 9600 0000 0000
                6002 1000 adee 0000 0204 05b4 0000
18:59:03.276579 hosta.my.dom.1021 > hostb.my.dom.login: tcp 0
                4500 0028 1ded 0000 3c06 5847 8012 0427
                8012 0451 03fd 0201 359d 9601 355f 162c
                5010 1000 7a10 0000 bffc 8090 0017
18:59:03.280703 hosta.my.dom.1021 > hostb.my.dom.login: tcp 1
                4500 0029 1df0 0000 3c06 5843 8012 0427
                8012 0451 03fd 0201 359d 9601 355f 162c
                5018 1000 7a07 0000 00fc 8090 0017
[.....]

18:59:03.700280 hosta.my.dom.1021 > hostb.my.dom.login: tcp 12
                4500 0034 1e6d 0000 3c06 57bb 8012 0427
                8012 0451 03fd 0201 359d 9617 355f 162f
                5018 1000 05fd 0000 ffff 7373 0023 0050
                0000 0000
[.....]

18:59:05.403451 hosta.my.dom.1021 > hostb.my.dom.login: tcp 1
                4500 0029 1fbf 0000 3c06 5674 8012 0427
                8012 0451 03fd 0201 359d 9626 355f 1639
                5018 1000 35d5 0000 4400 0204 05b4
[.....]
```

In this example, we tell tcpdump to print out all packets destined for the *login* port (used by the rlogin program) on host *hostb*. In this particular example we see the beginning of a connection (i.e., someone on *hosta* has typed rlogin hostb), which would normally include the user's login name and password. The output from tcpdump is in hexadecimal and includes header information from the TCP packets used by rlogin, but with a little work this can easily be deciphered into useful information by an attacker.

Network Spoofing

Another problem with networks of workstations is *network spoofing*, which was described in Chapter 4. Network spoofing involves using one host on the network to impersonate another host, either for the purposes of intercepting information destined for the impersonated host or for providing bogus information requested from the impersonated host. On most workstations the facilities used in this sort of attack are the same as those used to monitor the network, since the interfaces are often bidirectional. However, programs are not generally available to perform network spoofing and must be developed from scratch. The sophisticated nature of this task may place it beyond the abilities of most attackers.

Defenses

Defending against these sorts of attacks is difficult, since by their very nature workstations require network access. Although in most environments it is unlikely that an attacker will be able to connect his own machine to the network, this is often unnecessary since he can simply break into an existing host and then use the facilities it provides for such access. Some facilities such as Sun Microsystems' Network Interface Tap and Digital Equipment Corporation's Packetfilter require super-user access to be used effectively, while others such as the Berkeley Packet Filter will allow any user to make use of them subject to permissions on a device file.

Most vendors whose systems provide access to the network through a UNIX device file allow this ability to be configured into (or out of) the kernel via a configuration option. Sun uses the lines

```
pseudo-device    snit          # streams NIT
pseudo-device    pf            # packet filter
pseudo-device    nbuf          # NIT buffering module
```

in SunOS 4.x configuration files, and the line

```
options          NIT
```

in SunOS 3.x configuration files. This option is enabled by default, and a new kernel must be built in order to disable it. Digital Equipment uses the line

```
options PACKETFILTER
```

in ULTRIX 4.x kernels. This option is disabled by default, and a new kernel must be built in order to enable it. The Berkeley Packet Filter is enabled using the line

```
pseudo-device    bpfilter 16
```

in the configuration file. This option is also disabled by default (since the BPF was released after 4.3 BSD), and a new kernel must be built in order to enable it. By placing kernels without network monitoring capabilities on all workstations that do not require the capability, and by not installing the files required to build new kernels, much of the problems these features present can be avoided.

6.4 The PROM Monitor

One additional feature provided by most workstations is a PROM monitor. This monitor is entered when a special keyboard sequence is typed (such as L1-A on a Sun), when the system is shut down, and when the machine is initially turned on. One of the commands provided by all PROM monitors is the one to boot the operating system. But most PROM monitors also provide other commands that allow the user to examine and change memory contents, configure boot devices and other hardware, perform hardware diagnostics, and so on. Some PROM monitors provide the ability to continue the system where it left off when the monitor was first entered (via a keyboard sequence).

This last ability, to enter the PROM monitor while UNIX is running, examine and change memory, and then continue the system where it left off, presents a serious security problem. One of the things stored in memory when UNIX is running is the effective user id of each user (and hence each process). If an attacker can figure out **where** in memory this information is stored, and then change it, she can become the super-user even if other avenues (such as single-user booting) are protected.

Defending against this attack is extremely difficult. If you have a complete source license, it may be possible to modify the code for the PROM monitor and then make new PROMs for each workstation. Even if this is possible, it is extremely time-consuming, as well as very expensive. Some vendors provide a password that can be set in the PROM monitor, and then require this password to be entered to gain access to the commands that allow memory to be examined or changed, but these are few and far between, and often are an added-cost option.

The OPENPROM EEPROM monitor on Sun SPARCstation systems is one of the few that allows a password to be specified. The EEPROM variable `security-password` is used to store the password; this may be set either from the monitor using the `setenv` command, or from UNIX using the `eeprom` command. The EEPROM variable `security-mode` can be set to one of three values: `none`, indicating that no security is enabled, `command`, indicating that all commands other than "b" (boot) and "c" (continue) require a password, or `full`, indicating that only the "c" command may be entered; even booting requires a password.

6.5 Screen Access

A final security problem presented by workstations is one of access to the screen. Most workstations provide some sort of monochrome or color *frame buffer*, which is special memory that contains the entire contents of the screen. They also provide, either directly or through the auspices of a window system, a method to obtain the current contents of the frame buffer and place them into a file. The intent of this mechanism is to allow the contents of the screen to be sent to a printer.

There are two primary methods of obtaining the screen contents. The first, and most basic, is a program that reads the frame buffer directly, dumping its contents to a file. The advantage of this method is that it works regardless of whether or not a window system is in use. The problem is that any user who can log in to the workstation (via `rlogin` or whatever) can execute the program to obtain a copy of the screen, allowing him to "steal" the contents of another user's screen. For example, on a Sun workstation, the simple command

```
% rsh victim-workstation screendump > screen.out
```

can be used to obtain a copy of any other user's screen. This can then be displayed on the local workstation using the command

```
% screenload screen.out
```

Other workstation vendors provide similar software.

The other method of obtaining screen contents requires that the victim be running a window system, and that the thief know which window system is in use. For example, if the victim is running the X Window System, the command

```
% xwd -display victim-workstation:0 -root > screen.out
```

can be used to obtain a copy of any other user's screen. This can then be displayed on the local workstation (which must also be using the X Window System) with the command

```
% xwud -in screen.out
```

Other window systems provide similar features.

Defenses

Defending against these sorts of attacks is difficult. The frame buffer method can typically only be prevented by disallowing other users permission to log in to the workstation. While this is possible in environments in which each workstation is installed in a private office and hence is only used by one person, it is not practical in environments where workstations are shared among several users. Some workstations may allow the frame buffer device file to be protected so that only the user using the frame buffer may access it, but this is not common.

Defending against the window system attack is sometimes easier, since some window systems provide methods to control access to the display. For example, the X Window System by default does not allow other hosts to access the display, unless access is granted using the xhost command. The X Window System, Version 11 Release 4 and above also provides an authorization protocol, enabled using the xauth command, which enables more fine-grained access control. However, these mechanisms can still be circumvented if the thief can log into the victim workstation, since by their nature the access control mechanisms must provide access to the local host. The standard version of the xwd program will ring the workstation bell once when the screen dump begins and twice when it completes, which may alert the user that her screen is being copied. Of course, it is trivial for the thief to create a different version of xwd that does not ring the workstation bell.

6.6 Summary

In this chapter we described the special problems workstations present and how to defend against them:

- If possible, make sure that workstations cannot be taken into single-user mode without providing the *root* password.

- Do not allow untrusted workstations to mount file systems via NFS or RFS with *root* access enabled.

- If your system supports diskless workstations, make sure that the directories on the server that contain client root partitions are accessible only by the super-user.

- Wherever possible, disable any packet monitoring packages in the kernel, and do not provide the ability to rebuild the kernel on these systems.

- If possible, install a version of the PROM monitor that either does not provide or at least password-protects the commands to examine and change memory contents.

- Make use of any access control mechanisms provided by the operating system and window system to prevent theft of workstation display contents.

These measures can help protect your network from an attacker who breaks into one of your workstations.

Chapter 7
Terminals, Modems, and UUCP

Most large UNIX systems, such as those provided by university computer centers, are accessed via terminals rather than workstations. Most systems also provide some mechanism to allow users to access the system via dial-up modem as well, enabling them to work from home or while traveling. In addition to dial-up terminal access, all versions of UNIX provide a rudimentary form of networking called UUCP. This software allows files and electronic mail to be transferred, as well as remote command execution. UUCP is based entirely on dial-up modem access (although new versions of UUCP can also make use of local- and wide-area networks).

This chapter discusses the security issues pertaining to terminals, dial-up modems, and UUCP. Proper configuration of these features is vital to making your system secure.

7.1 Terminals

Terminals are typically used to provide access to large UNIX systems such as those in university computer centers. A terminal differs from a workstation in that it does not run its own copy of the operating system, and it is rarely connected to a network. Instead, it is simply a keyboard and screen connected to a large computer somewhere by a serial line which allows characters to be transferred back and forth. The VT-100 manufactured by Digital Equipment Corporation is an example of the type of terminal we are referring to.

Generally, terminals themselves do not present much of a security problem. They do not run a copy of the operating system, do not have a network connection, and do not have PROM monitors accessible to the user (although some terminals provide a "setup mode" which allows various parameters to be changed), so they cannot be subverted in the ways that a workstation can. However, there are a few precautions that can be taken in order to make terminals even more secure.

Secure Terminals

In 4.3BSD, the concept of a *secure* terminal was introduced. The term "secure" is perhaps a misnomer, since really all this means is that the user *root* is not allowed to log in directly on this terminal, even if the proper password is given. (Authorized users may still log in and then become the super-user using the `su` command, however.) The file */etc/ttys* is used to designate secure and insecure terminals. (On some Berkeley-based vendor systems this file has been renamed */etc/ttytab*.) This file usually looks like the following:

```
console "/etc/getty std.9600"     vt100       on   local  secure
tty00    "/etc/getty std.9600"     unknown     on   local
tty01    "/etc/getty std.9600"     unknown     on   local
tty02    "/etc/getty std.9600"     unknown     off  local
tty03    "/etc/getty std.9600"     unknown     off  local
.....
ttyp0    none                      network     off  secure
ttyp1    none                      network     off  secure
ttyp2    none                      network     off  secure
ttyp3    none                      network     off  secure
ttyp4    none                      network     off  secure
.....
```

The first column shows the name of the terminal as given in the */dev* directory. The second column shows the program and arguments which are to be executed on this terminal by the `init` process; usually this program is responsible for prompting the user for a login name and password. The third column shows the terminal type to be passed into the user's environment at login time. The fourth column indicates whether the terminal is "off" or "on," which determines whether the program in the second column will be started or not. The keyword "local" is used to indicate a directly connected terminal (i.e. one with a piece of hardware associated with it) as opposed to a remote (network or dial-up) terminal. The "secure" keyword, if present, means that *root* may log in directly to this terminal. If this keyword is not present, then *root* may not log in even if the correct password is given. In the example above, *root* may log in on the console or via the network (using `rlogin` or `telnet`), but may not log in on the directly connected terminals *tty00*, *tty01*, etc.

Usually, the best way to configure the *ttys* file is to delete the "secure" keyword from all but the console terminal. This prevents an attacker from logging in as the super-user on any public terminal, as well as preventing him from logging in as *root* via the network. For added security, the console terminal can be marked as insecure as well; this means that the only way a super-user can log in is to log in as herself first, and then use the `su` program. This effectively means that to become super-user requires an attacker to know two passwords rather than one.

On some UNIX systems (such as Sun's), marking the console terminal as "insecure" has the added side effect of requiring the *root* password to be entered when the system is booted in single-user mode (see Chapter 6).

"Smart" Terminals

Terminals are typically divided into two broad categories, "dumb" terminals and "smart" terminals. The difference is largely one of features; "smart" terminals provide features such as local editing and the ability to transmit data on the screen to the computer. In 1981, students at the University of California at Berkeley discovered that some "smart" terminals can be used to compromise system security (Wood et al., 1981).

Some terminals provide a feature called *block mode transmission*, which enables the terminal to transmit the contents of its display memory back to the host computer when a special code sequence or control command is received. This feature is often provided in several forms, usually described as "send line," "send line unprotected," or "send page." This feature can be used by an attacker if she can access the terminal remotely, by printing the commands she wants executed on the screen, sending special code sequences to cause the terminal to "back up" over these commands, and then using the block mode transmit code sequence to send the commands to the computer. The commands will then be executed just as if the victim had typed them.

A related feature, although not quite as generally useful to an attacker, is programmable function keys provided by most terminals. If an attacker can program a terminal's function keys remotely to send strings of his choosing when the keys are pressed, then he can execute any command he chooses as if he were the victim. The only problem arises in waiting for the victim to press the function key; some terminals eliminate this obstacle as well by providing special code sequences to transmit the contents of the function keys.

Defense against this attack is simple. An attacker must be able to write to the terminal device file in order to send the special code sequences. Write permission on a terminal device is typically called "message permission," since it allows the use of programs such as `talk` and `write` to communicate with other users. UNIX provides a command called `mesg` which enables or disables message permission. By executing the command

```
% mesg n
```

message permission can be turned off, protecting yourself from attack.

There is another method for an attacker to send special code sequences to a smart terminal: electronic mail. When the user reads his mail, the sequences are interpreted by the terminal, with sometimes devastating effects. This method of attack is more difficult, since many mail programs do not pass non-printing characters. It can be guarded against by always using a program such as `more` or `less` to page through mail messages; these programs display non-printing characters in a printable format rather than sending them directly to the terminal.

X Terminals

So-called "X terminals" are special terminal-like devices which plug into a network and run the X Window System. Although these terminals are not truly workstations in the sense of running their own copy of the operating system, they don't really behave like normal terminals either. Protecting these terminals involves many of the same procedures described in Chapter 6.

The large number of X terminal vendors makes discussing each terminal in detail impossible, but there are some general procedures to follow when securing these devices. Most of these devices provide some sort of setup mode that is used to tell the terminal its network address and so on. Some setup modes also allow you to set a password that will "lock out" changes unless the password is supplied; this password should always be set. Many of the terminals also allow a `telnet`-like mode of operation; this should be disabled or limited to local hosts and "standard" ports if at all possible.

7.2 Dial-Up Modems

Dial-up modems allow users to access the system from home or while traveling. They also allow anyone who knows the correct telephone number to access the system and try to break into it.

Proper Set-Up

The most common problem with dial-up modems is one of configuration. If improperly configured, dial-up modems may allow an attacker to call your system and obtain access to an already logged in line which someone else carelessly left behind. Explaining how to properly configure every brand of modem and every type of UNIX system would require a separate book in itself. However, the object of the configuration is to obtain the following behavior:

- If a user dialed up via modem hangs up the telephone, the system should automatically log him out. If it doesn't, check the hardware configuration of the modem and serial ports, as well as the kernel configuration of the serial ports connected to modems.

- When a user dialed up via modem logs out of her account, the system should force the local modem to hang up. Again, check the hardware configuration of the modem and serial ports, as well as the kernel configuration of the serial ports connected to modems, if this doesn't work.

Some systems, such as SunOS and ULTRIX, allow modems to be configured in the */etc/ttytab* file rather than in the kernel.

The Dial-Up Password

Some versions of UNIX, notably System V Release 4, have introduced the concept of a *dial-up password*. This is a second password that must be entered when logging in on a dial-up terminal port. The dial-up password is controlled by the system administrator, rather than by individual users.

On System V Release 4, the dial-up password is enabled by two files. The file */etc/dialups* contains a list of terminal devices on which a dial-up password will be required. This file might look like

```
/dev/term/21
/dev/term/22
/dev/term/23
```

The file */etc/d_passwd* contains the encrypted passwords and login programs that require the user to enter a password before they can be invoked. This file might look like

```
/usr/lib/uucp/uucico::
/usr/bin/csh:encrypted-password:
/usr/bin/ksh:encrypted-password:
/usr/bin/sh:encrypted-password:
```

When a user attempts to log in on any one of the ports listed in */etc/dialups*, her login shell as listed in the password file is looked up in */etc/d_passwd*, and if present, the password for that program is prompted for. The password for */usr/bin/sh* is considered the default password; if the user's login shell is not found in the file, this password will be used.

Dial-Back Modems

Dial-back modems offer security by requiring a known telephone number for each user who dials up to the system. When the user dials up, he enters his login name and password as usual. However, rather than giving the user a shell, the system logs him off. It then looks that user up in a database, obtains a telephone number for the user, and calls it. The user then logs in again, and receives his shell.

This scheme provides a great deal of security, since even if an attacker discovers a user's password, she cannot log in via dial-up. When the system tries to call back, it will call the telephone number listed for that user (usually his home telephone number), rather than the telephone number used by the attacker. Unfortunately, this scheme also has its disadvantages; the primary one is that it is usually not possible (without the system administrator's intervention) for a user to dial-up from a different telephone, for example one in a hotel room.

Most versions of UNIX do not provide dial-back software. However, several implementations are available from the source archive sites described in Chapter 11.

Some modems also implement dial-back within the modem; these are usually fairly easy for an attacker to circumvent.

Challenge-Response Boxes

Challenge-response boxes, described in Chapter 9, can also be used to provide additional security on dial-up connections. These boxes force the user to enter a special key sequence in response to a challenge from the host computer.

7.3 Terminal Servers

Terminal servers are used to concentrate terminals or modems in a single place where they may be shared. Usually, the terminal server is a host connected to the network from which dial-up users may connect to other systems using `rlogin` or `telnet`. Older systems, usually called terminal switches or terminal concentrators, are actually connected to the serial ports of several machines, and simply connect an incoming dial-up port to a port on one of the hosts.

There are two primary security issues associated with terminal servers and terminal switches. The first is one of hardware configuration to ensure that the modems behave properly. Modems connected to a terminal server or terminal switch should exhibit the following behavior:

- If a user dialed up via modem hangs up the telephone, the system should automatically log him out. If it doesn't, check the hardware configuration of the modem and serial ports, as well as the software configuration of the serial ports connected to modems.

- When a user dialed up via modem logs out of her account or the terminal server, the system should force the local modem to hang up. Again, check the hardware configuration of the modem and serial ports, as well as the software configuration of the serial ports connected to modems, if this doesn't work.

- If the connection from a terminal server or terminal switch is broken, the system should log the user off.

- If the user hangs up the telephone, the terminal server or terminal switch should inform the system that the user has hung up, so that he can be logged out.

Most terminal servers that connect to a network can be configured to prompt the user for his login name and password before granting access to the network, or at least to prompt for a single dial-up password. Additionally, some terminal servers can be configured so that network connections may only be established to certain hosts (usually local ones) as opposed to any host that can be reached from the network. The first configuration option (passwords) should be enabled to protect your systems from unauthorized use. The second option (restricted network access) should be used to protect *other people's* systems from unauthorized use.

Some terminal servers also allow outbound `telnet` connections to other TCP ports such as those used by SMTP, FTP, and so on. This feature should be disabled, either completely or at least for "regular" users.

7.4 The UNIX-to-UNIX Copy Program (UUCP)

UUCP (Nowitz and Lesk, 1979) is a collection of programs that allow UNIX systems to communicate via dial-up telephone lines or other paths. UUCP includes software to transfer files between systems, execute commands on remote systems, and send electronic mail to users on remote systems.

At specified times, a system running UUCP invokes the `uucico` program to place a telephone call to another system also running UUCP. When the remote system answers, the local `uucico` logs in (usually as *uucp*), provides a password, and the remote system invokes `uucico` as well. The two `uucico` processes then communicate with each other in order to effect file and electronic mail transfers, and remote command executions. When all files have been transferred, all mail sent, and all commands executed, the two processes terminate the connection.

There are two main versions of UUCP in use today. *Version 2* UUCP is based on the original version distributed with Seventh Edition UNIX in 1977. It has been modified many times over the years, primarily in releases of UNIX from Berkeley, and is hence often referred to as "Berkeley UUCP." *HoneyDanBer* UUCP was developed from scratch in 1983 by Peter Honeyman, David A. Nowitz, and Brian E. Redman. This version of UUCP is shipped with most versions of System V UNIX, where it is often called "Basic Networking Utilities (BNU)," as well as with SunOS 4.0 and later releases. Although the two versions are compatible in the sense that they can "talk" to each other, the configuration files and administration procedures differ greatly between the two systems. To determine which version of UUCP your system has, look in the directory *usr/lib/uucp*. If you see a file called *L.sys*, your system is running Version 2 UUCP. If instead you see a file called *Systems*, your system is using HoneyDanBer.

One method of increasing the security of UUCP works for both versions. Normally, there is only a single user for all UUCP connections, called *uucp*. This account is used to log in whenever a remote system calls your system, and thus all remote systems use the same password when logging in. In order to make your system somewhat more secure, you can create multiple accounts with the same user id (that of *uucp*) and different passwords, one for each remote system that will be calling you. This not only allows you to determine which remote systems are logged in at any given time, but also allows you to prevent a single system from logging in simply by changing the password for that system.

Other security measures can be taken, but they differ between Version 2 and HoneyDanBer. These procedures are described in the following sections.

Version 2 UUCP

Four files are important when securing Version 2 UUCP: */usr/lib/uucp/L.sys*, */usr/lib/uucp/L.cmds*, */usr/lib/uucp/SQFILE*, and */usr/lib/uucp/USERFILE*.

The *L.sys* File

The file */usr/lib/uucp/L.sys* is where remote system telephone numbers, login names, and passwords are stored. In order to protect the security of the other systems your site calls, this file should always be owned by *uucp* and set to mode 600.

The *L.cmds* File

The list of commands that may be executed by a remote system is contained in the file */usr/lib/uucp/L.cmds* (sometimes called *L-cmds*, or occasionally *uuxqtcmds*). If a command is not listed in this file, it cannot be executed by a remote system. The only two commands which really need to be listed in this file are `rmail` and `rnews`, which enable the receipt of mail and news respectively. Other commands should generally not be allowed, since they may allow an attacker to circumvent security. If this file exists but is empty, remote commands cannot be executed on your system.

The *SQFILE*

The file */usr/lib/uucp/SQFILE*, if present, is used to maintain conversation sequences with remote hosts. *SQFILE* contains one entry for each remote host you have agreed to perform sequence checks with. The remote system must also have an entry for your system in its *SQFILE*. Each entry contains the number of conversations with that host, and the date and time of the last conversation:

```
sun 12 11/19-16:42
```

There have been 12 conversations so far with host `sun`; the last one was on November 19 at 4:42 p.m.

When one system using conversation sequences calls another, the `uucico` program compares the sequence information for the two systems. If they match, things continue as they normally would. If they do not match, the login fails. This can be used to protect your system against an attacker who has somehow stolen the password to one of your UUCP logins and is masquerading as another system.

Since *SQFILE* contains sensitive information, it should be owned by user *uucp* and set to mode 600.

The *USERFILE*

The file */usr/lib/uucp/USERFILE* is used to set local file access permissions. The configuration of this file is unfortunately complex, and a good book on UUCP administration such as (O'Reilly and Todino, 1990) should be consulted for all the details. However, the basic idea will be presented below. *USERFILE* contains lines of the form

> *user , system*   [*c*]   *pathname(s)*

user specifies the login name of either a local user or one of the UUCP logins you have set up. *system* specifies the system name of the remote system (which is not necessarily the same as the login name). The character *c*, if present, specifies that the local system should terminate the UUCP connection after the initial login, and then call back the remote system, in the same way as described in section 7.3. *pathname(s)* is a list of absolute path names, separated by blanks, from which the remote system may access files.

A line in which the *user* field is empty is used to define the files that can be transferred from your system by local users (i.e., the files that local users can "send"). A line in which the *system* field is empty is used to define the files that can be requested from your system by a remote UUCP. Intuitively one would think that a single line in which both the *user* and *system* fields are omitted could be used, but most versions will actually only accept this as if only the *user* field were omitted. A second line with anything in the *user* field and a blank *system* field must also be used.

A sample *USERFILE* is shown below:

```
,                 /usr/spool/uucppublic
uucp,             /usr/spool/uucppublic
uusun,sun         /usr/spool/uucppublic /usr/spool/news
uudec,dec   c     /usr/spool/uucppublic
```

The first line requires that local users place files they want to send to remote systems into the */usr/spool/uucppublic* directory. By using a line of the form

```
,                 /
```

instead, you can allow them to send files from anywhere on the system. The second line indicates that any remote system calling yours may only transfer files from the */usr/spool/uucppublic* directory. This is desirable, since it prohibits an attacker from using UUCP to obtain copies of system files such as */etc/passwd*. The third and fourth lines specify the login names and system names used by two UUCP neighbors, Sun and DEC. Sun is allowed to transfer files to and from the news directory as well as the UUCP public area. The line for DEC shows that call-back is required.

Because the *USERFILE* contains sensitive information, it should be owned by the user *uucp* and set to mode 600.

HoneyDanBer UUCP

One of the major improvements made in HoneyDanBer UUCP was in how security is controlled. There are two important files when securing HoneyDanBer UUCP: */usr/lib/uucp/Systems*, and */usr/lib/uucp/Permissions*.

The *Systems* File

The file */usr/lib/uucp/Systems* is where remote system telephone numbers, login names, and passwords are stored. In order to protect the security of the other systems your site calls, this file should always be owned by *uucp* and set to mode 600.

The *Permissions* File

The file */usr/lib/uucp/Permissions* allows you to define permissions for individual remote systems using two types of entries:

- LOGNAME entries allow you to grant permissions for each UUCP login on your system. These permissions are used when a remote system calls your system.

- MACHINE entries allow you to grant permissions for each system your system calls. These permissions are used when your system calls a remote system.

Each line in the *Permissions* file consists of a number of name/value pairs, separated by spaces. If the name has more than one value, colons (":") are used to separate the values. Each entry begins with either LOGNAME or MACHINE. A single entry may be continued onto multiple lines by using the backslash character ("\") at the end of a line. Comments may be introduced with a "#" character and continue until the end of the line. Within each entry, Table 7.1 shows the name/value pairs which may be used. In the *Class* column, an L or M is used to show whether the name/value pair may be used in a LOGNAME entry, a MACHINE entry, or both.

An example *Permissions* file is shown below:

```
LOGNAME=udec  MACHINE=dec \
  READ=/  WRITE=/  COMMANDS=rmail:who:lp:uucp \
  SENDFILES=yes  REQUEST=yes

LOGNAME=usun  MACHINE=sun \
  READ=/usr/spool/uucppublic:/usr/spool/news \
  WRITE=/usr/spool/uucppublic \
  SENDFILES=call REQUEST=no
```

Table 7.1

Option	Class	Description
LOGNAME	L	Specifies the login ids that can be used by remote sites to log into the local system.
MACHINE	M	Specifies machines that the local system can call with the specified conditions in effect.
REQUEST	M, L	Specifies whether the remote system can request to set up file transfers from your computer. Default is "no."
SENDFILES	L	Specifies whether the called site can execute locally queued requests during a session. "Yes" means that your system may send jobs queued for the remote system as long as it is logged in as one of the names in the LOGNAME option. Default is "call"—the queued files are sent only when the *local* system calls the remote machine.
READ	M, L	Specifies the directories that `uucico` can use for requesting files. Default is the *uucppublic* directory.
WRITE	M, L	Specifies the directories that `uucico` can use for depositing files. Default is the *uucppublic* directory.
NOREAD	M, L	Exceptions to READ options or defaults.
NOWRITE	M, L	Exceptions to WRITE options or defaults.
CALLBACK	L	Whether or not the local system must call back the calling system before transactions can occur. Default is "no."
COMMANDS	M	Commands that the remote system can execute locally. This defaults to the command list in the *parms.h* header file, which is compiled into `uuxqt`. The COMMANDS option overrides the default command list. The keyword ALL grants access to all commands.
VALIDATE	L	Used to verify calling system's identity. Can be used with COMMANDS when specifying commands that may be potentially dangerous to your system's security.
MYNAME	M	Used to link another system name to the local system.
PUBDIR	M, L	Specifies the directory for local access (e.g., */usr/spool/uucppublic/loginA*). Default is the public directory.

Source: O'Reilly and Todino, 1990.

The system *dec* may log in as *udec*, and will be allowed to read or write files in any directory on the system. It can request or send files regardless of whether it initiated the call, and it can execute the commands `rmail`, `who`, `lp`, and `uucp`. The system *sun* may log in as *usun*, and will only be allowed to read files from */usr/spool/uucppublic* and */usr/spool/news*, and will only be allowed to write files to */usr/spool/uucppublic*. It may send files when it initiates the call, but will have requests to receive files denied. The *sun* system is only allowed to execute the default list of commands.

7.5 Summary

In this chapter we discussed terminals, modems, and UUCP, and ways to make them more secure:

- If your system provides the capability, designate all public and network terminals as "insecure" in the *ttys* or *ttytab* file. If desired, designate the console terminal as insecure as well.

- Disable message permission using the `mesg` command if you are using a terminal with block mode transmission features or remotely programmable function keys.

- If your system provides the capability, install dial-up passwords on all modem ports.

- Consider the use of dial-back modems or dial-back software.

- Use separate logins and passwords for each system that accesses yours via UUCP.

- Make sure that the file */usr/lib/uucp/L.sys* or */usr/lib/uucp/Systems* is owned by *uucp* and mode 600.

- Define permissions for all remote systems logging in via UUCP using the *USERFILE* and *L.cmds* or using the *Permissions* file.

- If supported, enable passwords on terminal servers.

These measures will make your system more secure against attacks over the telephone.

Chapter 8
Responding to Attacks

Part of handling a break-in is being ready to respond before one actually occurs. This includes protecting yourself as much as possible using the procedures described in the previous chapters. It also includes preparing guidelines to use for handling the incident and its aftermath. A written plan can eliminate much of the confusion that arises when everything seems to be happening at once. It is also important to establish guidelines for notifying people of a break-in. This chapter describes some of the more common types of attack, how to recognize them, and how to respond to them.

8.1 Detection

There are several common forms of attack on a computer system, and with a little vigilance, most of them are easy to detect. However, it is important to realize that many of these events may not be symptoms of an attack, but simply normal occurrences in the face of hardware failures, programming mistakes, and so on. It is important that you investigate these events without overreacting.

System Crashes

Systems may crash, or go down unexpectedly, for any number of reasons. Some of these include hardware failures (such as memory parity errors), running out of memory, and corrupted data on a disk. Typically however, unless the crash is due to a hardware failure, it won't repeat itself very often. If your system is crashing repeatedly (more than once a week), you may suspect that something is wrong.

When a UNIX system crashes, it normally prints a "panic" message on the console indicating its reason for giving up the ghost. After the system has rebooted, you should check the reason for the crash. If it is hardware-related, the obvious course of action is to repair the hardware. If the reason is not hardware-related, you should make a note of the reason, and watch for future crashes for the same reason. If possible, you should try to figure out what is causing the crash, in case it is a bug in the operating system. This is often difficult to do, since the meanings of UNIX "panic" messages are usually not documented anywhere. Some of the UNIX-related mailing lists and newsgroups described in Chapter 12 may help you here. If the system appears to be crashing for some reason that cannot be explained away by outside factors such as a hardware failure or a known bug in the operating system, or if the system seems to be crashing at the same time of day each time, you should begin to suspect that someone may be crashing the system intentionally.

New Accounts

One of the favorite techniques of many attackers, once they have broken in and obtained super-user permissions, is to create a new account for themselves. Many times, this account will be created with a user id of zero, giving it super-user permissions. (There is nothing special about the login name *root*. The important part of the super-user account is its user id, zero.) In this way, the attacker can log in using his "own" account, and he is not affected by anything that happens to stolen accounts he was using, such as password changes.

Detecting new accounts is simply a matter of examining the password file for unauthorized changes on a regular basis. If you are the only person authorized to add or delete accounts, this is a fairly simple task. However, if several people are allowed to add and delete accounts, differentiating between "authorized" and "unauthorized" changes becomes more difficult. The COPS program, described in Chapter 11, can help with the specific task of finding accounts other than *root* with user ids of zero. Another way to help find unauthorized changes is to establish an unusual or nonstandard method of updating the password file. For example, if you use RCS or SCCS to control revisions of the password file, and the attacker is unaware of this, then his change will be obvious just because he didn't follow the established procedure. It is important to realize however, that these techniques are not fool-proof.

New Files

The appearance of new files in the file system, often in directories such as /, /etc, /usr, and so on may indicate that someone has broken into your system. These files will often have novel or strange file names (such as *data.xx*, or a single letter), or will have the set-user-id or set-group-id bits set on them. In particular files whose names begin with "." should be searched for, since the standard ls program, unless called with the −a option, will not display these names. One favorite trick of many attackers is to create a directory called "...", since it won't show up in a regular ls listing, and even if the −a option is given, many people won't notice it since they're so used to mentally skipping over the entries for ".". and "..". The checklist tools described in Chapter 3 can be helpful in detecting files that have been created in system directories.

Data Modification

Another method used by attackers is that of changing data, usually by modifying some common system program such as `login`, `sh`, `csh`, or one of the */etc/rc* files. If an attacker can replace a standard system program (especially one that the super-user will execute) with one of her own, she can leave "trap doors" that allow her to log in at any time, have commands of her choosing executed by the super-user, or any number of other possible scenarios. If she can modify the */etc/rc* files, which are executed with super-user permissions whenever the system is rebooted, she can re-install any programs, modifications, or files that may have been deleted when the system was shut down. Again, the checklist tools described in Chapter 3 can be helpful in detecting unauthorized modifications to system files.

Poor Performance

Poor system performance, characterized by long response times, can be a sign of a break-in, if the attacker is executing programs. These programs may be attempting to break passwords, searching through every file in the file system, and so on. However, it is important to realize that poor performance can also be due to perfectly innocent problems such as users running several large "number crunching" jobs.

If your system is performing poorly, utilities such as `ps` can be used to examine the list of running processes. Look for processes that have accumulated a large amount of CPU time or are accumulating it rapidly, processes which have large in-core memory sizes, and processes which have large overall memory sizes (in-core plus swapped-out). Other symptoms include a large number of processes being run by the same user (most UNIX systems limit each user to around 20 simultaneous processes), or processes that appear and disappear quickly. Other programs that can help you in tracking down performance problems include `iostat`, `pstat`, `sar`, `vmstat`, and several programs available from the source archive sites described in Chapter 11.

Denial of Service

A denial of service attack is one in which an attacker consumes all of a resource so that nobody else may access it. One of the simplest denial of service attacks is to fill up a file system, so that no new data can be written there. This effectively "shuts down" all users working in that file system. Filling up the root file system or */tmp* can effectively stop all users from accomplishing anything. The `df` command can be used to locate file systems that are full, and the `du` command can often be used to find the offending user. However, it is possible to create a file, open it for writing, and then delete it. As long as a process still has the file open, the space on the disk will not be released. Because the file has been removed however, utilities such as du will not locate this space. If executing du on the entire file system does not account for all the space in use in the file system, you should suspect this as the reason. Sometimes the quot command can be used to determine which user has taken all the space, although it will not indicate which process is doing it, or what file the data is stored in. There are utilities available from the source archive sites described in Chapter 11 that can detect these types of files (one of them is called ofiles). However, if you do not have access to these programs, you can simply shut down and reboot the system. When the system is shut down, all processes are terminated, and this will terminate the process taking all the space, allowing the space to be freed.

UNIX systems also make use of several tables in the operating system, to store information about processes, open files, inodes (files in use on the disk), and so on. These tables normally have fixed sizes, and filling one up can deny service to others. If the process table is filled (which usually requires more than one user id to accomplish, since each user is limited to a smaller number of processes), nobody will be able to execute new programs. This essentially means that no new work can be done. If the file table is filled, nobody will be able to open any files, which also prevents any work from being done. Each file system has a fixed number of inodes (file entries), and when this number is exceeded no new files can be created. Sometimes, tables will fill up simply because they are too small to allow all of your users to work at the same time. In this case, you can often build a new version of the operating system with larger tables. However, if this does not seem to cure the problem, you may suspect a denial of service attack. These types of attack are difficult to pinpoint; the ps, pstat, and ofiles commands may help you.

Another attack that can deny service to all users of the system is to run the system out of swap space. Virtual memory implementations require a place on the disk where unused pages of memory can be stored, to make room in memory for the pages that are in use. On UNIX systems, this is usually called the swap area. Generally speaking, a swap area should be anywhere from two to four times the size of the system's memory. An attacker can start up several very large programs, which will fill up the swap area. When this happens, nobody can execute any new programs, since there is no more room in the swap area. The ps command can be used to find large programs, by looking at the SIZE and RSS fields.

A fourth type of denial of service attack is one that denies network service. This can be done by rapidly issuing connection requests to services on your system, or by swamping your system with useless network packets. Although easy to recognize (the network stops working), this type of attack is difficult to defend against, since it is being mounted from another system, possibly not under your control. Unplugging the system from the network, or turning off the network interface by using the ifconfig command can temporarily protect the system from further abuse, but eventually network service will have to be restored.

Suspicious Probes

Many attackers will try to probe your system, looking for "easy" accounts to log in to. These are typically accounts that are known to be on many systems, such as *guest*, *user*, *bin*, *root*, *sys*, and so on. Most versions of `login` now log bad login attempts (or multiple bad login attempts) to the console or a system log file; you should periodically check for these messages.

Suspicious Browsing

After an attacker has broken into your system, unless she has a particular purpose in mind, she will often begin browsing through the system. She will systematically go through each directory, looking at each file, with the goal of finding something "interesting."

Each time a file is accessed under UNIX, its access time is updated. The `-u` option of the `ls` command, when used with `-l`, will display access times. You should periodically use these options on some directories, searching for directories where each file has been accessed within a few minutes of the others. Don't be too suspicious if you find a few directories like this, since many users will execute commands that will read all files in a directory. However, if you find that every file in a file system has been accessed in a seemingly consecutive manner, this is suspicious.

One reminder—if you use a program such as `cpio` or `tar` to do backups, or any other program that reads the file system rather than reading the raw disk device, these programs will update the file access times. In this case, examining the file system in this manner will not tell you much of anything.

Accounting Discrepancies

Finally, if you run process accounting on your system, and you actually examine or use the output for billing purposes, discrepancies in the accounts can be a clue to an attacker's presence. For example, if the amount of CPU time used by a user suddenly increases dramatically, this user's account may have been compromised. You can also maintain a list of the types of commands typically used by each user. If a secretary whose most often-used command is the text editor suddenly begins executing the C compiler over and over again, it may be that her account has been stolen.

8.2 Response

It is important to bear in mind that all of the symptoms of attack described above also have normal, innocent explanations. Just because you notice something that may indicate an attack, don't assume that it **is** an attack. Carefully investigate the situation, trying to locate a reasonable explanation. If you can't find a reasonable explanation, then it's time to suspect an attack.

Finding the Attacker

The first step in responding to an attack is to try to locate the attacker. This doesn't necessarily mean identifying the actual person involved, or even figuring out where he is. Instead, it means determining how the attacker is accessing your system, what account or accounts he is using, and so on.

The `cron` Program

A simple way to find an attacker, if you can determine the time of his attacks (either in advance or afterward), is to make use of the `cron` utility. This program executes other programs repeatedly at given time intervals. To identify your attacker, construct a shell script that checks who is logged in, what processes are running, and other similar information, such as the one shown in Example 8.1. Now set up the `cron` program (consult the manual page for how to do this, since the procedure differs from system to system) to execute this program as often as necessary. This may be once an hour, once every half hour, or even once every ten or fifteen minutes.

After a while, you should have enough data that you can begin to narrow things down. Certain users will always be logged in when the break-ins occur. Certain processes may always be running. From here, you can take actions such as changing passwords or deleting accounts, or otherwise locking the attacker out. After doing so however, you should continue to run your shell script (perhaps at longer intervals) for a few days, to make sure that the attacker doesn't break in again using another account.

One problem with this approach is that attackers can "hide" themselves if the files you are monitoring are writable (or they have super-user permissions). There is no good way to counter this, other than running your checks as often as possible to attempt to catch the attacker before he can delete the traces of his presence, or sending all logging information to a hard-copy output device (such as a line printer or teletype) that is stored in a secure room.

Accounting

The system accounting files, described in Chapter 2, can also be a valuable means of finding an attacker. By examining these files for suspicious command executions, you can determine which users are executing these commands. Again, because attackers can delete references to themselves from these files, this is not a fool-proof technique.

Network Monitors

If your system is being attacked from the network, network monitoring tools such as `etherfind`, `tcpdump`, and `netstat` can help you determine where the attack is

Example 8.1   checksys.sh

```sh
#!/bin/sh

LOGFILE=path to the file you want to save the information in

echo -n "================================== " >> $LOGFILE
date >> $LOGFILE

who >> $LOGFILE

ps -axlww >> $LOGFILE

exit 0
```

coming from. Unfortunately, most network monitors are not really designed for this purpose, and so you have to capture more data than you need, and then sift through it manually. This is a time-consuming procedure, but is arguably better than nothing.

Containment

After it has been determined that your system has been broken into, it is necessary to contain the break-in to keep it from spreading to other systems. This may involve removing the attacked host from other hosts' *.rhosts* and *hosts.equiv* files, turning off any software distribution originating from the affected host, and so on. Because there are often many ways for an attack to spread from one host to another, containment should be the subject of a predetermined procedure. In this way you can be sure that you have thought of everything, since even a single path for the attack to spread is enough to ruin your whole day.

Eradication

Once the attack has been contained, and you are reasonably sure that it cannot spread, it is time to eradicate the cause of the break-in. If an account was broken into, delete it or change its password. If a bug in some piece of software was used to gain access, either disable the program or install a fixed version.

Recovery

After the cause of the attack has been disposed of, you must recover from the attack. This involves returning the system to normal. If you installed modified versions of some programs to enable extra logging, the original programs should be restored. Files which were created by the attacker should be saved to a backup medium for future reference, and then deleted. Files modified by the attacker should likewise be saved, and then known-good versions should be restored from backup tapes.

Documentation

From the moment you suspect that a break-in or attack is occurring, it is extremely important to document all details related to the incident. This will ultimately save you time—if you don't write down everything you discover, and everything you try to thwart the attack, you are likely to forget things. At the same time, documentation will aid you in determining exactly what happened after it is all over, and may also aid you in prosecution of the attacker, if you elect to do so.

At a minimum, you should record

- all system events (audit records),

- all actions you take, with time notations, and

- all telephone or electronic mail conversations, including the name of the person you talked to, the date and time, and the content of the conversation.

The simplest way to keep track of all this is to maintain a log book. This provides you with a single, chronological source of information, rather than requiring you to sort through a pile of paper scraps and scribbled notes to yourself. Should you elect to prosecute your attacker, this log book may become important evidence in the proceedings.

One additional note to remember is that if someone has broken into your system, it is highly likely that she can make changes to any file stored on the system. For this reason, any evidence that you save (your log book, output from monitoring commands, system log files, etc.) should **not** be stored on-line. Print it out as soon as possible, and store the hardcopy in a safe place. Otherwise, you may be surprised when you go back to examine your logs that all traces of the attacker have disappeared.

When you begin handling a security incident, you probably won't know whether or not the resolution of the incident will result in a prosecution. Therefore, you should take care to maintain your log book in a proper fashion so that it can be used as evidence in a court of law. The investigative agencies you establish contacts with (see below) will be able to provide detailed information on the procedures necessary, but at a minimum, the following procedures should be followed (Wack, 1991):

- At the end of each day, make a photocopy of your log book.

- Sign and date the photocopy and submit it to a document custodian.

- Accept and retain the receipt from the custodian.

- The document custodian must store the photocopy in a secure area.

8.3 Notification

Once you have determined that some type of attack is taking place, the appropriate personnel must be notified. Who must be notified and when is important to determine beforehand, in order to keep the incident under control, both from a technical and an emotional standpoint.

Any notifications that you give should be both factual and explicit. Attempting to hide things, either by omitting them from your notification message or by trying to couch them in inexact language, may actually hurt you in the long run. This is especially true if asking the system administrators from other sites (for example, in a network attack from another host) for assistance.

Systems Personnel

The first group of people to be notified of an attack should be those people responsible for maintaining the systems involved and other systems that may potentially be attacked. It may be desirable to create a single point of contact who can be notified of any security problem, and then make this person responsible for notifying others. This serves two purposes. First, it lets you devote your time to dealing with the attacker, rather than calling several people on the phone and explaining things to each of them. Second, the point of contact can serve as a clearinghouse for information; forwarding important information to all persons who need to be aware of it.

Response Teams

Now that several organizations have formed some type of incident response team to deal with security problems, you (or the point of contact for your site, if you have one) should decide whether or not to inform the response team of the break-in. If the break-in to your site could have implications on other sites, you should definitely inform the response team, so that they can inform the other sites. Additionally, many response teams will be able to help you deal with the attack on your site, either by lending personnel, or by suggesting methods of detection and containment.

Existing response teams, and procedures you can use to create your own response team, are discussed in Chapter 12.

Law Enforcement

It is important to establish contacts with personnel from investigative and law enforcement agencies such as the FBI, the Secret Service, your local city or campus police department, and your corporate security department as soon as possible. Cooperating with these agencies in a manner that will foster a good working relationship, and one that is consistent with the normal operating procedures of these agencies, will help you in the future. By being aware of the agencies' normal procedures and expectations in advance, you will be able to provide them with the type of information that they need in a timely manner. Find out who the representatives from these agencies responsible for computer crimes in your area are, and meet with them before an attack occurs. You can find out what types of incidents they are responsible for, what type of information they need from you, and the procedures they expect you to follow when collecting that information. This also has the advantage of informing the agencies that you are the point of contact for your site, if they should find out about an attack on or from your site that you are not yet aware of.

Although less true today than it was several years ago, many law enforcement personnel do not know very much about computers, or the forms of attack on them. This can be frustrating for both you and them, since you will each be speaking an entirely different language. When you make contact with your local law enforcement personnel, invite them for a tour of your site. Explain to them the types of computers you have, how they are linked together on the network, what other systems on-site you are (and are not) linked to, how your site is linked to the outside world, and so on. The purpose here is to instill in the officer at least a basic understanding of how your system operates, and the types of problems you face. In some cases, it is also necessary to point out what your system **cannot** do (for example, your system cannot directly affect the campus telephone system).

If your policies permit, and an officer seems especially interested, consider giving him an account on your system to play with. You may also offer yourself as a technical contact for the agency; indicate that you are willing to help with problems at other sites, or answer any technical questions the agency may have. This is simply applying the same principle that fast-food and donut shops have used for years by giving police officers reduced prices or free coffee. If you show that you are willing to cooperate, be friendly, and make an officer's life easier, you can expect that he'll be that much more responsive to your problems than if you refuse to tell him anything.

If your organization has legal counsel, they should be consulted as well. These people can provide you with invaluable advice about what you can and cannot do when tracking an intruder. They can also assist you in preparing any case against the attacker, should you decide to prosecute. Finally, legal counsel may be able to assist you in your interaction with law enforcement agencies.

Press

One final group to consider is the press. Chances are, if your site is either a large one or a principal employer in your town, the press will eventually find out about any serious attack on your system. First, you must decide when and how much information to provide. Whatever the information is however, whether it be brief or detailed, it should be factual. Otherwise, your information will not be corroborated by other sources, and you will come out looking bad.

If your site has a public relations office, it is important to make use of it. The public relations officers are trained in the type and wording of information to be released, and can also help insulate you from the press. This will allow you to concentrate on handling the attack, rather than answering telephone calls from reporters. If you do not have a public relations office, designate a single point of contact to talk to the press. This person can serve as the buffer between the reporters and you, and can insure that information is released in a consistent manner.

8.4 Summary

Responding to a security violation, attack, or break-in is not a simple procedure. It can rapidly become confusing and even overwhelming, as events begin to take place faster than you can deal with them. Outside interruptions from users, management, and the press can cause you to lose track of what you are doing. The most important thing to do is plan things beforehand as much as possible. Develop procedures for responding to an attack, notifying those people involved in the response, working with law enforcement, documenting the attack and your response, and interfacing with the press. For some real-life examples of responding to an attack, consult the Internet worm references (Seely, 1988; Spafford, 1988; Eichin and Rochlis, 1989) or Cliff Stoll's book on the Lawrence Berkeley Laboratory attack (Stoll, 1989).

When an attack occurs, follow these procedures as much as possible, inventing new procedures where existing ones break down. After things have settled down, evaluate your procedures against the reality of the situation. Where your procedures broke down, devise new procedures that will work better the next time. Where procedures did not exist, develop them. There is no way to plan for every contingency. But by planning ahead as much as possible, you can concentrate your efforts on responding to the incident, instead of figuring out what to do next.

Chapter 9
Encryption and Authentication

This chapter discusses issues related to UNIX security, but not generally considered "part" of the system itself. The first half of the chapter, on encryption, discusses methods of protecting information by transforming it into something useless to a data thief. The second half of the chapter, on authentication, discusses methods of insuring that a user accessing the system is really who she says she is.

9.1 Encryption

Before discussing encryption techniques, it is necessary to define several terms. Cryptology is a science unto itself, and like most other sciences, has its own special vocabulary (much of which is borrowed from the fields of mathematics and statistics). The definitions in this section are adapted from Denning (1983) and Kahn (1967).

A *cipher* is a secret method of writing by which *plaintext* is transformed into *ciphertext*. This process is called *encryption*; the reverse process of transforming ciphertext into plaintext is called *decryption*. Both processes are controlled by a cryptographic *key* (or keys).

There are two basic types of ciphers: transpositions and substitutions. A *transposition* cipher rearranges bits or characters in the plaintext to produce the ciphertext. For example, the plaintext "SECRET MESSAGE" might be enciphered as "CTSGEEEASRMSE." A *substitution* cipher replaces bits, characters, or blocks of characters with substitutes. A simple type of substitution cipher, called a *Caesar substitution*, shifts the alphabet forward by K positions; K is the key to the cipher. For example, if K is 3, then plaintext "A" becomes ciphertext "D," "B" becomes "E," and so forth with "Z" becoming "C." Substitutions do not have to be based on letters however; the word "PRIVATE" could also be enciphered as "23 17 9 11 4 13 1" if some system of numbering the letters of the alphabet is used. Substitutions and transpositions can also be combined into a single cipher.

A Caesar cipher is called a *monoalphabetic* substitution cipher, since it uses only a single "alphabet" of substitution characters. A *polyalphabetic* substitution cipher is a substitution cipher which uses more than one ciphertext alphabet, in some prearranged order, to encipher the plaintext. For example, two Caesar ciphers, one with K equal to 3 and the other with K equal to 8, can be used as a polyalphabetic cipher. The first letter of the plaintext is enciphered using the first alphabet, the second plaintext letter is enciphered using the second alphabet, the first alphabet is used again for the third plaintext letter, and so on. Modern substitution ciphers utilize millions of ciphertext alphabets.

Cryptanalysis is the science and study of methods of breaking ciphers. If it is possible to determine the plaintext or key from the ciphertext, or to determine the key from plaintext-ciphertext pairs, a cipher is *breakable*. There are three basic methods of attacking a cipher. A *ciphertext-only attack* requires a cryptanalyst to determine the key (or the plaintext) solely from intercepted ciphertext. He may know things such as the method of encryption, the plaintext language, and certain probable words in the plaintext. In a *known-plaintext attack*, the cryptanalyst knows some plaintext-ciphertext pairs (for example, she may know that plaintext "E" is ciphertext "G"). These can often be determined if the cryptanalyst knows something about the plaintext; for example, if she knows that all plaintexts begin with "Dear sir," she can easily determine those pairs. Then, by substituting these known values into the ciphertext, and by making guesses about other probable words in the text (e.g., "Sincerely yours"), she can determine the key. The last type of attack, a *chosen-plaintext attack*, supposes that the cryptanalyst is able to obtain enciphered copies of plaintext that he chooses. By observing the changes in the ciphertext as the plaintext is changed, the cryptanalyst can learn a great deal about the cipher.

The UNIX Crypt Program

A *rotor machine* consists of a number of rotors, or wired wheels, as shown in Figure 9.1. The outside edge of each rotor has 26 electrical contacts (one for each letter of the alphabet) on both its front and rear. Each contact on the front face is wired to some other contact on the rear face, producing a simple substitution cipher. Multiple rotors are used to perform multiple substitutions. After enciphering a character or block of characters, the rotors can be turned, producing a new set of substitutions. The key to the cipher is the wiring of the rotors and their initial positions.

The `crypt` program provided with most UNIX systems implements a one-rotor machine designed along the lines of the Enigma machine used by the Germans in World War II. The rotor has 256 contacts to allow for the encipherment of 8-bit bytes. After each character is enciphered, the rotor is rotated one position (changing the mapping associated with each letter). After each block of 256 characters is enciphered, the basic transformation (which letters go to which inputs on the rotor) is changed again, producing a new substitution. The methods for breaking systems such as this are well

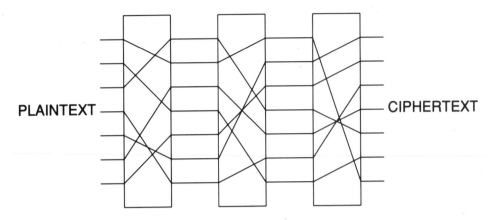

Figure 9.1 A Three-Rotor Machine

known, and the methods for breaking `crypt` in particular have been documented several times (Bishop, 1983; Reeds and Weinberger, 1984).

The statistical analysis of `crypt`'s algorithm is beyond the scope of this book. However, the procedures for a ciphertext-only attack are briefly described here. It is assumed that the attacker has a stock of probable words or phrases that might occur in the plaintext; for example, programming language keywords would be useful if the plaintext is suspected to be a program or shell script. It is also assumed (for simplicity) that the plaintext consists entirely of ASCII characters.

The first step is to try to place a likely word in each possible position in a block of ciphertext. Since most of these placements cannot work, either because they imply that some characters are not ASCII or because they contradict with earlier placements of likely words, this process can easily be automated by an interactive program. The program accepts words from the user, places them in all possible locations, presents the user with all successful placements of all the words, and allows him to select the decipherment he considers best. The process is then repeated with the user giving the program additional probable words. Such a technique can be used to decrypt a completely unknown C language program in a few hours or less (Reeds and Weinberger, 1984).

An additional attack, developed by Robert Morris (Robert Tappan Morris' father), uses statistical analysis to generate lots of probable plaintext. The attack applies the ideas above to the 20 one-letter probable words formed by the 20 most common ASCII characters. The results of placing these "words" in each of their possible positions is scored, and the placements with the highest scores are accepted. This process produces a partially deciphered block which can then be used as a starting point for probable word guessing, as described earlier.

In combination with the above attacks, statistical methods can be used to recover the rotor settings used to encrypt a given block of text. As mentioned previously, `crypt` turns the rotor once every 256 characters. Once the rotor setting for any single block of ciphertext, and the number of positions the rotor is turned between each block are known, the rest of the rotor settings can be recovered, and the problem is solved. Thus, cryptanalyzing the ciphertext produced by `crypt` begins rather slowly using probable word guesses, but finishes rapidly once enough guesses have been made to figure out the rotor settings.

The Crypt Breaker's Workbench

In 1987, Robert Baldwin released the *Crypt Breaker's Workbench* (CBW) (Baldwin, 1986). CBW is an interactive, multi-window system for mounting ciphertext-only attacks on files encrypted with the UNIX `crypt` command. The user interacts with the workbench by choosing assorted tools and setting parameters; CBW carries out the work and displays the results. The general procedure is as follows:

1. Enter a few characters, indicating a guess at what the first few characters of plaintext might be. This will produce several other characters throughout the first ciphertext block.

2. Use CBW to determine a list of possible characters for other positions, based on the characters you have already chosen. CBW provides this list sorted by most likely value.

3. When you're gotten as much as you think you can by guessing, use CBW to search for probable words. This is done by giving CBW a list of words you expect in the plaintext.

4. Use CBW to try bigram and trigram guesses. Bigrams and trigrams are sequences of two and three characters occurring often in the language of the plaintext; e.g., "ed," "qu," "the," and "ing" for English.

5. After a while at this, you will have a few partially decrypted blocks. Now CBW can be used to determine the relationships between the blocks (how much the rotor turned between each block).

6. Once the inter-block relationships are known, the entire file can be decrypted.

The basic cryptanalytic techniques used by CBW are exactly those described by Reeds and Weinberger. Initial probable word guesses are made, followed by statistical "guesswork" based on likely letters. Next comes recovery of the rotor setting for one block of ciphertext, followed by determination of the amount of rotor rotation between blocks, and finally, the entire ciphertext can be decrypted.

Use of Crypt

The point of all this is that `crypt` is not very secure. Although `crypt` may be useful to simply dissuade "prying eyes," it should **never** be used when the security of the plaintext is an issue. It should be noted that one of the well-known suggestions for using `crypt` is to compress the plaintext (using `compress`, `pack`, or whatever) before encrypting, thus eliminating the possibility of a probable-word attack. Unfortunately this logic is misguided, since most compression programs place some type of header on the front of their output, and the contents of this header are well known. Thus the probable-word attack can be made easier, since the attacker need not even worry that his guess is incorrect.

The Data Encryption Standard

The Data Encryption Standard (DES) (National Bureau of Standards, 1977) combines several substitution and transposition ciphers to produce a secure encryption. To date, no claims that DES has been completely broken have been made publicly, although many cryptanalysts have expressed concern over the security of various parts of the algorithm. Cryptologists Adi Shamir and Eli Biham have claimed that, using a chosen-plaintext attack, they have been able to break full DES (Markoff, 1991). However, since a chosen-plaintext attack is not likely to be available to attackers in the "real world," it will not be clear what this means to the overall security of DES until Shamir and Biham publish their work.

DES enciphers 64-bit (eight byte) blocks of data with a 56-bit key. The algorithm used by DES is complex, and the details are beyond the scope of this book. But generally, the cipher works as follows.

An input block is first transposed using an initial permutation called IP. After the result has been through 16 passes of an encryption function f that combines transposition and substitution, it is transposed under the inverse permutation $font R size 11 IP sup -1$ to produce the final result, as shown in Figure 9.2.

In each iteration of f, the 64-bit block is broken into left and right halves. The left half receives the right half of the previous iteration, while the right half receives the left half of the previous iteration exclusive-ored with the output of a function g of the right half of the previous iteration and the current key, as shown in Figure 9.3.

In each iteration, the 32-bit right half of the previous iteration is expanded to a 48-bit block using a bit-selection table called E, which selects some bits more than once. This block is then exclusive-ored with the 48-bit key for the current iteration, and the result broken into eight 6-bit blocks. Each block is then used as input to one of eight selection functions, called *S-boxes*. The S-boxes return a 4-bit substitution encipherment of their input. The eight 4-bit blocks are concatenated together and transposed again using a table called P. This result is exclusive-ored with the left half of the previous iteration to produce the right half of the current iteration. This is shown in Figure 9.4.

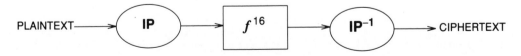

PLAINTEXT   **IP** f^{16} **IP⁻¹**   CIPHERTEXT

Figure 9.2 Basic DES Flow

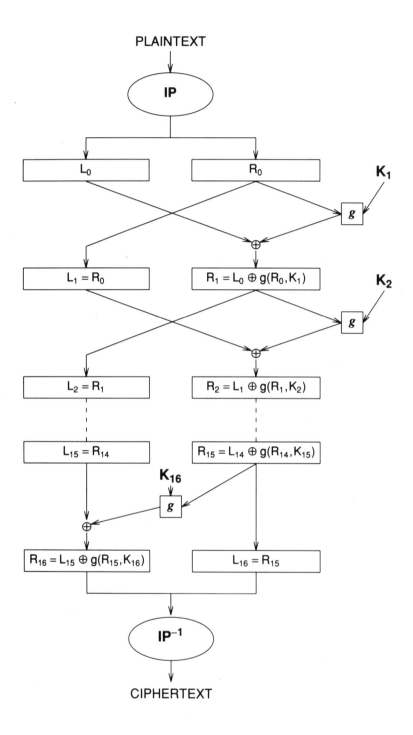

Figure 9.3   The Function f

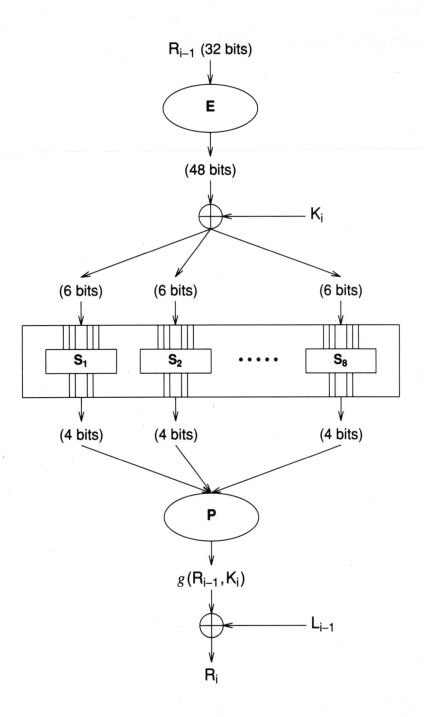

Figure 9.4   Calculation of R_i

Each of the 16 iterations through function f uses a different 48-bit key derived from the original 56-bit key. This is done by passing the original key through a transposition table called PC-1, as shown in Figure 9.5. This output is divided into two halves called C and D, which are then shifted left (bits shifted off the end wrap around to the right) by a number of places determined by the iteration, and the result is passed through a second transposition, PC-2.

Decipherment is performed using the same algorithm, except that the 16 iterative keys are used in reverse order (i.e., K_{16} is used in the first iteration, followed by K_{15}, and so on).

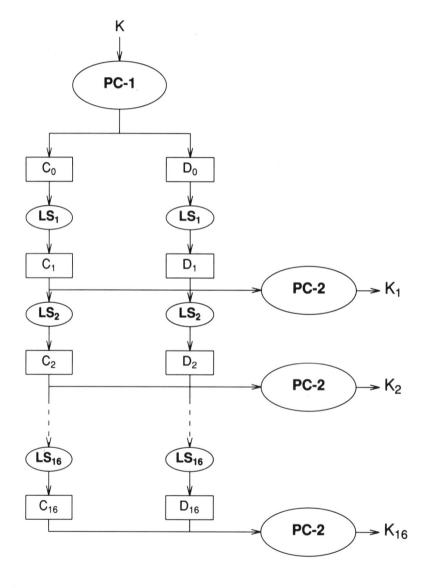

Figure 9.5   Calculation of Keys

There are two principal areas of concern about DES: First, cryptology experts Diffie and Hellman (1977), believe that the 56-bit key is too short, allowing known-plaintext attacks and brute-force searches to be used. Although this is a valid concern, and they point out that the easiest way to do this would be to construct a custom machine to do it, it is still very computationally intensive to make such an attack on general-purpose computers. Second, Hellman (1979) and others have questioned the security of the S-boxes. There is concern that they may have hidden "trap doors" allowing cryptanalysts aware of them to easily break the cipher. The rationale behind the design of the S-boxes is still classified, instilling them with a sense of "magic." Although the trap door theory has never been proven, it has been demonstrated that different S-boxes make the cipher significantly less secure (Hellman, 1979), leading to speculation about how the configuration of the S-boxes was determined.

Use of DES

Many vendors are now providing software implementations of DES on their domestic systems as an alternative to `crypt`. Publically available implementations are also available from the software archive sites described in Chapter 11. Because export of DES implementations outside of the United States is restricted, vendors cannot ship it out of the country. However, one of the publically available implementations was developed in Europe, and is thus available to non–U.S. sites.

The DES is significantly more secure than `crypt` and most other publically available forms of encryption (which are usually based on easily broken techniques). However, the absolute security of the system has never been proven (and also never disproven), so some small risk may still be present.

Password Encryption

Password encryption on UNIX is based on a modified version of the DES. Contrary to popular belief, the typed password is **not** encrypted. Rather, the password is used as the key to encrypt a block of zero-valued bytes. The process is shown in Figure 9.6.

To begin the encryption, the first seven bits of each character in the password are extracted to form the 56-bit key. This implies that no more than eight characters are significant in a password. Next, the E table is modified using the *salt*, which is the first two characters of the encrypted password (stored in the password file). The purpose of the salt is to make it difficult to use hardware DES chips or a precomputed list of encrypted passwords to attack the algorithm. The DES algorithm (with the modified E table) is then invoked for 25 iterations on the block of zeros. The output of this encryption, which is 64 bits long, is then coerced into a 64-character alphabet (A-Z, a-z, 0-9, "." and "/"). Because this coercion involves translations in which several different values are represented by the same character, password encryption is essentially one-way; the result cannot be decrypted.

When a user logs in and types a password, this password and the encrypted value from the password file are passed to the `crypt` library function (not to be confused

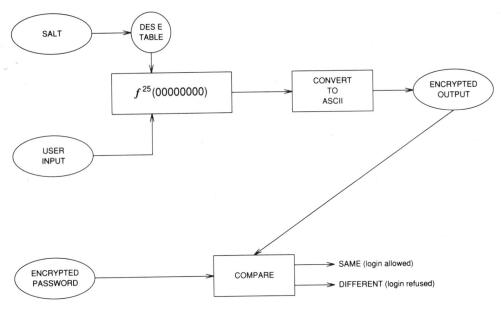

Figure 9.6   UNIX Password Encryption

with the `crypt` program described earlier). The encrypted value is needed to determine the proper salt to use when modifying the E table. The password entered by the user is then used to encrypt the block of zeros, and the output is compared to the output stored in the password file. If the results are the same the user is allowed to log in; otherwise login is refused. When a user changes her password, a new salt is generated for the new password. This is done by generating two pseudo-random characters, using the current time of day and process id of the password-changing program as a seed.

9.2 Authentication

Authentication is the process of verifying something. This may be a user's identity, a workstation's network address, or the integrity of a file. There are several approaches to authentication; some of them are described in this section.

Authenticating File Integrity

The integrity of data stored on a computer system can be important for several reasons. In a hospital, the integrity of patient records is vital to providing correct treatment, since incorrect data may result in the injury or death of the patient. The integrity of the system itself (its programs, configuration files, and so on) is no less important. If the changes made to a system program by a virus or a human attacker cannot be detected, then the attack cannot be defended against.

As described in Chapter 3, the usual method of verifying the integrity of a file is by using a checksum, such as that calculated by the sum command. However, checksum algorithms can be fooled, and a file can be modified in such a way that its checksum is not altered. A more secure method of verifying a file's contents uses a *message-digest*, also called a one-way hash function, cryptographic checksum, or manipulation detection code. (A checksum is also a one-way hash function, but not a very good one.) This section describes two message-digest functions available in the public domain for UNIX systems.

Snefru

Snefru (Merkle, 1990) is a message-digest function developed by Ralph C. Merkle, a researcher at Xerox's Palo Alto Research Center. The fundamental design criteria for Snefru were good security and the ability to hash data rapidly on a 32-bit RISC processor. For an arbitrary size input file, Snefru produces a 128- or 256-bit fixed-size output. The design of the algorithm is such that it is computationally infeasible to produce two inputs which will produce the same output, and it is also computationally infeasible to design an input that will produce a prespecified output. Multiple passes of the algorithm are used to provide additional security. In April 1990, a method of producing two inputs that produce the same output in two-pass Snefru was found, and an attack on four-pass Snefru has been suggested as well. As of this writing, Merkle is suggesting using eight passes.

Dan Bernstein of New York University has developed an encryption algorithm based on Snefru, called *Snuffle*. Although the cryptographic security of Snuffle has not been verified, Bernstein claims that it is easy to prove that certain measures of cryptographic algorithm security are much higher for Snuffle than for DES. The keys used with Snuffle are certainly much less vulnerable to brute-force attack: the primary key uses at least 128 bits. Snuffle is available from the public archive sites described in Chapter 11.

MD4

MD4 (Rivest, 1991a) is another message-digest function, proposed by one of the inventors of the RSA public-key encryption algorithm. Its design goals were similar to those of Snefru, although the implementation is quite different. MD4 accepts an arbitrarily large file as input, and produces a 128-bit output. The primary purpose of MD4 is to verify the integrity of a file before being encrypted with a private key under a public-key encryption system (see section 9.3). The cryptographic integrity of MD4 has not been held up to public scrutiny as much as that of Snefru has; this is primarily because MD4 is newer.

A newer function, MD5 (Rivest, 1991b), has recently been released. This function is similar to MD4, but provides a little more security in the face of cryptanalytic attack at the sacrifice of some speed.

Authenticating Users

Authenticating users is extremely important; this is the primary purpose of password protection. However, a password only serves to initially authenticate the user (ignoring for the moment the possibility of stolen passwords) to the system. Once the user is logged in, he can attempt to impersonate other users in order to gain added permissions. Or, he can attempt to convince a workstation or personal computer to impersonate another host, allowing him to attack the system as well.

The focus of the first half of this book has been on preventing users from impersonating other users or other network hosts. The object is to make each UNIX system as secure as possible, preventing impersonations from taking place.

Kerberos

At MIT's Project Athena, a different approach has been taken. Project Athena, because of the large number of workstations it controls (over 1,000), has adopted the position that it is impossible to make sure that every workstation is secure. Thus, rather than attempting to make the system as secure as possible against impersonation, they have assumed that impersonation **will** take place, and set as their goal defending against it. This is done by making each and every network service, from electronic mail to the Network File System, require that both the user and the workstation authenticate themselves before any service is granted. This authentication is provided by a system called *Kerberos* (Kohl and Neuman, 1990). A brief overview of how Kerberos is used is provided here; for more detailed information, as well as information about **why** Kerberos works the way it does, consult Appendix C.

Kerberos is a trusted third-party authentication service, based on the model developed by Needham and Schroeder (1978). Each of its clients accepts Kerberos' judgement that the identity of each of its other clients is accurate. As Kerberos views things, a client is anything using the authentication system, be it a user or a network server. There may be more than one network server providing a given network service (for example, one on each machine), just as there may be more than one user requesting a given service.

The primary part of Kerberos is a master database which maintains a list of each of its clients and their private keys. These keys are known only to Kerberos and the clients they belong to. Because it knows these keys, Kerberos can create messages which convince one client that another is really who it claims to be. This is done by encrypting information about one client with the other client's key. If a client can decrypt the message using its key, it will accept that the information in the message is valid (since only Kerberos could have encrypted it), otherwise it will refuse the information as being invalid.

Kerberos uses two types of credentials, called *tickets* and *authenticators*. Both are based on private key encryption, but are encrypted with different keys. A ticket is used to pass the identity of the person to whom the ticket was issued between the authentication server and the network server. A ticket also contains information that can be used to verify the person using it. The authenticator contains the additional information that, when compared against the information in the ticket, proves that the client presenting the ticket is the one to whom the ticket was issued.

When a user logs in, she enters her login name as usual. A request is then sent to the authentication server, which looks up the user in the database. The user's password (key) is then used to encrypt a ticket for use with the *ticket-granting* service, and the encrypted ticket is returned to the login program. The login program now prompts the user for her password, which is used to decrypt the ticket. If the ticket is successfully decrypted, the user is allowed to log in, otherwise login is not permitted. The ticket-granting ticket is saved for future use in obtaining tickets to use other network services. Its primary purpose is to allow operation without having to continually prompt for the password each time a new network service is requested.

A ticket is only good for a single server. Thus each time a service is requested from a new network server, a new ticket must be obtained. Tickets are obtained from the ticket-granting service, for which a ticket was given when the user logged in. The client program executed by the user sends a request to the ticket-granting service which contains the name of the server for which the ticket is being requested, the ticket-granting ticket, and an authenticator containing the user's name, the network address of her workstation, and the current time. The authenticator is encrypted using a special session key that was returned in the ticket-granting ticket. Provided everything "checks out," the ticket-granting service returns a ticket for the requested network service. The client program then builds another authenticator, and sends it along with the service ticket to the network server, which will provide the service if everything is correct.

In order to reduce network traffic, tickets may be reused. Timeouts are used to prevent *replay*, by which an attacker steals tickets off the network and then retransmits them at a later time. When the user logs out, all saved tickets are deleted. If a user stays logged in past a ticket timeout (currently eight hours), she must re-enter her password to the authentication system.

Kerberos significantly improves the security of a network by making it much more difficult for an attacker to impersonate another user (including the super-user). Even if he can obtain access to another user's privileges in the ways alluded to in earlier chapters, he cannot access network services without providing the password of the user he is impersonating to the authentication service. However, Kerberos is not a cure-all for UNIX security. Perhaps the most obvious problem is that Kerberos still relies on well-chosen passwords and the secrecy of those passwords. If an attacker can gain access to another user's password, there is no way for Kerberos to distinguish between the user and the attacker.

There are several other possible problems (or limitations) associated with Kerberos (Bellovin and Merritt, 1991). One of the most serious is that the Kerberos master authentication server must store all the keys in plaintext so that it can use them. This means that if the security of the Kerberos machine is compromised, so is the entire Kerberos system. A second problem is that Kerberos is not as secure against replay attacks (an attacker retransmitting packets intercepted from the network) as it could be. This is because authenticators have timeouts associated with them which are large enough to accommodate machines with slightly unsynchronized clocks, meaning that an authenticator could conceivably be intercepted and retransmitted quickly enough to "scrape by" this timeout. This could be solved (although not easily) by maintaining a cache of all "used" authenticators, so that no timeouts are necessary. Related to this problem is that if a host can be misled about the current time, replay attacks become simple. This could be prevented by use of a (yet to be developed) secure time service. Another problem is that Kerberos uses untrusted workstations that are not "reset" between user sessions. This means that the ability of an attacker to use Trojan horses and other subterfuge to gain access is not adequately dealt with. Several other problems have been identified as well by Bellovin and Merritt, although the latest version of the protocol (Version 5 Draft 4) has solved most of them.

All this is not to say that Kerberos isn't useful. Perhaps its biggest drawback is not even related to its security, but rather to its implementation. Because network services must now perform authentication, this means that every network program which makes use of authentication must be modified to use Kerberos. While the modifications are not difficult, they do require source code. The Kerberos distribution comes with the most common Berkeley utilities (`rlogin`, `rsh`, etc.) already modified, allowing at least the "common" services to make use of authentication, but sites without a UNIX source license are somewhat out of luck. This may change in the future; several versions of UNIX are scheduled to contain Kerberos, including the next release of Berkeley UNIX (usually referred to as 4.4BSD), the Open Software Foundation's Distributed Computing Environment, and a future version of Digital Equipment Corporation's ULTRIX operating system. The current implementation of Kerberos may be obtained from the archive sites described in Chapter 11.

Challenge-Response Boxes

A challenge-response box is a small calculator-like device with buttons (numbers and letters) and a display. When logging in, a user types his login name and password as usual. The system then presents a challenge to the user by prompting him with a string of numbers and/or letters. The user enters this string into his challenge-response box, and it prints another string in the display. He enters this second string to the computer, which then allows him to log in. An alternative type of box requires that the user enter a special sequence into the box before it will produce the response; this effectively serves as the password, and no password is necessary on the host system.

Challenge-response boxes are basically just encryption devices that share an encryption algorithm with the host computer. Each challenge-response box implements the same encryption algorithm, but with a different key. Each time someone logs in, the system looks up the user to see which box is registered to him, and then prints a random string. The user enters this string into the box, and obtains the result of encrypting that string. The computer encrypts the string with the same key, and compares the results.

The advantage of challenge-response boxes is obvious: even if an attacker can obtain a user's password, she cannot log in as that user unless she possesses his challenge-response box. If on the other hand she obtains the box, she cannot log in without knowing his password. An additional benefit is that challenge-response boxes can be used over dial-up phone lines and insecure networks to eliminate the need for transmitting unencrypted passwords. Unfortunately, for sites with a large number of users, the cost of implementing a challenge-response system may be prohibitive. Inexpensive boxes are priced at around $50.00 each in small quantities.

9.3 Encrypting and Authenticating Electronic Mail

As the use of electronic mail becomes more widespread, the need for both secrecy and authentication of messages sent electronically is becoming more evident. Although assorted proprietary methods for accomplishing this exist, it is much more convenient to have a system which can work with any existing mail system.

Secret Mail

Most UNIX systems provide a rudimentary system called *secret mail*. This is implemented by the commands `enroll`, `xsend`, and `xget`. Secret mail is built around the `crypt` command, whose problems were described earlier. Although the idea of secret mail is interesting, the implementation has nothing but curiosity value, and will not be discussed further.

Public-Key Encryption

Most encryption systems are *symmetric*, meaning that the enciphering and deciphering keys are the same (or easily determined from one another). For example, in order to decrypt a file encrypted with DES, the original key must be supplied. Although this is sufficient for most applications, it has a disadvantage when several people must share the ability to encrypt and decrypt; they must all know the same key. The problem here lies in transmitting the key to all users without revealing it to anyone else. (A similar problem exists in the UNIX world: it makes no sense to change the *root* password if you distribute it to everyone using electronic mail!)

In 1976, Diffie and Hellman introduced a new method of encryption, called *public-key* encryption. This is an *asymmetric* system involving more than one key.

In a public-key system, each user has a *private key*, known only to himself, used for decryption, and a *public key*, known to everyone, used for encryption. The public key is derived from the private key by a one-way transformation, and it is computationally infeasible to determine the private key from the public key. Secrecy and authenticity are provided separately or together by different uses of these keys.

If a user A wishes to send B a message in secrecy, he encrypts the message using B's public key and transmits it. When B receives the message, she decrypts it using her private key. Because nobody but B knows B's private (deciphering) key, the message is secure.

For authentication, A instead encrypts the message using his private key, and then transmits it to B. B decrypts the message using A's public key. This guarantees authenticity, since only A could have sent a message that can be decrypted using his public key. Secrecy is not preserved however, since anyone intercepting the message can apply A's public key to it.

To achieve both secrecy and authenticity, two encryptions (and two decryptions) must be performed. First, A enciphers the message using his private key, which will guarantee authenticity of the message. Next, he takes the result of this encipherment and encrypts it using B's public key, which will preserve secrecy. The result is sent to B. When B receives the message, she first decrypts it using her private key, and then deciphers that result using A's public key.

Although several public-key systems exist which can be used either for secrecy or authentication, the ability to use the same keys for both purposes as described in the previous paragraph requires that the keys have special properties. The only two systems currently available which have these properties are RSA (Rivest et al., 1978), invented by three researchers at MIT, and ElGamal (ElGamal, 1985), invented by a researcher at Stanford University.

Privacy-Enhanced Mail

Privacy-enhanced mail (Linn, 1989a, 1989b; Kent and Linn, 1989) is a draft standard elective protocol for the Internet community. It defines message encipherment and authentication procedures for electronic mail, allowing users to send private mail readable only by the intended recipients, and to send mail whose sender can be unquestionably authenticated. The integrity of a message (that the contents are complete and unchanged) can also be verified. The procedures defined in this standard are compatible with both symmetric (one-key) and asymmetric (two-key) cryptosystems.

Authentication and integrity checks are always applied to the entirety of a message's text. Encryption however, may be applied selectively to parts of a message or to the entire message. Headers required for delivery of the mail (sender and recipient names, addresses, etc.) cannot be encrypted, since the service is intended to operate transparently with existing Internet mail systems. This allows intermediate systems used in the delivery of the message to process it without having to implement the privacy enhancements.

Although nearly any cryptosystem can be used to implement privacy-enhanced mail, there are only two standards presently defined for this purpose. The first uses the Data Encryption Standard in various forms for all parts of the message (encryption, authentication, and message integrity), and will not be discussed further. The second uses the RSA public-key encryption algorithm supplied by RSA Data Security, Inc. (RSADSI).

In this scheme, RSADSI will offer a service in which it will sign an electronic "certificate" (using a digital signature, their private key) which has been generated by a user and vouched for either by an organization or a Notary Public (this is for purposes of authentication). This service carries (at the time of this writing) a $25.00 bi-annual fee, which includes a license to use the RSA algorithm for the purposes of privacy-enhanced mail.

The certificate consists of the user's public key, various information that serves to identify the user, and the identity of the organization (or Notary Public) vouching for the user. In signing the certificate, the organization (or RSADSI, in the case of a Notary Public) vouches for the identity of the user, especially as it relates to the affiliation of the user with the organization. Once generated, the certificate may be stored anywhere, since its contents are not secret.

Prior to sending a privacy-enhanced message, the originator must obtain a certificate for each recipient (from some type of directory yet to be defined) and validate these certificates by decrypting them using the public key of the issuer of the certificate. Once a certificate has been validated, the recipient's public key is extracted from the certificate and used to encrypt the message. Upon receiving the encrypted message, the recipient uses his private key to decipher it.

In order to provide the message authentication and integrity checks, the originator generates a message integrity code, and signs (encrypts) it using his private key. This value, and the originator's certificate, are then transmitted with the message. Upon receiving the message, the recipient validates the sender's certificate as described above, extracts the originator's public key, and uses it to decrypt the message integrity code. The message's contents are then checked against this code.

The message integrity code is generated using the MD2 message-digest function, also developed by RSADSI. This algorithm is a predecessor of MD4, described previously.

9.4 Summary

In this chapter, we discussed encryption and authentication mechanisms. The salient points raised here include

- The `crypt` command is not secure.

- The Data Encryption Standard is a much more secure algorithm, although there are doubts about its security as well.

- Checksums are not totally secure ways to determine file integrity. Message-digest functions such as Snefru and MD4 should be used instead.

- User authentication can be performed using systems such as Kerberos or challenge-response boxes.

- UNIX "secret mail" is not very secure, and thus not very secret.

- Public-key encryption techniques can be used to implement both secrecy and authentication, and are used in Internet privacy-enhanced mail.

Perhaps the most important point to be learned from this chapter is that both data security and user authentication are extremely difficult problems to solve. When the security or integrity of data is required, and users of that data cannot be unquestionably authenticated, it may be safer to remove that data from the computer, or remove the computer from external access by disconnecting it from any networks and locking it up in a secure location.

Chapter 10
Security Policies

A comprehensive security policy can be as important in protecting your system from unauthorized access or abuse as any of the procedures described in earlier chapters. This chapter examines security policies: why they are important, how to create them, and what they should contain.

10.1 Establishing Policies and Why

Many universities include a "code of conduct" section in their student handbooks that details the university's expectations for student behavior. These policies typically include the university's definitions of offenses such as plagiarism, cheating, racism, and so on, and the penalties for these offenses. By publishing the code of conduct in the student handbook, which presumably all students are required to read, the university has established a means by which it can enforce certain standards of behavior. Violators of the policy face disciplinary action ranging from notations in the infamous "permanent record" to expulsion from the university.

A security policy is a code of conduct for use of the computer system. This policy details the activities that are and are not allowed, steps users must take to protect their accounts and data, how users may access other users' files, the rights of the system administrators, and so on. Additionally, the security policy explains what penalties may be imposed if violations occur. In the case of a university, penalties may be similar to those for violating the code of conduct; students can face appropriate disciplinary action, including probation and expulsion. In the case of a corporation, penalties may include loss of or restricted access to the computer, or termination of employment.

Just writing a security policy and filing it away is not enough. The most important step is making sure that each and every user of the system is aware of the policy and agrees to abide by it. In a university environment for example, it is just as important that the faculty users of the system adhere to the policy as it is that students do. In a corporation, it does no good to require every secretary to choose a good password if the president is allowed to use her husband's name.

The easiest way to make sure that every user is aware of the security policy is to give each user a copy of that policy when he receives his computer account. To ensure that the user agrees to abide by the policy, a signature may be required: no signature, no account. If your organization publishes a code of conduct, student or employee handbook, or something similar, publishing the security policy there is another step that can be taken. The policy should also be available on-line, accessible to all users.

The remainder of this chapter describes specific topics that a security policy should cover. Where appropriate, examples are given from computer security and use policies of various universities, collected by Dave Grisham of the University of New Mexico. These are available for anonymous FTP from the host *ariel.unm.edu* in the *ethics* directory.

10.2 Access to the System

One of the most important parts of the security policy are the sections that describe who may have access to the system, and who may grant access to the system.

Authorized Access

The first question a security policy must answer is: Who is allowed to use the system? Or, if multiple systems are involved: Who is allowed to use each system? For example, undergraduate students may be allowed to use the terminals in the terminal room, but the workstations are restricted for use by graduate students only. Answering this question is typically a good way to begin your statement of security policy. Some examples are shown below:

- The computing facilities at the University are provided for the use of students, faculty, and staff in support of the programs of the University. All students, faculty, and staff are responsible for seeing that these computing facilities are used in an effective, efficient, ethical, and lawful manner. The following policies relate to their use.

- The Computing Center is maintained by the University as an educational and research facility for its faculty, research staff, and students. It also supports the data processing requirements of its administrative offices. Usage of the facility is allowed to other organizations by special permission and upon the payment of appropriate fees.

- Computer facilities operated by the University are available for the use of students, faculty, and staff without charge. Students, faculty, and staff are encouraged to use University computer facilities for research and instruction. In order to facilitate the ethical and responsible use of computers, the following guidelines are established for students, faculty, and staff. Instructors or departments may impose additional requirements or restrictions in connection with course or departmental work.

In larger facilities, such as those at universities, it may be necessary to divide this section into multiple parts, covering each type of facility (e.g., student, faculty, administrative) separately.

Granting Access

After indicating who may have access to the computers, it is important to indicate who may grant that access, and what types of access they are permitted to give. Controlling who is allowed to grant access to the computers is the only way you can control who is using your system. There are several approaches to granting access. Accounts can be distributed from a centralized point, in which case only one or two people will be granting access. Alternatively, accounts can be distributed from several points (for example, each department could distribute its own accounts), in which case there will be several people granting access. The trade-off is one of security versus convenience.

Regardless of which method you choose, there should be a specific, written procedure for creating accounts. This procedure should cover what files should be edited, how to choose a login name and user id number that are unique across all systems involved, what mode to make the new account's home directory, how to select an initial password for the account, and so on. This procedure should be given to all people who have the authorization to create accounts.

With regard to the security policy, you should include text which describes who may grant access to the system, and also include a section which prohibits others from granting access. This section will typically prohibit users from sharing their passwords with others, using other people's accounts, and so on. In some cases, it may be necessary to make exceptions to this rule; for example, company procedures may be simplified if a secretary and her boss can share their passwords. These exceptions should be fully documented in the security policy.

Some examples of paragraphs describing the access-granting procedure are shown below:

- Computer facilities and accounts are owned by the University and are to be used for university-related activities only. All access to central computer systems, including the issuing of passwords, must be approved through the Computer Center. All access to departmental computer systems must be approved by the department chairman or an authorized representative.

- You must use only those accounts which have been authorized for your use by the University. The unauthorized use of another's account, as well as the providing of false or misleading information for the purpose of obtaining access to computing facilities is prohibited. You may not authorize anyone to use your account for any reason.

- Only persons properly authorized may access the computer facilities. Proper authorization is provided by computer center staff or their designate in the form of an account issued in the name of the authorized person. Users may not permit other persons to access the computer facilities via their account.

- Computer accounts will be given to all employees, to outside collaborators with written agreements, and to guests who are collaborating with a project. All outsiders must be sponsored by a member of the technical staff. All guest accounts will be closed after the project termination date unless the account sponsor renews the agreement. Account holders should not share their accounts or passwords with others.

It is not normally a good idea to list the names of those people who can grant access in your policy document; this requires the document to be updated whenever someone resigns or a new person is hired. It may be possible, however, to list persons by office or title.

10.3 Password Policies

Since passwords are typically the first line of defense against unauthorized use of the computer system, it is important that your security policy cover them. There are three elements to a good password policy.

First, users should be instructed on how to choose a secure password. This should take the form of a list of guidelines to follow when choosing a password; the list provided in Chapter 2 is a good start. If you have installed a proactive password checker, users should be told to use this program to determine that their chosen password is reasonably secure.

Second, it is important to impress on the users the need to keep their passwords secret. Passwords should never be written down on desk blotters, calendars, and the like. Storing passwords on-line is also a bad idea, and should be discouraged.

Third, users cannot be allowed to share their passwords with others. This overlaps with the section on granting access, but because it is such a seemingly common practice, bears repeated discussion. It is a good idea to tell users not to give out their passwords over the phone if a "system administrator" calls and asks for it—system administrators, since they have super-user privileges, do not need to know a user's password.

A final suggestion is that you include instructions for changing a password, if practical. This will perhaps motivate those users who read the password policy and then ignore it because they don't know how to change their password. A sample description for the UNIX system is shown below:

- You may change your password at any time using the `passwd` command. You will be prompted for your old password, and then your new password.

You will be asked to retype the new password, to ensure that you did not make a typing mistake.

Obviously, techniques such as this become cumbersome if your site uses many different operating systems. In that case, you might consider attaching a separate instruction sheet to the policy when giving it out with new computer accounts.

If your site has other password-related policies, such as requiring users to change their passwords at specified intervals, these should be included in this section as well.

10.4 Proper Use

Now that the policies governing access have been completed, it is important to define exactly what activities are and are not allowed on the computer system. This section may have several parts; some of the more common ones are described shortly. Typically, the section will begin with a broad statement of the purpose of the computing facility. This statement will usually allow the use of the computer system only for activities directly relating to the educational, research, or operational goals of the organization. After this broad statement has been made, it is usually necessary to cover specific topics in detail.

Profit-Making Activities

One of the most commonly prohibited activities, particularly in university and research environments, is the use of the computer systems for personal gain. This is often necessary due to the nature of the software licenses used by the organization; educational licenses rarely allow commercial use.

When prohibiting profit-making activities, it is often useful to mention some of the more common ones. For example,

• Do not make use of any University computing facilities for any activity that is commercial in nature without first obtaining written approval to do so. Commercial activities include: consulting, typing services, developing software for sale, and in general any activity for which you are paid from non-University funds.

You may also wish to include other activities, such as writing articles and books, developing public-domain software, and so on in this section.

Recreational and Personal Use

In environments where resources are limited; it may be desirable to include text that regulates the use of the computer system for recreational and personal uses. Typically, recreational uses (game-playing) are either allowed, allowed but restricted to "off" periods of use, or prohibited entirely. This policy should be set forth in the policy document.

Personal use of the computer system includes using it to balance your checkbook, maintain address lists, store recipes, and so on. If disk space or printing resources are scarce, a policy should be formed that restricts this use to something tolerable, such as "no more than ten percent of disk usage may be for personal files," or "personal files may not be printed on the laser printer."

License to Hack

In many environments, some users will be interested in computer security, and may want to experiment with breaking the security of your system. Other users may be interested in worms or viruses, and will want to experiment with those types of programs. Needless to say, these users can pose a serious security threat to your system, since they may inadvertently open your system to outside attack, or damage the system when experimenting with worms and viruses.

It is therefore necessary to recognize that there are valid reasons for experimenting with the security of the system, and to require that the users inform the system staff of their intentions to experiment with security, and that they conduct their experiments only under closely supervised conditions. This is typically called a "license to hack." Some examples of how to allow (or prohibit) this activity include

- Loopholes in computer security systems or knowledge of a special password should not be used to damage computer systems, obtain extra resources, take resources from another user, gain access to systems, or use systems for which proper authorization has not been given.

- Actions taken by users intentionally to interfere with or to alter the integrity of the system are improper. Such actions include unauthorized use of accounts, impersonation of other individuals in communications, attempts to capture or crack passwords, attempts to break encryption protocols, compromising privacy, and destruction or alteration of data or programs belonging to other users. It is unacceptable to create worm or virus programs. It is unacceptable to conduct experiments that demonstrate network vulnerabilities without the prior permission of network authorities. It is unacceptable to engage in acts that would restrict or deny access by legitimate users to the system.

- Users shall not intentionally develop or use programs which harass other users of the facility or infiltrate the system and/or damage the software or hardware components of the system.

- A user who feels that he or she has legitimate reason to experiment with security-related aspects of the computer facilities should discuss the project with systems staff before embarking on the experiment.

The license to hack is designed to protect you and your system. If necessary, it may be necessary to install special systems or isolated networks to facilitate the users' needs in this regard; if you do this, these systems (or the ability to construct them) should be described in the policy statement.

Super-User Privileges

When granting super-user privileges, it is important to recognize that the super-user is not bound by file access permissions. This allows the super-user to access any file on the system, regardless of its protection. Your policy should acknowledge this fact, and specifically require those users with super-user permissions to respect the privacy of other users' files (however, see the next section). A good start for a super-user policy are the rules for operating as *root* set forth in section 2.7.

10.5 System Staff Rights and Responsibilities

It is important to realize that under some circumstances, it may be necessary for the system administrator to examine users' private files in the course of normal system administration duties, or when investigating a security violation. Your policy should explain this to the user population, in order to avoid embarrassing situations later. This can be done with text such as the following:

- In the normal course of system administration, the staff may have to examine files, mail, and printer listings to gather sufficient information to diagnose and correct problems with system software, or to determine if a user is acting in violation of the policies set forth in this document. The staff has the right to do this. The staff also has an obligation to maintain the privacy of a user's files, mail, and printer listings.

- To protect the integrity of the computer system against unauthorized or improper use, and to protect authorized users from the effects of unauthorized or improper use of the system, the system staff reserves the rights to: limit or restrict any account holder's usage, and to inspect, copy, remove, or otherwise alter any data, file, or system resources which may undermine the authorized use of that system without notice to the user. The system staff disclaims responsibility for loss of data or interference with files resulting from its efforts to maintain the privacy and security of the computer facilities.

The purpose of this section is not to give the system administrators license to do anything they want. However, it is appropriate to inform the user population of the actions that may be taken by the system staff if events warrant them.

10.6 Copyrights and Licenses

Software copyrights and licenses have become especially important over the last several years. It is important to explain to users that some or all of the software in use on the computer system is copyrighted or licensed, and that the users may not violate the terms of these agreements. This can be done with statements such as the following:

- United States copyright and patent laws protect the interests of authors, inventors, and software developers in their products. Software license agreements serve to increase compliance with copyright and patent laws, and to help insure publishers, authors, and developers of return on their investments. It is against federal law and University policy to violate the copyrights or patents of computer software. It is against University policy and may be a violation of state or federal law to violate software license agreements.

- The University acquires a substantial portion of its computer software from third-party vendors under license agreements which restrict the use of the software to specific computer systems and which require the University to limit the use and copying of the software. It is a violation of University policy and may be a violation of state or federal laws for individuals using the computing facilities to use or copy any software except as specifically authorized.

Violation of copyrights and software licenses is a serious offense, often punishable by large fines or other penalties. Every step should be taken to avoid these violations.

10.7 Ethics

One of the last sections of your security policy document should contain something about the ethical use of computing resources. This section tends to "fill in" any gaps left in the previous sections, by encouraging the responsible and proper use of your computer system. Your statement on ethics may be a simple one, such as

- You must not use the system irresponsibly, or needlessly affect the work of others. This includes transmitting or making accessible offensive, annoying, or harassing material; intentionally damaging the system; intentionally damaging information not belonging to you; or intentionally misusing system resources or allowing misuse of system resources by others. You are responsible for reporting to systems staff any violation of these guidelines by another individual.

Alternatively, you may wish to make a longer statement, listing individual points. This list may include such items as not reading other users' files, even if they are accessible to you, not altering files that do not belong to you even if access permissions allow you to, not overloading the system with background jobs, relinquishing licensed software when done with it so that others may use it, relinquishing resources such as dial-up modems when not in use, and so on.

10.8 Guidelines for the Secure Operation of the Internet

As a final element of security policy, any organization whose systems are connected to the Internet should be aware of Request for Comments Number 1281, *Guidelines for the Secure Operation of the Internet* (Pethia et al., 1991). These guidelines address the entire Internet community, and encompass six main points. The points are

1. Users are individually responsible for understanding and respecting the security policies of the systems (computers and networks) they are using. Users are individually accountable for their own behavior.

2. Users have a responsibility to employ available security mechanisms and procedures for protecting their own data. They also have a responsibility for assisting in the protection of the systems they use.

3. Computer and network service providers are responsible for maintaining the security of the systems they operate. They are further responsible for notifying users of their security policies and any changes to these policies.

4. Vendors and system developers are responsible for providing systems which are sound and which embody adequate security controls.

5. Users, service providers, and hardware and software vendors are responsible for cooperating to provide security.

6. Technical improvements in Internet security protocols should be sought on a continuing basis. At the same time, personnel developing new protocols, hardware, or software for the Internet are expected to include security considerations as part of the design and development process.

The document goes on to expand upon these points, providing more detail and presenting the rationale behind them. It is available for anonymous FTP from the site *nic.ddn.mil*, as well as other archive sites around the Internet.

10.9 Summary

Your security policy is an important document for protecting your system from abuse. As has been shown above, the policy covers more than just the topics presented in earlier chapters; it also describes the proper use of the system, sets forth policies on access, and indicates the users' rights and responsibilities.

Once you have constructed your policy, it is important to make the policy as "official" as possible; the best way to do this is to have it signed by the president of the company or university. This gives the policy as much weight as possible, and demonstrates that the organization as a whole is committed to the policy.

Finally, each user should be asked to sign the policy when given an account; this ensures that the policy has been read and understood by every user of the system.

A complete security policy that encompasses all of the points covered in this chapter is shown in Appendix D.

Chapter 11
Security Software

Because security is of great concern to many sites, a wealth of software has been developed for improving the security of UNIX systems. Much of this software has been developed at universities and other public institutions, and is available free for the asking. This chapter describes how to obtain this software, and mentions some of the more important programs available, including those described in earlier chapters of this book.

11.1 Obtaining Fixes and New Versions

Several sites on the Internet maintain large repositories of public-domain and freely distributable software, and make this material available for "anonymous" FTP. A host which allows anonymous FTP allows anyone to connect to the host using the login *anonymous*, and transfer files from a restricted directory. A sample anonymous FTP session is shown below.

```
$ ftp ftp.uu.net
Connected to uunet.UU.NET.
220 uunet FTP server (V. 5.100 Mon Feb 11 17:13:28 EST 1991) ready.
Name (ftp.uu.net:huey): anonymous
331 Guest login ok, send ident as password.
Password:          enter your mail address, yourname@yourhost, here
230 Guest login ok, access restrictions apply.
ftp> cd sun-dist
250 CWD command successful.
ftp> dir
200 PORT command successful.
150 Opening ASCII mode data connection for /bin/ls.
total 2798
-r--r--r--  1 76    21    601779 May  6 17:18 100100-01.tar.Z
-r--r--r--  1 76    21      3830 May 14 16:46 100103-06.tar.Z
```

```
-r--r--r-- 1 76   21    148497 May  6 17:18 100108-01.tar.Z
.....
-r--r--r-- 1 76   21    529589 Aug  2 18:37 100305-05.tar.Z
-r--r--r-- 1 76   21       557 Mar 21 17:38 README.sendmail
226 Transfer complete.
1006 bytes received in 0.1 seconds (9.8 Kbytes/s)
ftp> type image
200 Type set to I.
ftp> get 100100-01.tar.Z
200 PORT command successful.
150 Opening BINARY data connection for 100100-01.tar.Z (601779 bytes).
226 Transfer complete.
local: 100100-01.tar.Z remote: 100100-01.tar.Z
601779 bytes received in 18 seconds (32 Kbytes/s)
ftp> bye
221 Goodbye.
$
```

After connecting to the host, log in with the special login *anonymous*. As a password, enter your electronic mail address. The `cd` command can be used to change directories; most sites place their distributions in a subdirectory called *pub*. The `dir` command lists the current directory. Many sites compress their distributions to conserve disk space; files which have been compressed have names which end in ".Z". These files must be transferred in "binary" mode to avoid corruption; the `type image` FTP command tells FTP to perform binary transfers instead of ASCII transfers (ASCII files may usually be transferred in binary mode also, at least between systems of the same type). The `get` command copies a remote file to a local file of the same name. Finally, the `bye` command closes the connection. For more information on the use of FTP, consult the manual page for the `ftp` command on your system.

UUNET

UUNET Communications Services, Inc. makes large volumes of software and other information available for anonymous FTP and also "anonymous" UUCP. Some of the directories which may be of interest to readers of this book include

athena   The MIT Project Athena software distribution, including Kerberos.

bsd-sources   The sources to much of 4.3BSD, including most of the utility programs, and the TCP/IP networking code. If you want to make a modified version of a standard program such as `login` for your site, the sources here are often a good place to start.

*comp.sources.**   The USENET newsgroups *comp.sources.** are all archived here. There are directories for several varieties of home computer and workstation, as well as more general directories such as *comp.sources.unix* and *comp.sources.misc*. The software in these directories is divided into volumes; indexes are contained in the top-level directories.

ietf Minutes of meetings of the various working groups of the Internet Engineering Task Force, which is responsible for adopting new Internet standard protocols. Working groups exist for almost any topic imaginable, including several on security-related subjects.

internet-drafts Copies of all Internet Drafts, which are the predecessors to Request for Comments (see below). These documents specify proposed protocols and policies, and are available for public review and comment.

rfc Copies of all Internet Request for Comments documents, which specify the protocols and procedures used on the Internet. The protocol specifications for all "official" Internet services, including IP, TCP, UDP, SMTP, FTP, and TELNET are contained here. The file *rfc-index* contains an index to the documents.

sun-dist Official security-related patches from Sun Microsystems. Other patches (non-security-related) must be obtained through the normal Sun channels.

ucb-fixes Official patches (both security-related and non-security-related) for 4.3BSD from the University of California at Berkeley.

The above list is only a small fraction of the material available from UUNET; the best way to find out what is available is to log in via FTP and browse around.

To connect to UUNET via anonymous FTP, contact the host *ftp.uu.net*. To connect via "anonymous" UUCP, call (900) 468-7727 and use the login *uucp* with no password. Standard modem speeds from 300 to 9600 bps, as well as Telebit PEP (18,000 bps) are supported. The file *~/help* contains instructions. The file *~/ls-lR.Z* contains a complete list of files available and is updated daily. You will be charged $0.40 per minute (as of August 1991) on your next telephone bill; this equates to approximately $7/megabyte at 9600 bps or PEP speeds.

Berkeley

The University of California at Berkeley makes fixes available for anonymous FTP. These fixes pertain primarily to the current release of BSD UNIX (currently release 4.3-Reno). However, even if you are not running their software, these fixes are still important, since many vendors (Sun Microsystems, Digital Equipment, Hewlett-Packard, etc.) base some or most of their software on the Berkeley releases.

The Berkeley fixes are available for anonymous FTP from the host *ucbarpa.berkeley.edu* in the directory *4.3/ucb-fixes*. The file *INDEX* in this directory describes what each fix contains.

Berkeley also distributes new versions of `sendmail` and `named` from this host. New versions of these programs are stored in the *4.3* directory, usually in the files *sendmail.tar.Z* and *bind.tar.Z*, respectively.

SIMTEL-20

The host *wsmr-simtel20.army.mil* is a TOPS-20 system operated by the U.S. Army at White Sands Missile Range, New Mexico. Its primary purpose is to make repositories of UNIX, MS-DOS, and Ada software available to the military organizations connected to the MILNET, although access is open to anyone, military or not.

The directory *PD6:<UNIX-C>* contains a large amount of UNIX software, primarily taken from the USENET *comp.sources* newsgroups. The file *000-MASTER-INDEX.TXT* contains a description of each file contained in the repository. The file *000-INTRO-UNIX-SW.TXT* contains information on the mailing list used to announce new software in the repository, and also contains detailed instructions for transferring the software with FTP. Because the TOPS-20 file formats differ from those of UNIX systems, this file should be consulted before transferring any software.

SUN-SPOTS

The SUN-SPOTS mailing list, and the USENET newsgroup *comp.sys.sun* are used for discussing software and hardware issues associated with workstations from Sun Microsystems, Inc. A repository of software for Sun workstations, including security-related software, is accessible for anonymous FTP from the host *titan.rice.edu*.

comp.sources

The USENET newsgroups *comp.sources.unix* and *comp.sources.misc* provide a wealth of UNIX software for every conceivable purpose. The sources posted to these groups are archived in several places around the Internet, both in the United States and Europe. A related group, *alt.sources*, also contains some useful software.

Vendors

Some UNIX vendors make bug fixes for their systems available over the Internet. These fixes are announced through various channels.

Sun Microsystems

Security problems in Sun's operating system are reported through the *cert-advisory* mailing list (see section 12.1), as well as via Sun's Customer Warning System (see section 12.3).

Fixes for security-related bugs in Sun Microsystems' version of UNIX can be obtained via anonymous FTP or anonymous UUCP from UUNET Communications Services (described above) in the directory *sun-dist*. Each file contains instructions for installing the fix, and files for all Sun architectures affected by the fix. The fixes usually apply only to Sun's most recent operating system releases.

Digital Equipment Corporation

Digital Equipment Corporation makes software for its version of UNIX, such as new versions of `sendmail`, available for anonymous FTP from the host *gatekeeper. dec.com* in the directory *pub/DEC*. These are **unofficial** distributions provided as a service by DEC's Western Research Laboratory.

For official patches to Ultrix, contact your Digital sales representative.

Hewlett-Packard

At the end of 1990, Hewlett-Packard announced that it would be making its support service available over the Internet for its customers with support contracts. Contact your sales representative for information on how to obtain this service.

11.2 Publicly Available Software

A large amount of software has been developed in the UNIX community, and much of it is available free for the asking, or for a nominal distribution fee. This section describes how to obtain many of the programs described in this book.

NPASSWD

The `npasswd` command, developed by Clyde Hoover at the University of Texas at Austin, is intended to be a replacement for the standard UNIX `passwd` command, as well as the Sun `yppasswd` command. The `npasswd` program makes passwords more secure by refusing to allow users to select insecure passwords. The following capabilities are provided by `npasswd`:

- Configurable minimum password length

- Configurable to force users to use mixed case or digits and punctuation

- Checking for "simple" passwords such as a repeated letter

- Checking against the host name and other host-specific information

- Checking against the login name, first and last names, and so on

- Checking for words in various dictionaries, including the system dictionary

The `npasswd` distribution is available for anonymous FTP from the host *emx.utexas.edu* in the directory *pub/npasswd*.

COPS

The `COPS` package (Farmer and Spafford, 1990), developed by Dan Farmer of Sun Microsystems, is a security tool for system administrators that checks for numerous common security problems on UNIX systems, including most of the things described in this book. A collection of shell scripts and C programs (a new version uses PERL instead of C), COPS can be easily run on almost any UNIX variant. Among other things, it checks the following items and sends the results to the system administrator:

- Checks */dev/kmem* and other devices for world read/writability

- Checks special/important files and directories for "bad" modes (world-writable, etc.)

- Checks for easily-guessed passwords

- Checks for duplicate user ids, invalid fields in the password file, etc.

- Checks for duplicate group ids, invalid fields in the group file, etc.

- Checks all users' home directories and their *.cshrc*, *.login*, *.profile*, and *.rhosts* files for security problems

- Checks all commands in the */etc/rc* files and *cron* files for world-writability

- Checks for bad *root* search paths, NFS file systems exported to the world, etc.

- Includes an expert system that checks to see if a given user (usually *root*) can be compromised, given that certain conditions exist

- Checks for *changes* in the set-user-id status of programs on the system

The COPS package is available for anonymous FTP from the host *cert.sei.cmu.edu* in the directory *pub/cops*. It is also distributed periodically via the *comp.sources.unix* USENET newsgroup.

CRACK

The `crack` program is a password cracking utility developed by Alec David Muffett of the University College of Wales. It comes with a fast version of the UNIX password encryption function, called `fcrypt`; this function is approximately 13 times faster than the standard UNIX `crypt` function. It also includes the ability to use multiple systems to parallelize the cracking. The general procedure used by `crack` is to first base guesses on the contents of the GECOS field, and then to use several pre-processed dictionaries. Additional dictionaries may be added. The `crack` distribution version 4.0a was posted in Volume 25 of the *comp.sources.misc* newsgroup in November 1991; it is also available from the host *wuarchive.wustl.edu* in the *packages* directory.

NFSWATCH

The `nfswatch` program, developed by the author, which monitors NFS packets by host, network, or file system, is available for anonymous FTP from the hosts *harbor.ecn.purdue.edu*, *ftp.erg.sri.com*, and *gatekeeper.dec.com*. It is also available from the SUN-SPOTS archives on *titan.rice.edu*.

TCPDUMP

The `tcpdump` packet monitoring program is available for anonymous FTP from the site *ftp.ee.lbl.gov* in the file *tcpdump-2.0.tar.Z* It generally requires a Berkeley or Berkeley-based TCP/IP implementation, such as those used in SunOS and ULTRIX.

GATED

The `gated` program, which has a more configurable implementation of the Routing Information Protocol (RIP), is available for anonymous FTP from the host *gated.cornell.edu* in the directory *pub/gated*. The current `gated` implementation also contains support for the HELLO, BGP, and OSPF routing protocols.

Kerberos

The Kerberos package, developed by the Massachusetts Institute of Technology's Project Athena and described in Chapter 9, is available for anonymous FTP from the host *athena-dist.mit.edu* in the directory *pub/kerberos*. The other software developed by Project Athena, as well as various conference papers describing the project and its software, are available from this host as well.

UCSF System Manager's Toolkit

The UCSF System Manager's Toolkit (SMT), developed at the University of California, is a collection of software to automate routine administrative functions on a network of UNIX machines. It includes software to manage accounting, security audits, unattended file system backups, file system clean-up, user account installation and deletion, as well as other major components. It was developed on Sun systems, and should work with only minor modification on other Berkeley-based systems. System V systems are not supported.

The SMT is available for a modest license fee. For more information, contact

Claire LeDonne, Manager
Campus Software Office
2320 Shattuck Avenue, Suite B
Berkeley, CA 94704

(415) 643-7201
ledonne@violet.berkeley.edu

Shadow Password Implementation

John F. Haugh has written a set of routines to implement shadow password files and password aging. The distribution also includes replacement versions of `login`, `passwd`, and `su`, a program to be run when booting in single-user mode to prompt for the *root* password before invoking a shell, and several other utilities. Version 3 of the distribution was posted in Volume 26 of the *comp.sources.misc* newsgroup in November 1991 and is available from the *comp.sources* archive sites.

Password Cracking Dictionaries

The password cracking dictionaries used by Dan Klein in his experiments that were described in section 2.1 are available for anonymous FTP from the host *ftp.uu.net* in the file *pub/dictionaries.tar.Z*.

Henk Smit of Vrije Universiteit, Amsterdam, has made available a collection of dictionaries he has obtained from several sources. Included are Dan Klein's dictionaries, and lists of words from Dutch, English, French, German, and Italian. The files are available for anonymous FTP from the host *ftp.cs.vu.nl* in the directory *pub/dictionaries*.

Obvious Password Detector

John Nagle of Stanford University has developed a library routine that can be used to detect "obvious" passwords by searching for English language triples (such as "ing," "the," and so on). Although a complete password changing program is not included in the distribution, the routine may still prove useful as a tool to allow users to verify that their password choices are secure. The software was posted in Volume 16 of the *comp.sources.unix* newsgroup in November 1988 and is available from the *comp.sources* archive sites.

Snefru Message-Digest Function

A C-language implementation of the Snefru message-digest function, described in Chapter 9, is available for anonymous FTP from the host *arisia.xerox.com* in the directory *pub/hash*.

An alternative version, written by Rich Salz, is available from the *comp.sources.unix* archives. The two versions are compatible (they compute the same results), but the implementations differ slightly.

Snuffle Encryption Program

The Snuffle encryption program, developed by Dan Bernstein of New York University, and based on the Snefru message-digest function, is available from those sites that archive the *alt.sources* newsgroup. It uses the version of Snefru written by Rich Salz, not the version available from Xerox.

MD4 and MD5 Message-Digest Functions

The MD4 and MD5 message-digest functions, described in Chapter 9, along with the documents describing them, are available for anonymous FTP from the host *rsa.com* in the files *pub/md4.doc* and *pub/md5.doc*.

Data Encryption Standard Software

Several implementations of the Data Encryption Standard (DES), described in Chapter 9, are available from sites on the Internet. Many UNIX vendors include implementations of DES with their products, at least in the United States. Current U.S. export restrictions prevent the distribution of DES software outside the United States.

Phil Karn, author of the popular KA9Q implementation of TCP/IP for packet radio and personal computers, offers a freely distributable implementation of DES as part of this package. It is available for anonymous FTP from *ucsd.edu* in the file */hamradio/ka9q/des/des.tar.Z*.

Dave Barrett of the University of Colorado at Boulder has written a fast DES-compatible encipherment program, along with material to send enciphered material through electronic mail. It is available for anonymous FTP from the host *ftp.uu.net* in the file *pub/fast-des.shar.Z*.

To counter the U.S. export restrictions, Antti Louko of the Helsinki University of Technology in Finland has created an implementation of DES suitable for use with Kerberos. Because this implementation was not created in the U.S., the export restrictions do not apply. This implementation was posted in Volume 18 of the *comp.sources.unix* newsgroup in March 1989, and may be obtained from any of the *comp.sources* archive sites. It is also available for anonymous FTP from the site *kampi.hut.fi*.

A public domain implementation of DES suitable for use with Kerberos has been written by Eric Young of Bond University in Australia. It is available for anonymous FTP from the host *gondwana.ecr.mu.oz.au* in the file *pub/athena/eBones-p9-des.tar.Z.* He has a newer version in the works which can be gotten from *ftp.psy.uq.oz.au* in the file *pub/DES/libdes.tar.Z.*

The next version of Berkeley UNIX (following 4.3 Reno) will probably have a copyrighted but freely available implementation of DES.

There are several other versions of DES available, but many of them are designed explicitly for speed, for use in research on password crackers and the like. These versions are not typically available via anonymous sources, and must be obtained from the authors.

11.3 RSA Privacy-Enhanced Mail

RSA Data Security, Inc. offers an implementation of Internet Privacy-Enhanced Mail, as described in Chapter 9. The product, called the Toolkit for Interoperable Privacy-Enhanced Mail (TIPEM), enables you to

*   generate RSA Public/Private key pairs for encryption/decryption,

*   create Internet certificate requests,

*   add authentication and privacy to mail with digital signatures and envelopes,

*   receive, process, and format Privacy-Enhanced Mail messages, and

*   check certificates (identification) for authenticity.

The TIPEM package includes modules for the Data Encryption Standard, RSA key generation and management, RSA encryption and decryption, the MD2 and MD4 message-digest functions, and more. It requires that you supply an interface to your database and file structure.

For more information, contact

RSA Data Security, Inc.
10 Twin Dolphin Drive
Redwood City, CA 94065
(415) 595-8782

11.4 The National Computer Security Center

The National Computer Security Center (NCSC) was formed in January 1981. Its purpose is to encourage the widespread availability of trusted computer systems for use by those who process classified or other sensitive information (NCSC, 1985b).

The best-known publication of the NCSC is the *Trusted Computer System Evaluation Criteria* (TCSEC), commonly known as the "Orange Book" because of the color of its cover. This document defines seven classes of computer security which may be used to evaluate existing computer systems and to construct new ones. These classes are briefly described below.

The Evaluated Products List

Part of the TCSEC involves an exhaustive evaluation process. Vendors submit a specific combination of hardware and software to the NCSC for evaluation, and the NCSC then checks this system for conformance to the criteria. If the system passes, it receives an official certification that it is secure at a given security class. Systems that have been evaluated and rated are listed in the *Evaluated Products List*, available from the NCSC.

Several vendors (e.g., Sun) provide software that claims to increase the security of a system to one of the classes in the TCSEC. However, these products have **not** been evaluated by the NCSC (an extremely costly and time-consuming process). This is not to say that the products are useless; in fact, many of them are quite valuable. However, you should be aware that unless a system has been evaluated by the NCSC, it is not "officially" secure at any particular TCSEC class.

Classes in the TCSEC

There are seven classes, or levels, in the TCSEC. Each level builds on its predecessors; for example, class B1 includes all the requirements of class C2, as well as new requirements.

D – Minimal Protection

This class is provided for those systems that have been evaluated but fail to meet the requirements for a higher evaluation class. Systems at this level have little or no security protections; this includes systems such as MS-DOS.

C1 – Discretionary Security Protection

Systems at this level provide some form of discretionary access control, allowing access to files to be limited on an individual basis. Generally speaking, "plain" UNIX falls into this class.

C2 – Controlled Access Protection

Systems in this class enforce more fine-grained access control than those at level C1, making users individually accountable for their actions through login procedures, auditing of security-related events, and resource isolation. Versions of VMS (Digital Equipment), AOS/VS (Data General), VM/SP with CMS and RACF (IBM), MVS with RACF (IBM), and NOS (Control Data) have all been certified at level C2. Increasing a UNIX system's security level to C2 is relatively easy to do, and several vendors offer software to do so, although most of it has not been evaluated by the NCSC.

B1 – Labeled Security Protection

Systems at this level require all features required for C2 systems. Additionally, they require an ability to label data at different levels (e.g., confidential, secret, top secret), and an ability to enforce mandatory access control (a user cleared for "secret" cannot access "top secret" data). UNIX systems can be made to operate at this security level, but it is typically only offered as a separate product, because of the major changes involved. In the UNIX marketplace, B1 systems are usually referred to as MLS systems; MLS stands for Multi-Level Secure. AT&T offers System V/MLS, which has been evaluated at the B1 level.

B2 – Structured Protection

This level requires everything in level B1, as well as a clearly defined and documented formal security policy model that provides discretionary and mandatory access control for all objects in the system. In addition, "covert channels," the ability to signal information via unusual means (for example, sending information by utilizing system resources in a timed manner), are addressed. Security at levels of B2 and above cannot easily be implemented entirely in software; hardware assistance is usually required. Multics, from Honeywell Information Systems and Trusted XENIX, from Trusted Information Systems are the only general-purpose operating systems currently evaluated at the B2 security level.

B3 – Security Domains

At this level, the part of the operating system that implements security must eliminate code not essential to security enforcement, must be tamper-proof, and must be small enough to be subjected to analysis and tests.

A1 – Verified Design

At this level, the systems are functionally equivalent to class B3; there are no new architectural features. However, systems in this class must have formal design specifications, and formal verification techniques must be used to determine that the system is secure. Loosely speaking, the system must be "proven," using mathematic-style proofs, to be secure. The only way to successfully implement a system at this level is to design it from the ground up with the intent of an A1 verification; this level cannot be retrofitted onto existing systems such as UNIX.

The Rainbow Collection

The "Orange Book" is actually just one publication in a whole series from the NCSC. This series is usually called the "Rainbow Collection," because of the brightly colored covers on the books. A single complimentary copy of these documents can be obtained from the NCSC by writing or calling

> National Computer Security Center
> 9800 Savage Road
> Ft. George G. Meade, MD 20755-6000
> (301) 859-4458

Additional copies can be ordered from the U.S. Government Printing Office. The "Rainbow Collection" includes

- *Department of Defense Trusted Computer System Evaluation Criteria* (Orange), December 1985, DOD 5200.28-STD

- *Trusted Network Interpretation of the Trusted Computer System Evaluation Criteria* (Red), July 1987, NCSC-TG-005

- *PC Security Considerations* (Light Blue), 1985, NCSC-TG-002-85

- *Department of Defense Password Management Guideline* (Light Green), April 1985, CSC-STD-002-85

- *Guidance for Applying the Department of Defense Trusted Computer System Evaluation Criteria in Specific Environments* (Yellow), June 1985, CSC-STD-003-85

- *Technical Rationale Behind CSC-STD-003-85: Computer Security Requirements* (Yellow), June 1985, CSC-STD-004-85

- *A Guide to Understanding Audit in Trusted Systems* (Tan), June 1988, NCSC-TG-001

- *A Guide to Understanding Discretionary Access Control in Trusted Systems* (Red), September 1987, NCSC-TG-003

- *A Guide to Understanding Configuration Management in Trusted Systems* (Orange), March 1988, NCSC-TG-006

- *A Guide to Understanding Design Documentation in Trusted Systems* (Burgundy), October 1988, NCSC-TG-007

- *A Guide to Understanding Trusted Distribution in Trusted Systems* (Lilac), December 1988, NCSC-TG-008

- *Computer Security Subsystem Interpretation of the Trusted Computer System Evaluation Criteria* (Light Grey), September 1988, NCSC-TG-009

- *Rating Maintenance Phase Program Document* (Pink), June 1989, NCSC-TG-013

- *Guidelines for Formal Verification Systems* (Purple), April 1989, NCSC-TG-014

- *Trusted UNIX Working Group (TRUSIX) Rationale for Selecting Access Control List Features for the UNIX System* (Grey), August 1989, NCSC-TG-020-A

- *Glossary of Computer Security Terms* (Green), October 1988, NCSC-TG-004

11.5 Summary

The large amount of software development on "the net" as a whole has made it possible to find a program for almost any purpose. Several pieces of software have been developed that can help you increase the security of your system; it is important that you investigate the distribution sources of these programs.

One caution about obtaining software from "the net" bears mentioning, however. It is important to realize that most of the software out there is offered on an as-is basis, and that there **are** unethical people who will create versions of these programs that contain viruses, Trojan horses, or other problems. Before installing and executing any program obtained from the network, either via anonymous FTP or from one of the source newsgroups, carefully examine the code to be sure it does only what you expect it to.

Chapter 12
Obtaining Security Information

One of the hardest parts of keeping systems secure is finding out about security problems before the "bad guys" do. To combat this, there are several sources of information you can and should make use of on a regular basis.

12.1 Computer Security Incident Response Capabilities

Several organizations have formed special groups of people to deal with computer security problems. These teams, called Computer Security Incident Response Capabilities (CSIRCs) or Computer Emergency Response Teams (CERTs), collect information about possible security holes and distribute it to proper people. They also track intruders and assist in recovery from security violations. Most of the teams have both electronic mail distribution lists and special telephone "hot line" numbers that can be called for information or to report a problem. Many of these teams are members of the Forum of Incident Response and Security Teams (FIRST), which is coordinated by the National Institute of Standards and Technology (NIST), and exists to facilitate the exchange of information between the various teams.

The descriptions in this section are taken from Holbrook and Reynolds (1991).

DARPA Computer Emergency Response Team

The Computer Emergency Response Team/Coordination Center (CERT/CC) was established in 1988 by the Defense Advanced Research Projects Agency (DARPA) to address computer security concerns of research users of the Internet. It is operated by the Software Engineering Institute (SEI) at Carnegie-Mellon University (CMU). The CERT/CC can immediately confer with experts to diagnose and solve security problems, and also establish and maintain communications with the affected computer users and government authorities as appropriate.

The CERT/CC serves as a clearinghouse for the identification and repair of security vulnerabilities, informal assessments of existing systems, improvement of emergency response capability, and both vendor and user security awareness. In addition, the team works with vendors of various systems in order to coordinate the fixes for security problems.

The CERT/CC sends out security advisories to the *cert-advisory* mailing list whenever appropriate. They also operate a 24-hour hotline that can be called to report security problems (e.g., someone breaking into your system), as well as to obtain current (and accurate) information about rumored security problems.

To join the *cert-advisory* mailing list, send a message to *cert@cert.sei.cmu.edu* and ask to be added to the mailing list. The material sent to this list also appears in the USENET newsgroup *comp.security.announce*. Past advisories are available for anonymous FTP from the host *cert.sei.cmu.edu*. The 24-hour hotline number is (412) 268-7090.

The CERT/CC also maintains a *cert-tools* mailing list to encourage the exchange of information on tools and techniques that increase the secure operation of Internet systems. The CERT/CC does not review or endorse the tools described on the list. To subscribe, send a message to *cert-tools-request@cert.sei.cmu.edu* and ask to be added to the mailing list.

The CERT/CC maintains other generally useful security information for anonymous FTP from the host *cert.sei.cmu.edu*. Get the *README* file for a list of what is available.

For more information, contact

CERT
Software Engineering Institute
Carnegie-Mellon University
Pittsburgh, PA 15213-3890

(412) 268-7090
cert@cert.sei.cmu.edu

DDN Security Coordination Center

For users of the Defense Data Network (DDN), the Security Coordination Center (SCC) serves a function similar to the CERT/CC. The SCC is the DDN's clearinghouse for host/user security problems and fixes, and works with the DDN Network Security Officer. The SCC also distributes the DDN *Security Bulletin*, which communicates information on network and host security exposures, fixes, and concerns to security and management personnel at DDN facilities.

Issues of the DDN *Security Bulletin* are available on-line, via `kermit` or anonymous FTP, from the host *nic.ddn.mil* in the directory *SCC:*. The files are named *DDN-SECURITY-yy-nn.TXT*, where *yy* is the year and *nn* is the bulletin number.

The SCC provides immediate assistance with DDN-related host security problems;

call (800) 365-3642 (7:00 am to 7:00 pm Eastern Standard Time) or send electronic mail to *scc@nic.ddn.mil*.

NIST Computer Security Resource and Response Center

The National Institute of Standards and Technology (NIST) has responsibility within the U.S. Government for computer science and technology activities. NIST has played a strong role in organizing the FIRST and is now serving as the FIRST Secretariat. NIST also operates a Computer Security Resource and Response Center (CSRC) to provide help and information regarding computer security events and incidents, as well as to raise awareness about computer security vulnerabilities.

The CSRC team operates a 24-hour hotline, at (301) 975-5200. For individuals with access to the Internet, on-line publications and computer security information can be obtained via anonymous FTP from the host *csrc.ncsl.nist.gov*. NIST also operates a personal computer bulletin board that contains information regarding computer viruses as well as other aspects of computer security. To access this board, set your modem to 300/1200/2400 bps, eight data bits, one stop bit, no parity, and call (301) 948-5717. All users are given full access to the board immediately upon registering.

NIST has produced several special publications related to computer security and computer viruses in particular; some of these publications are downloadable. For further information, contact

Computer Security Resource and Response Center
A-216 Technology
Gaithersburg, MD 20899

(301) 975-3359
csrc@nist.gov

DOE Computer Incident Advisory Capability

The U.S. Department of Energy (DOE) Computer Incident Advisory Capability (CIAC) is a four-person team of computer scientists from the Lawrence Livermore National Laboratory (LLNL) charged with the primary responsibility of assisting DOE sites faced with computer security incidents (e.g., intruder attacks, virus infections, worm attacks, etc.). This capability is available to DOE sites on a 24-hour basis.

The CIAC was formed to provide a centralized response capability (including technical assistance), to keep sites informed of current events, to deal proactively with computer security issues, and to maintain liaisons with other response teams and agencies. The CIAC's charter is to assist sites (through direct technical assistance, providing information, or referring inquiries to other technical experts), serve as a clearing house for information about threats, known incidents, and vulnerabilities, develop guidelines for incident handling, develop software for responding to events and incidents, analyze events and trends, conduct training and awareness activities, and alert and advise sites about vulnerabilities and potential attacks.

The CIAC's business-hours telephone number is (415) 422-8193 or FTS 532-8193. They can be reached via electronic mail at *ciac@tiger.llnl.gov*.

NASA Ames Computer Network Security Response Team

The Computer Network Security Response Team (CNSRT) is NASA Ames Research Center's local version of the DARPA CERT/CC. Formed in August 1989, the team has a constituency that is primarily Ames users, but is also involved in assisting other NASA Centers and federal agencies. The CNSRT maintains liaisons with the DOE CIAC team and the DARPA CERT/CC. It is also a charter member of the FIRST. The team may be reached by 24-hour pager at (415) 694-0571, or by electronic mail at *cnsrt@ames.arc.nasa.gov*.

12.2 Forming a CSIRC

The National Institute of Standards and Technology has produced a document which details the procedures to follow and issues to consider when establishing a Computer Security Incident Response Capability (Wack, 1991). Some of these issues include

- determining the goals of the incident response capability,
- defining the constituency, those people the CSIRC is supposed to help,
- determining the structure of the CSIRC,
- acquiring management support and funding,
- creating a charter,
- creating a CSIRC Operations Handbook, and
- staffing issues.

Also discussed are the procedures to follow once the CSIRC is in operation, including

- communicating with the constituency,
- logging information,
- incident notification issues,
- legal issues,
- working with the media,

- post-incident analysis, and

- measuring the CSIRC's effectiveness.

The document, *Establishing a Computer Security Incident Response Capability*, is available for anonymous FTP from the host *csrc.ncsl.nist.gov* in the directory *pub/first*. This host archives several other documents relating to computer security as well.

12.3 Vendor Security Notification

Many vendors are now making security information available to their customers directly. This is an important benefit, since you can receive information on security problems and their fixes before they become common knowledge. Unfortunately, most vendors have not announced these notification channels, and so very few of their customers are aware of them. Contact your sales representative to find out if your vendors have implemented these notification mechanisms, and how to receive information from them.

Sun Customer Warning System

In August 1990, Sun Microsystems announced their Customer Warning System (CWS) via the *cert-tools* mailing list. The CWS is a formal process within Sun which includes having a well-advertised point of contact within Sun for reporting security problems, proactively alerting customers to security problems with Sun systems, and distributing patches and work-arounds as quickly as possible.

Sun has established a position of "Security Coordinator" who is responsible for manning the CWS electronic mail and telephone hotlines and evaluating the security problems reported to them. They have also established a team of knowledgeable senior people within Sun Corporate who are committed to being available to meet whenever necessary and who are empowered to make all necessary decisions with regard to handling a security threat.

To contact the Security Coordinator to report a bug or security problem in Sun products, send electronic mail to *security-alert@sun.com*, or call (415) 688-9081. The telephone line has a voice mail backup, but electronic mail is preferred. Non-security-related bugs and problems should be reported through normal Sun channels.

To be placed on the list which receives notification from the CWS, contact your Sun sales representative, who can fill out the proper form.

12.4 Mailing Lists

Several Internet mailing lists pertain directly or indirectly to computer security issues.

Zardoz

The "Zardoz" list is a restricted-access UNIX security mailing list run by Neil Gorsuch. It exists to notify system administrators of serious security dangers **before** they become public knowledge. Most of the traffic on the list has been explanations of, and fixes for, specific UNIX security problems. Because the list contains detailed information about UNIX security problems, access is restricted and it is difficult to join. The procedure is as follows:

To apply for membership, send a message to *security-request@cpd.com* requesting that Neil contact one of the following persons:

- For UUCP sites with a UUCP map entry, the listed electronic mail contact, the map entry writer, or *root*.

- For Internet sites, the NIC WHOIS-listed site contact, or *root*.

Neil will contact one of these people to verify your credentials (in other words, if you're a random undergraduate student at Podunk U., you're not likely to get on the list). Include the following information in addition to the name of the contact:

- The UUCP map entry and name of the map to find it in, or the WHOIS response from the NIC and the request handle.

- The actual electronic mail destination you want material sent to. It can be a person or an alias, but must be on the same machine cited as a reference, or in a sub-domain of that machine.

- Indicate whether you want immediate reflected postings, or the weekly moderated digests.

- The electronic mail address and voice telephone number of the administrative contact if different from the above.

- Your organization name, address, and voice telephone number if not already provided.

Also, Neil asks that you do not waste his time by sending requests from *root* on *machine_17.basement.podunk_u.edu*, requests from *machine_at_my_house.uucp*, or hosts on networks other than UUCP or the Internet (since he has no way to verify them). He also cannot deal with requests asking him to verify your credentials by telephoning so-and-so; this is too time-consuming and expensive.

The above restrictions may seem at first glance to be more trouble than they're worth. However, it is exactly these restrictions that make the list so useful, by providing a reasonable certainty that "bad guys" are not receiving the information.

RISKS

The RISKS digest is a component of the ACM Committee on Computers and Public Policy, moderated by Peter G. Neumann. It is a discussion forum on risks to the public in computers and related systems, and along with discussing computer security and privacy issues, has discussed such subjects as the Stark incident, the shooting down of the Iranian airliner in the Persian Gulf (as it relates to computerized weapons systems), the failure of the Patriot anti-missile system in the attack on the U.S. barracks in Saudi Arabia, problems in air and railroad traffic control systems, software engineering, and so on. To join the mailing list, send a message to *risks-request@csl.sri.com*. This list is also available in the USENET newsgroup *comp.risks*.

TCP-IP

The TCP-IP list is intended to act as a discussion forum for developers and maintainers of implementations of the TCP/IP protocol suite. It also discusses network-related security problems when they involve programs providing network services, such as `sendmail`. This was one of the first places that notification of the Internet worm's detection, as well as the eventual bug fixes from Berkeley, appeared. To join the list, send a message to *tcp-ip-request@nic.ddn.mil*. This list is also available in the USENET newsgroup *comp.protocols.tcp-ip*.

VIRUS-L

The VIRUS-L list is a forum for the discussion of computer virus experiences, protection software, and related topics. Most of the information is related to personal computers, although some of it may be applicable to larger systems. To subscribe, send the line

```
SUB VIRUS-L your full name
```

to the address *listserv%lehiibm.bitnet@mitvma.mit.edu*.

SUN-SPOTS, SUN-NETS, SUN-MANAGERS

The SUN-SPOTS, SUN-NETS, and SUN-MANAGERS lists are all discussion groups for users and administrators of Sun Microsystems products. SUN-SPOTS is a fairly general list, discussing everything from hardware configuration to simple UNIX questions. To subscribe, send a message to *sun-spots-request@rice.edu*. This list is also available in the USENET newsgroup *comp.sys.sun*.

SUN-NETS is a discussion list for items pertaining to networking on Sun systems. Much of the discussion is related to NFS, NIS, and name servers. To subscribe, send a message to *sun-nets-request@umiacs.umd.edu*.

SUN-MANAGERS is a discussion list for Sun system administrators and covers all aspects of Sun system administration. To subscribe, send a message to *sun-managers-request@eecs.nwu.edu*.

12.5 USENET Newsgroups

In addition to the mailing lists already mentioned, the following USENET newsgroups also contain information directly or indirectly related to UNIX security.

alt.security	Computer security issues
comp.admin.policy	Discussions of site policies and issues
comp.bugs.4bsd	Berkeley UNIX bug reports and fixes
comp.bugs.4bsd.ucb-fixes	Official bug fixes from Berkeley
comp.bugs.misc	General UNIX bug reports and fixes
comp.bugs.sys5	System V bug reports and fixes
comp.protocols.kerberos	Discussions about Kerberos
comp.protocols.tcp-ip	Gatewayed to the TCP-IP mailing list
comp.risks	Gatewayed to the RISKS mailing list
comp.security.announce	Announcements from CERT
comp.sys.apollo	Apollo computer systems
comp.sys.att	AT&T computer systems
comp.sys.dec	Digital Equipment computer systems
comp.sys.hp	Hewlett-Packard computer systems
comp.sys.next	NeXT computer systems
comp.sys.sgi	Silicon Graphics computer systems
comp.sys.sun	Gatewayed to the SUN-SPOTS mailing list
comp.unix.aix	IBM version of UNIX
comp.unix.aux	Apple version of UNIX
comp.unix.ultrix	Digital Equipment version of UNIX
comp.unix.xenix	UNIX for IBM personal computers
comp.virus	Computer viruses and security
sci.crypt	Cryptology

12.6 Suggested Reading

A great deal of information has been published on computer security, although not much of it pertains directly to UNIX security. The references listed at the end of this book comprise a large part of the material written about UNIX security. For more information on any of the topics presented in this book, the cited references should be consulted.

Some references however, are worthy of special mention and are recommended reading for anyone interested in computer security issues. These references are listed, with brief descriptions, below:

• The *Site Security Handbook*, Request for Comments Number 1244, is the product of the Site Security Policy Handbook Working Group of the Internet

Engineering Task Force. It is a first attempt at providing guidance on how to deal with security issues, including how to protect a system, how to develop security policies, and how to handle security incidents. It is available for anonymous FTP from the site *nic.ddn.mil*, as well as other archive sites around the Internet.

- The *Guidelines for the Secure Operation of the Internet*, Request for Comments Number 1281, provides a set of guidelines, listed in Chapter 10, for the entire Internet community. The document also elaborates on these guidelines, providing justification for each one of them. It is available for anonymous FTP from the site *nic.ddn.mil*, as well as other archive sites around the Internet.

- In early 1991, the National Research Council published *Computers at Risk: Safe Computing in the Information Age*. This document is the end result of the System Security Study Committee of the Computer Sciences and Technology Board, which was charged with developing a "national research, engineering, and policy agenda to help the United States achieve a more trustworthy computing technology base by the end of the century." *Computers at Risk* is available from

    National Academy Press
    2101 Constitution Avenue N.W.
    Washington, D.C. 20418

- *Computers Under Attack: Intruders, Worms, and Viruses*, edited by Peter J. Denning, the editor-in-chief of *Communications of the ACM*, collects a number of papers and articles about computer security incidents including the Internet worm, the Lawrence Berkeley Labs attack discovered by Cliff Stoll, and numerous virus attacks. *Computers Under Attack* is published through Addison-Wesley by the ACM Press.

- *The Cuckoo's Egg*, by Clifford Stoll, provides a first-hand account of the attack on the Lawrence Berkeley Labs systems described in Chapter 1. Written for the general public, the book provides an excellent account of the incident and presents a good picture of how to catch an attacker, without becoming bogged down in computer jargon. Stoll is an excellent story teller, and this book is required reading for friends and family members who ask, "Just what is it you do, anyway?"

- *Legal Issues: A Site Manager's Nightmare*, by Steve Hansen, details some of the legal issues in security incident handling, especially procedures for handling electronic information. The paper focuses on the Electronic Communications Privacy Act of 1986 and some of the problems involved in interpreting the law. The document is available in *Proceedings of the Second Invitational Workshop on Computer Security Incident Response* (June 1990), or via anonymous FTP from the host *csrc.ncsl.nist.gov*.

- The *Bibliography of Selected Computer Security Publications January 1980 – October 1989*, NIST Special Publication 800-1, cites selected articles and books on computer security published during the 1980s. Selection criteria required that an article be substantial in content and published in professional or technical journals, magazines, or conference proceedings. English language from foreign journals was also included. A category for pre-1980 publications is also provided, as well as an appendix containing the addresses of all journals and magazines cited. The bibliography is available for sale from the United States Government Printing Office, Washington, D.C. 20402, (202) 783-3238, reference number 003-003-03060-1. It is also available for anonymous FTP from the host *csrc.ncsl.nist.gov*.

12.7 Summary

The only way to stay ahead of the "bad guys" is to obtain as much information as possible about things that affect the security of your system. This means subscribing to mailing lists, reading appropriate newsgroups, and so on. It's a time-consuming task, but it is easily justified when you realize that whether you read these things or not, the "bad guys" are absorbing every word.

Glossary

This section provides definitions for some of the terms used in this book. Terms specific to the UNIX operating system are not described here. Readers who are not familiar with the operation of UNIX or the terminology associated with UNIX may wish to consult *A Practical Guide to the UNIX System, Second Edition* by Mark G. Sobell, published by Addison-Wesley. Readers who would like to learn more about UNIX system administration should consult the *UNIX System Administration Handbook* by Evi Nemeth, Garth Snyder, and Scott Seebass, published by Prentice Hall.

$PATH An environment variable used by the shell to determine in which directories to look for commands, and the order the directories should be searched. Placing the current directory (".") in the search path can make you vulnerable to Trojan horse programs.

.cshrc A startup file, stored in a user's home directory, that is read by the C shell (csh) upon invocation. This file is used to set the search path and other variables, and to define aliases. Leaving this file writable by others can make you vulnerable to attack.

.emacs A startup file, stored in a user's home directory, that is read by the EMACS text editor. This file is used to define various editor modes and functions. Leaving this file writable by others can make you vulnerable to attack.

.exrc A startup file, usually stored in a user's home directory, that is read by the edit, ex, vi, and view text editors. This file is used to define various editor modes and functions. Leaving this file writable by others can make you vulnerable to attack.

.forward A file, stored in a user's home directory, that can be used to forward electronic mail addressed to the user to other addresses. Leaving this file writable by others can result in an attacker stealing your mail, or breaking into your account.

.login A startup file, stored in a user's home directory, that is read by invocations of the C shell (csh) that are login shells. This file is used to execute commands that should only be executed at login time, such as establishing the terminal type, starting window systems, etc. Leaving this file writable by others can make you vulnerable to attack.

.mailrc A file, stored in a user's home directory, used to define mail aliases and set configuration options for the Mail and mailx commands.

.netrc A file, stored in a user's home directory, used to define login names and passwords to be used when logging into remote hosts via FTP. Passwords are stored in this file in **unencrypted** form, making it a serious security problem.

.profile A startup file, stored in a user's home directory, that is read by the Bourne and Korn shells (sh, ksh) upon invocation. This file is used to set the search path and other variables, and to define shell functions. Leaving this file writable by others can make you vulnerable to attack.

.rhosts A file, stored in a user's home directory, that lists host and login names that are allowed to log into the user's account without a password. Leaving this file writable by others can make you vulnerable to attack.

a.out An executable file produced as output from a language compiler, assembler, or loader. The file may be renamed using options to these programs, but this is the default name.

Access control list A method of specifying access permissions for files that is more fine-grained than standard UNIX access permissions. A list is created that enumerates exactly who may and may not access the file. This form of access control is provided by many versions of UNIX that provide "Orange Book" security.

ACL See *access control list*.

Anonymous FTP A part of the File Transfer Protocol that allows users to connect to a host using the special login *anonymous*, and transfer files from a restricted area.

Authentication The process of determining the authenticity of a user or message, often using cryptographic techniques such as passwords, digital signatures, or public-key encryption. The Kerberos system provides authentication of users requesting network services.

BNU An installation option on many System V UNIX systems, the Basic Networking Utilities include the software associated with *UUCP* and sometimes *USENET* news.

BSD An acronym for Berkeley Software Distribution, this identifies the version of UNIX distributed by the Computer Science Research Group at the University of California, Berkeley. The current release is 4.3BSD-Reno, released in November 1990.

CERT An acronym for Computer Emergency Response Team, this also refers to the DARPA CERT/CC at Carnegie-Mellon University. See *CSIRC*.

Challenge-response box A small calculator-like device that can be used in combination with or in place of passwords. The user enters a number, given to him by the computer, into the box which then generates a response that the user types back to the computer.

Checksum An algorithm that computes a value based on the data stored in a file. The checksums of two files may be compared to determine whether the files are the same or different.

Ciphertext The output of an *encryption* algorithm.

Crypt The library routine used on UNIX to encrypt passwords. It uses a modified implementation of the *DES* algorithm. Also a program on UNIX to encrypt files using a not-very-secure one-rotor machine.

CSIRC An acronym for Computer Security Incident Response Capability, a group of people responsible for responding to security incidents within an organization.

Decryption The process of turning *ciphertext* back into *plaintext*.

DES The Data Encryption Standard, a very secure *encryption* algorithm. A modified version of this algorithm is used to encrypt passwords on UNIX.

Device file A special file on a UNIX system that allows access to devices such as memory, disk drives, and tape drives using the same semantics as those used to access regular files.

DNS The Domain Name System, a distributed database of host names and network addresses controlled by name servers on the Internet.

Domain name A host name composed of components that allow hosts in different locales to have the same name. For example, *myhost.bigschool.edu* and *myhost.company.com*.

Dumb terminal A terminal that has output display capabilities but no ability to respond to queries from the host computer.

Encryption The process of turning *plaintext* into *ciphertext* by applying an algorithm that rearranges or changes its input into something unrecognizable.

Finger The Internet protocol used for finding information about users, such as their names, telephone numbers, and last login times.

Firewall A system that sits between the outside network and an organization's internal networks, stopping all packet flow between the two.

FIRST An acronym for Forum of Incident Response and Security Teams, an organization chaired by the National Institute of Standards and Technology for the purpose of fostering cooperation and information exchange between *CSIRC*s.

FTP An acronym for File Transfer Protocol.

Gateway A piece of network hardware or a computer system that forwards packets from one network to another, possibly performing protocol translations.

GECOS field The field of the password file where a user's full name, telephone number, and other information is typically stored. GECOS stands for General Electric Comprehensive Operating System, an operating system similar to IBM System/360 DOS. Later the name was changed to GCOS, for General Comprehensive Operating System, when Honeywell bought out GE's computer division. The field got its name because it was first used at Bell Laboratories to hold the information necessary for submitting batch jobs to their GCOS systems.

HDB An acronym for Honey-DanBer, the version of *UUCP* shipped with most *System V* UNIX systems and *SunOS*. It stands for the names of the authors, Peter Honeyman, David A. Nowitz, and Brian E. Redman.

HP-UX The version of UNIX provided by Hewlett-Packard Company, based primarily on System V Release 3.

Internet The collection of hosts connected to numerous regional networks around the United States and Canada, the NSFNet, the MILNET, and several networks in Europe. As of mid-1991, there were over 2,000 networks and over 500,000 hosts connected to the Internet.

IP An acronym for Internet Protocol, the primary protocol in use on the Internet.

Kerberos A software system developed by Project Athena at MIT that provides authentication of users requesting network services.

Key A part of an *encryption* algorithm that controls the behavior of the algorithm in some way. Without the key, *ciphertext* (hopefully) cannot be converted back into *plaintext*.

License to hack The part of a security policy that allows users to experiment with system security, worms, and viruses, possibly under controlled conditions.

Message-digest function A sophisticated *checksum* algorithm for which it is computationally infeasible to find two inputs that produce the same output, or to deduce the input that produces a specific output.

Modem Short for modulator-demodulator. A hardware device that allows two computers to communicate over ordinary telephone lines.

Multi-user mode The operating mode of a UNIX system in which all system services are running, and users may log in.

NFS An acronym for Network File System, software provided with *SunOS* and other systems that allows file systems on one host to be used over the network by other hosts.

NIS An acronym for Network Information Service, the software used by *SunOS* and other systems to provide distributed database access.

Password aging A process of expiring passwords, forcing users to change their passwords at specified intervals.

Password generator A program that generates passwords, requiring the user to pick one for use as his password, rather than letting him choose his own (possibly less secure) password.

Plaintext The input to an *encryption* algorithm.

Privacy-enhanced mail Electronic mail that has been made secure by the use of encryption software.

Proactive password checker A program that evaluates password choices for security before allowing them to be selected.

PROM monitor The command set provided by some workstations when they are not running UNIX. The monitor allows memory contents to be examined and changed, the system to be booted, and diagnostics to be run.

Public-key encryption A type of encryption in which each user has both a public key and a private key. A message from A to B is enciphered by A using B's public key, and is deciphered by B using B's private key. A message from B can be authenticated (proven to be from B) if it is first enciphered using B's secret key; it can then be deciphered using B's public key, thus proving it came from B. Some public-key systems such as *RSA* can be used for both secrecy and authentication, others can only be used for one or the other.

RFS An acronym for Remote File Sharing service, software provided with most *System V* systems that allows file systems on one host to be used over the network by other hosts.

Root The conventional login name for the UNIX super-user, the account that has unlimited powers over the system.

Route A piece of information that tells a host on one network where to send packets destined for a host on another network.

Router A piece of network hardware or a computer that forwards packets from one network to another.

RSA An acronym for Rivest, Shamir, and Adleman, the inventors of the public-key encryption system that bears their names.

Set-group-id A special mode on an executable file that temporarily grants the user executing the program the permissions associated with the group owner of the file.

Set-user-id A special mode on an executable file that temporarily grants the user executing the program the permissions associated with the owner of the file.

Seventh Edition The first version of UNIX generally available from Bell Laboratories circa 1977, Seventh Edition ran on Digital Equipment Corporation PDP-11 computers.

Shadow password file An alternative file, readable only by the super-user, in which encrypted passwords are stored. The passwords are not stored in the standard password file, which is accessible by non-privileged users.

Shell The program that reads commands from the keyboard or a file and executes them for the user.

Single-user mode The mode of operation of a UNIX system in which none of the standard system services are provided, and the system may only be accessed from the system console.

Smart terminal A terminal which contains special functions allowing it to transmit its memory contents to the computer, program function keys, and so on.

SMTP An acronym for Simple Mail Transfer Protocol, the protocol used to exchange electronic mail between hosts on the Internet.

SNMP An acronym for Simple Network Management Protocol, a protocol used to obtain statistical information from gateways, routers, and other network elements.

Sticky bit A special permission bit on a file that indicates that its text image should be maintained in the swap area for faster loading. On some systems, the sticky bit, when set on a directory, prevents users from removing files owned by other users from the directory.

Substitution cipher A method of encryption in which letters or words are replaced with other letters or words following some prearranged pattern.

SunOS The version of UNIX provided by Sun Microsystems, Inc., based primarily on 4.2 and 4.3BSD.

Super-user The account that has unlimited powers over a UNIX system. The super-user commonly has the login name *root*.

System V The version of UNIX provided by AT&T. The current release is System V Release 4, although many vendors sell versions still based on System V Release 3.

TCP An acronym for Transmission Control Protocol, one of the primary protocols in use on the Internet.

TFTP An acronym for Trivial File Transfer Protocol, a stripped-down version of *FTP* commonly used for booting diskless workstations from a server.

Transposition cipher A type of encryption in which the contents of the *plaintext* are rearranged in some prearranged fashion.

Trojan horse A program that masquerades as something it is not, usually for the purpose of breaking into an account or executing commands with another user's privileges.

Trusted host A host from which users are allowed to log in or execute commands on the local host without providing a password.

UDP An acronym for User Datagram Protocol, one of the primary protocols in use on the Internet.

ULTRIX The version of UNIX provided by Digital Equipment Corporation, based primarily on 4.2 and 4.3BSD.

umask A special value that controls which permission bits are turned off when a file is created.

USENET The "network news" system in which articles in newsgroups are forwarded from host to host, providing a world-wide bulletin-board system.

UUCP An acronym for the UNIX-to-UNIX Copy Program, a program that allows two UNIX systems to exchange files and electronic mail via dial-up telephone lines.

Virus A piece of a program that attaches itself to other programs and can be used to destroy files or perform other tasks with another user's privileges.

Worm A program which propagates by replicating itself on each host in a network, with the purpose of breaking into systems.

YP An acronym for Yellow Pages, the previous name for the Network Information Service, ***NIS***.

References

AT&T. 1986. *UNIX System V Release 3 System Administrator's Guide.* Part Number 305-558.

AT&T. 1990a. *UNIX System V Release 4 System Administrator's Guide.* Englewood Cliffs, NJ: Prentice Hall.

AT&T. 1990b. *UNIX System V Release 4 Network User's and Administrator's Guide.* Englewood Cliffs, NJ: Prentice Hall.

Baldwin, Robert W. 1986. *Crypt Breaker's Workbench Users' Manual.* Posted to *comp.sources.unix*, Volume 10, Issues 1-11, June 17, 1987.

Bellovin, S. M. 1989. ''Security Problems in the TCP/IP Protocol Suite.'' *ACM Computer Communications Review (SIGCOMM)* 19 (April): 32-48.

Bellovin, Steven M., and Michael Merritt. 1991. ''Limitations of the Kerberos Authentication System.'' *USENIX Conference Proceedings* Dallas (Winter): 253-67.

Bentley, Jon L., and Brian W. Kernighan. 1988. ''Tools for Printing Indexes.'' *Electronic Publishing* 1 (April): 3-17.

Bishop, Matt. 1983. *Breaking a Simple Rotor System.* Department of Computer Science, Purdue University.

Bishop, Matt. 1990. ''An Extendable Password Checker.'' *USENIX Security Workshop Proceedings* Portland (August): 15-16.

Carlin, Jerry M. 1990. ''Internet Gateway Security Checklist.'' *USENIX Security Workshop Proceedings* Portland (August): 145-7.

Case, J. D., M. Fedor, M. L. Schoffstall, and C. Davin. 1990. ''Simple Network Management Protocol (SNMP).'' Request for Comments 1157. DDN Network Information Center, Government Systems, Inc., Chantilly, VA.

Cheswick, Bill. 1990. ''The Design of a Secure Internet Gateway.'' *USENIX Conference Proceedings* Anaheim (Summer): 233-37.

CSRG. 1990. *UNIX Programmer's Reference Manual.* 4.3 Berkeley Software Distribution, Virtual VAX-11 Version. April 1986. Revised.

Curry, David A. 1990. *Improving the Security of Your UNIX System.* Technical Report No. ITSTD-721-FR-90-21. SRI International, Menlo Park, CA.

De Alvaré, Ana Marie. 1990. ''How Crackers Crack Passwords, or What Passwords to Avoid.'' *USENIX Security Workshop Proceedings* Portland (August): 103-12.

Denning, Dorothy E. R. 1983. *Cryptography and Data Security.* Reading, MA: Addison-Wesley.

Diffie, W., and M. Hellman. 1976. ''New Directions in Cryptography.'' *IEEE Transactions on Information Theory*, 22 (November): 644-54.

Diffie, W., and M. Hellman. 1977. "Exhaustive Cryptanalysis of the NBS Data Encryption Standard." *Computer* 10 (June): 74-84.

Digital Equipment Corporation. 1990. *ULTRIX Security Guide for Users and Programmers*. Order Number AA-PBKTA-TE.

Duff, Tom. 1989. "Viral Attacks on UNIX System Security." *USENIX Conference Proceedings* San Diego (Winter): 165-71. A revised and expanded version of this paper appears in *Computing Systems* 2 (Spring 1989): 155-71.

Eichin, Mark W., and Jon A. Rochlis. 1989. *With Microscope and Tweezers: An Analysis of the Internet Virus of November 1988*. Massachusetts Institute of Technology.

ElGamal, Taher. 1985. "A Public Key Cryptosystem and a Signature Scheme Based on Discrete Logarithms." *IEEE Transactions on Information Theory* IT-31 (July): 469-72.

Farmer, Daniel, and Eugene H. Spafford. 1990. "The COPS Security Checker System." *USENIX Conference Proceedings* Anaheim (Summer): 165-90.

Finlayson, R. 1984. "Bootstrap Loading Using TFTP." Request for Comments 906. DDN Network Information Center, Government Systems, Inc., Chantilly, VA.

Grampp, F. T., and R. H. Morris. "UNIX Operating System Security." *AT&T Bell Laboratories Technical Journal* 63 (October): 1649-72.

Hedrick, C. L. 1988. "Routing Information Protocol." Request for Comments 1058. DDN Network Information Center, Government Systems, Inc., Chantilly, VA.

Hellman, M. E. 1979. "DES Will Be Totally Insecure Within Ten Years." *IEEE Spectrum*, 16 (July): 32-9.

Hewlett-Packard Company. 1989a. *HP-UX Release 7.0 Reference*, Volume 3. Part Number 09000-90013.

Hewlett-Packard Company. 1989b. *HP-UX System Security*. Part Number 92453-90029.

Holbrook, P., and J. Reynolds, editors. 1991. "Site Security Handbook." Request for Comments 1244. DDN Network Information Center, Government Systems, Inc., Chantilly, VA.

Kahn, David. 1967. *The Codebreakers: The Story of Secret Writing*. New York, NY: Macmillan.

Kent, S., and J. Linn. 1989. "Privacy Enhancement for Internet Electronic Mail: Part II – Certificate-Based Key Management." Request for Comments 1114. DDN Network Information Center, Government Systems, Inc., Chantilly, VA.

Klein, Daniel V. 1990. " 'Foiling the Cracker': A Survey of, and Improvements to, Password Security." *USENIX Security Workshop Proceedings* Portland (August): 5-14.

Kohl, John, and B. Clifford Neuman. 1990. *The Kerberos Network Authentication Service*. Request for Comments Version 5, Draft 4.

Kramer, Steven M. 1988. ''On Incorporating Access Control Lists into the UNIX Operating System.'' *USENIX Security Workshop Proceedings* Portland (August): 38-48.

Leffler, Samuel J., Marshall Kirk McKusick, Michael J. Karels, and John S. Quarterman. 1989. *The Design and Implementation of the 4.3BSD UNIX Operating System*. Reading, MA: Addison-Wesley.

Linn, J. 1989a. ''Privacy Enhancement for Internet Electronic Mail: Part I – Message Encipherment and Authentication Procedures.'' Request for Comments 1113. DDN Network Information Center, Government Systems, Inc., Chantilly, VA.

Linn, J. 1989b. ''Privacy Enhancement for Internet Electronic Mail: Part III – Algorithms, Modes and Identifiers.'' Request for Comments 1115. DDN Network Information Center, Government Systems, Inc., Chantilly, VA.

Lynn, M. Stuart, Chair. 1989. *The Computer Worm: A Report to the Provost of Cornell University on an Investigation Conducted by the Commission of Preliminary Enquiry*. Cornell University.

McIlroy, M. Douglas. 1989. ''Virology 101.'' *Computing Systems* 2 (Spring): 173-81.

Markoff, John. 1991. ''Scientists Devise Math Tool To Break a Protective Code.'' *The New York Times* (National Edition) CXLI (October 3): A-16.

Merkle, Ralph C. 1990. ''A Fast Software One-Way Hash Function.'' *Journal of Cryptology* 3 (1): 43-58.

Mockapetris, P. V. 1987a. ''Domain Names – Concepts and Facilities.'' Request for Comments 1034. DDN Network Information Center, Government Systems, Inc., Chantilly, VA.

Mockapetris, P. V. 1987b. ''Domain Names – Implementation and Specification.'' Request for Comments 1035. DDN Network Information Center, Government Systems, Inc., Chantilly, VA.

Mogul, Jeffrey C. 1989. ''Simple and Flexible Datagram Access Controls for UNIX-based Gateways.'' *USENIX Conference Proceedings* Baltimore (Summer): 203-221.

Morris, Robert T. 1985. *A Weakness in the 4.2BSD TCP/IP Software*. Computing Science Technical Report No. 117. AT&T Bell Laboratories, Murray Hill, NJ.

Morris, Robert, and Ken Thompson. 1979. ''Password Security: A Case History.'' *Communications of the ACM*, 22 (November): 594-7.

National Bureau of Standards. 1977. *Data Encryption Standard*. FIPS PUB 46.

National Computer Security Center. 1985a. *Department of Defense Password Management Guideline*. Report No. CSC-STD-002-85.

National Computer Security Center. 1985b. *Department of Defense Trusted Computer System Evaluation Criteria*. Department of Defense Standard DOD 5200.28-STD.

Needham, R. M., and M. D. Schroeder. 1978. "Using Encryption for Authentication in Large Networks of Computers." *Communications of the ACM*, 21 (December): 993-999.

Neumann, Peter G., Moderator. *Forum on Risks to the Public in Computers and Related Systems*. ACM Committee on Computers and Public Policy. Internet mailing list. Issue 9.69, February 20, 1990.

Nowitz, D. A., and M. E. Lesk. 1979. "A Dial-Up Network of UNIX Systems." Reprinted in *UNIX System Manager's Manual*. 4.3 Berkeley Software Distribution, University of California, Berkeley, April 1986.

O'Reilly, Tim, and Grace Todino. 1990. *Managing UUCP and Usenet*. Sebastopol, CA: O'Reilly and Associates, Inc.

Ould, Andrew. 1990. "Internet Felon Gets Fine, Probation." *UNIX World* 7 (July): 13.

Pethia, Richard, Steve Crocker, and Barbara Fraser. 1991. *Guidelines for the Secure Operation of the Internet*. Request for Comments 1281. DDN Network Information Center, Government Systems, Inc., Chantilly, VA.

Postel, J. B. 1980. "User Datagram Protocol." Request for Comments 768. DDN Network Information Center, Government Systems, Inc., Chantilly, VA.

Postel, J. B. 1981a. "Internet Protocol." Request for Comments 791. DDN Network Information Center, Government Systems, Inc., Chantilly, VA.

Postel, J. B. 1981b. "Transmission Control Protocol." Request for Comments 793. DDN Network Information Center, Government Systems, Inc., Chantilly, VA.

Postel, J. B., and J. K. Reynolds. 1985. "File Transfer Protocol." Request for Comments 959. DDN Network Information Center, Government Systems, Inc., Chantilly, VA.

Quarterman, John S., and Josiah C. Hoskins. 1986. "Notable Computer Networks." *Communications of the ACM*, 29 (October): 932-71.

Reeds, J. A., and P. J. Weinberger. "File Security and the UNIX System Crypt Command." *AT&T Bell Laboratories Technical Journal* 63 (October): 1673-83.

Ritchie, Dennis M. "On the Security of UNIX." 1975. Reprinted in *UNIX System Manager's Manual*. 4.3 Berkeley Software Distribution, University of California, Berkeley, April 1986.

Rivest, R., A. Shamir, and L. Adleman. 1978. "A Method for Obtaining Digital Signatures and Public Key Cryptosystems." *Communications of the ACM* 21 (February): 120-26.

Rivest, R. 1991a. "The MD4 Message-Digest Algorithm." Internet Draft.

Rivest, R. 1991b. "The MD5 Message-Digest Algorithm." Internet Draft. DDN Network Information Center, Government Systems, Inc., Chantilly, VA.

Seely, Donn. 1988. *A Tour of the Worm*. Department of Computer Science, University of Utah.

Sollins, K. R. 1981. "TFTP Protocol (Revision 2)." Request for Comments 783. DDN Network Information Center, Government Systems, Inc., Chantilly, VA.

Spafford, Eugene H. 1988. *The Internet Worm Program: An Analysis*. Technical Report No. CSD-TR-823. Department of Computer Science, Purdue University.

Stoll, Clifford. 1988. "Stalking the Wily Hacker." *Communications of the ACM* 31 (May): 484-97.

Stoll, Clifford. 1989. *The Cuckoo's Egg*. New York: Doubleday.

Stoll, Clifford. 1990a. *NOVA: The KGB, The Computer, and Me*. NOVA television series (October 1990). WGBH, Boston.

Stoll, Clifford. 1990b. Electronic mail conversation with author, 28 December 1990.

Sun Microsystems. 1990. *System and Network Administration*. Part Number 800-3805-10, Revision A.

Thompson, Ken. 1984. "Reflections on Trusting Trust." *Communications of the ACM* 27 (August): 761-3.

Wack, John P. 1991. *Establishing a Computer Security Incident Response Capability*, NIST Special Publication, National Institute of Standards and Technology.

UNIX Today! 1991a. "Morris Appeals to Supreme Court." June 10, p. 5.

UNIX Today! 1991b. "Supreme Court Upholds Morris Conviction." October 14, p. 8.

Wood, Charles C., Scott Kramer, and Jerome A. Smith. 1981. *Terminal Security Vulnerability*. SRI International, Menlo Park, CA.

Zimmerman, D. P. 1990. "Finger User Information Protocol." Request for Comments 1194. DDN Network Information Center, Government Systems, Inc., Chantilly, VA.

This program is a simple password cracker. It reads password file lines one at a time and tries several guesses on each password. First, it extracts the login name and each word in the full name (GECOS) field from the password file entry. It then tries each of these words as they appear in the password file, in all lower case, in all upper case, and capitalized. Then it reverses each of those guesses, and tries them again. If this still doesn't succeed, the program starts trying the same combinations on words in the dictionary. As each password is discovered, it is printed out along with the login name of the account whose password was cracked.

```c
/*
 * crack - crack passwords
 *
 * Usage: crack [-w wordlist]
 */
#include <sys/param.h>
#include <sys/time.h>
#include <ctype.h>
#include <stdio.h>
#include <pwd.h>

#define DEF_WORDLIST    "/usr/dict/words"
#define MAXWORDS        32767
#define NW              64

int ndictwords = 0;

char *pname;
char *wordfile = DEF_WORDLIST;

char wordlist[MAXWORDS][9];
```

```
main(argc, argv)
char **argv;
int argc;
{
    char *try();
    register char *passwd;
    register struct passwd *pw;

    setlinebuf(stdout);
    pname = *argv;

    /*
     * Process arguments.
     */
    while (--argc) {
        if (**++argv != '-')
            goto usage;

        switch (*++*argv) {
        case 'w':
            if (--argc <= 0)
                goto usage;

            wordfile = *++argv;
            break;
        default:
usage:          fprintf(stderr, "Usage: %s [-w wordfile]\n", pname);
            exit(1);
        }
    }

    /*
     * Load in the list of words.
     */
    load_wordlist();

    /*
     * For each password file line...
     */
    while ((pw = getpwent()) != NULL) {
        /*
         * Look at the encrypted password.  If it's not 13
         * characters long, it's an impossible value.
         */
```

```
        switch (strlen(pw->pw_passwd)) {
        case 13:
            /*
             * Try to crack it.
             */
            if ((passwd = try(pw)) != NULL) {
                printf("%s was cracked, password = %s\n",
                        pw->pw_name, passwd);
            }
            break;
        case 0:
            printf("ZERO LENGTH PASSWORD: %s\n", pw->pw_name);
            break;
        default:
            break;
        }
    }


    exit(0);
}


/*
 * try - try to crack a password.
 */
char *
try(pw)
struct passwd *pw;
{
    char *crypt();
    char *words[NW];
    register char *s;
    static char buf[1024];
    register int i, nwords;


    /*
     * Build a list of words - the login name, plus every word
     * from the GECOS field.
     */
    words[0] = pw->pw_name;


    nwords = 1;
    s = pw->pw_gecos;
```

```
while (*s == ' ' || *s == '\t')
    s++;

while (*s != ',' && *s != '\0' && nwords < NW) {
    while (*s == ' ' || *s == '\t')
        *s++ = '\0';

    words[nwords++] = s;

    while (*s != ' ' && *s != '\t' &&
           *s != ',' && *s != '\0')
        s++;
}

*s = '\0';

/*
 * Now try all those words in various permutations.
 */
for (i = 0; i < nwords; i++) {
    if (!strcmp(pw->pw_passwd, crypt(words[i],
        pw->pw_passwd))) return(words[i]);
    reverse(words[i], buf);
    if (!strcmp(pw->pw_passwd, crypt(buf, pw->pw_passwd)))
        return(buf);
    lower(words[i], buf);
    if (!strcmp(pw->pw_passwd, crypt(buf, pw->pw_passwd)))
        return(buf);
    reverse(buf, buf);
    if (!strcmp(pw->pw_passwd, crypt(buf, pw->pw_passwd)))
        return(buf);
    upper(words[i], buf);
    if (!strcmp(pw->pw_passwd, crypt(buf, pw->pw_passwd)))
        return(buf);
    reverse(buf, buf);
    if (!strcmp(pw->pw_passwd, crypt(buf, pw->pw_passwd)))
        return(buf);
    capital(words[i], buf);
    if (!strcmp(pw->pw_passwd, crypt(buf, pw->pw_passwd)))
        return(buf);
    reverse(buf, buf);
    if (!strcmp(pw->pw_passwd, crypt(buf, pw->pw_passwd)))
        return(buf);
}
```

```
    /*
     * Now try the words in the dictionary.
     */
    for (i = 0; i < ndictwords; i++) {
        if (!strcmp(pw->pw_passwd, crypt(wordlist[i],
            pw->pw_passwd))) return(wordlist[i]);
        reverse(wordlist[i], buf);
        if (!strcmp(pw->pw_passwd, crypt(buf, pw->pw_passwd)))
            return(buf);
        lower(wordlist[i], buf);
        if (!strcmp(pw->pw_passwd, crypt(buf, pw->pw_passwd)))
            return(buf);
        reverse(buf, buf);
        if (!strcmp(pw->pw_passwd, crypt(buf, pw->pw_passwd)))
            return(buf);
        upper(wordlist[i], buf);
        if (!strcmp(pw->pw_passwd, crypt(buf, pw->pw_passwd)))
            return(buf);
        reverse(buf, buf);
        if (!strcmp(pw->pw_passwd, crypt(buf, pw->pw_passwd)))
            return(buf);
        capital(wordlist[i], buf);
        if (!strcmp(pw->pw_passwd, crypt(buf, pw->pw_passwd)))
            return(buf);
        reverse(buf, buf);
        if (!strcmp(pw->pw_passwd, crypt(buf, pw->pw_passwd)))
            return(buf);
    }

    return(NULL);
}

/*
 * load_wordlist - read the dictionary into memory.
 */
load_wordlist()
{
    FILE *fp;
    char word[BUFSIZ];

    if ((fp = fopen(wordfile, "r")) == NULL) {
        fprintf(stderr, "%s: cannot open %s.\n", pname, wordlist);
        exit(1);
    }
```

```
    while (ndictwords < MAXWORDS && fgets(word, BUFSIZ, fp) != NULL) {
        word[strlen(word)-1] = '\0';     /* strip newline */
        strncpy(wordlist[ndictwords], word, 8);
        wordlist[ndictwords++][8] = '\0';
    }


    fclose(fp);
}


/*
 * lower - convert s to lower case and store in t.
 */
lower(s, t)
register char *s, *t;
{
    while (*s) {
        *t++ = isupper(*s) ? tolower(*s) : *s;
        s++;
    }
}


/*
 * upper - convert s to upper case and store in t.
 */
upper(s, t)
register char *s, *t;
{
    while (*s) {
        *t++ = islower(*s) ? toupper(*s) : *s;
        s++;
    }
}


/*
 * capital - capitalize s and store in t.
 */
capital(s, t)
register char *s, *t;
{
    *t++ = islower(*s) ? toupper(*s) : *s;
    s++;
```

```
        while (*s) {
            *t++ = isupper(*s) ? tolower(*s) : *s;
            s++;
        }
    }


    /*
     * reverse - reverse s and store in t.
     */
    reverse(s, t)
    register char *s, *t;
    {
        register char *p;

        p = &s[strlen(s) - 1];

        while (p >= s)
            *t++ = *p--;
        *t = '\0';
    }
```

Appendix B
A File System Checker

Using the material presented in Chapter 3, a simple file system checker can be constructed, as shown below.

```
#!/bin/sh
#
# fscheck - check file system for insecurities
#
# This should be run as "root".
#

PATH=/usr/bin:/bin
export PATH

#
# Set CHECKDIRS to the list of directories you want to put in
# your check lists.
#
# Set MASTER_LS to the path of the master checklist generated
# with "ls".
#
# Set MASTER_SUM to the path of the master checklist generated
# with "sum".
#
CHECKDIRS="/bin /etc /usr/bin /usr/etc /usr/lib /usr/ucb"
MASTER_LS=ls.master
MASTER_SUM=sum.master

#
# Search the entire file system for set-user-id files.
#
```

```
echo "Set-User-Id files found:"
find / -type f -a -perm -4000 -exec ls -aslg {} \;
echo ""


#
# Search the entire file system for set-group-id files.
#
echo "Set-Group-Id files found:"
find / -type f -a -perm -2000 -exec ls -aslg {} \;
echo ""


#
# Search the entire file system for device files; strip out the
# ones we find in /dev.
#
echo "Device files not located in /dev:"
find / \( -type b -o -type c \) -print | grep -v '^/dev'
echo ""


#
# Search the entire file system for world writable files and
# directories.
#
echo "World writable files and directories:"
find / -perm -2 -exec ls -aslgd {} \;
echo ""


#
# Search the entire file system for files and directories owned by
# nonexistent users or groups.  This will only work on systems with
# the "-nouser" and "-nogroup" options to find.
#
echo "Files owned by nonexistent user or group:"
find / \( -nouser -o -nogroup \) -exec ls -aslgd {} \;
echo ""


#
# Generate a checklist using ls.
#
ls -alsgR $CHECKDIRS > /tmp/lschk.$$


#
# Generate a checklist using sum.
#
```

```
# The first find command should be used on Berkeley systems - that
# version of sum does not print the file name, so we need to print it
# using echo.  The second find command should be used on System V
# systems.
#
find $CHECKDIRS -type f -exec echo -n {} " " \; \
    -exec sum {} \; > /tmp/sumchk.$$
# find $CHECKDIRS -type f -exec sum {} \; > /tmp/sumchk.$$


#
# Compare the ls checklist with the master checklist.
#
echo "Files in $CHECKDIRS whose attributes have changed:"
echo "< = master check list, > = current listing"
diff $MASTER_LS /tmp/lschk.$$
echo ""


#
# Compare the sum checklist with the master checklist.
#
echo "Files in $CHECKDIRS whose checksums have changed:"
echo "< = master check list, > = current listing"
diff $MASTER_SUM /tmp/sumchk.$$


#
# Delete our temporary files and exit.
#
rm -f /tmp/lschk.$$ /tmp/sumchk.$$
exit 0
```

This shell script executes each of the find commands described in section 3.8 (except for the one that searches for *.rhosts* files), labeling the output appropriately. It also implements a fairly simplistic version of ls-based and sum-based checklists. This version of the script does not handle files in the checklists that are expected to change; it will report them just like any other file.

In order to use this script, first edit it and change the values of CHECKDIRS, MASTER_LS, and MASTER_SUM. Then generate initial versions of the checklists by using the find, ls, and sum commands shown in the script, redirecting the output to the master lists. You can then run this script as *root* periodically, to check up on the status of your file systems.

Appendix C
Kerberos Dialogue

This dialogue[1] provides a fictitious account of the design of an open-network authentication system called "Charon." As the dialogue progresses, the characters Athena and Euripides discover the problems of security inherent in an open network environment. Each problem must be addressed in the design of Charon, and the design evolves accordingly. Athena and Euripides don't complete their work until the dialogue's close.

When they finish designing the system, Athena changes the system's name to "Kerberos," the name, coincidentally enough, of the authentication system that was designed and implemented at MIT's Project Athena. The dialogue's "Kerberos" system bears a striking resemblance to the system described in Chapter 9. This dialogue was written by Bill Bryant, of MIT's Project Athena.

Dramatis Personae:

Athena, an up-and-coming system developer.

Euripides, a seasoned developer and resident crank.

Scene I

(A cubicle area. Athena and Euripides are working at neighboring terminals.)

Athena: Hey Rip, this timesharing system is a drag. I can't get any work done because everyone else is logged in.

Euripides: Don't complain to me. I only work here.

Athena: You know what we need? We need to give everyone their own workstation so they don't have to worry about sharing computer cycles. And we'll use a network to connect all the workstations so folks can communicate with one another.

Euripides: Fine. So what do we need, about a thousand workstations?

Athena: More or less.

Euripides: Have you seen the size of a typical workstation's disk drive? There isn't enough room for all the software that you have on a timesharing machine.

Athena: I figured that out already. We can keep copies of the system software on various server machines. When you log in to a workstation, the workstation accesses the system software by making a network connection with one of the servers. This setup lets a whole bunch of workstations use the same copy of the system software, and it makes software updates convenient. You don't have to trundle around to each workstation. Just modify the system software servers.

Euripides: All right. What are you going to do about personal files? With a timesharing system I can log in and get to my files from any terminal that is connected to the system. Will I be able to walk up to any workstation and automatically get to my files? Or do I have to make like a PC user and keep my files on diskette? I hope not.

Athena: I think we can use other machines to provide personal file storage. You can log in to any workstation and get to your files.

Euripides: What about printing? Does every workstation have its own printer? Whose money are you spending anyway? And what about electronic mail? How are you going to distribute mail to all these workstations?

Athena: Ah... Well obviously we don't have the cash to give everyone a printer, but we could have machines dedicated to print service. You send a job to a print server, and it prints it for you. You could do sort of the same thing with mail. Have a machine dedicated to mail service. You want your mail, you contact the mail server and pick up your mail.

Euripides: Your workstation system sounds really good Tina. When I get mine, you know what I'm going to do? I'm going to find out your username, and get my workstation to think that I am you. Then I'm going to contact the mail server and pick up your mail. I'm going to contact your file server and remove your files, and—

Athena: Can you do that?

Euripides: Sure! How are these network servers going to know that I'm not you?

Athena: Gee, I don't know. I guess I need to do some thinking.

Euripides: Sounds like it. Let me know when you figure it out.

Scene II

(Euripides' office, the next morning. Euripides sits at his desk, reading his mail. Athena knocks on the door.)

Athena: Well, I've figured out how to secure an open network environment so that unscrupulous folks like you cannot use network services in other people's names.

Euripides: Is that so? Have a seat.

(She does.)

Athena: Before I describe it, can I lay down one ground rule about this discussion?

Euripides: What's your rule?

Athena: Well suppose I say something like the following: "I want my electronic mail, so I contact the mail server and ask it to send the mail to my workstation." In reality I'm not the entity that contacts the mail server. I'm using a program to contact the mail server and retrieve my mail, a program that is a CLIENT of the mail service program.

But I don't want to say "the client does such-and-such" every time I refer to a transaction between the user and a network server. I'd just as soon say "I do such-and-such," keeping in mind of course that a client program is doing things on my behalf. Is that okay with you?

Euripides: Sure. No problem.

Athena: Good. All right, I'll begin by stating the problem I have solved. In an open network environment, machines that provide services must be able to confirm the identities of people who request service. If I contact the mail server and ask for my mail, the service program must be able to verify that I am who I claim to be, right?

Euripides: Right.

Athena: You could solve the problem clumsily by requiring the mail server to ask for a password before I could use it. I prove who I am to the server by giving it my password.

Euripides: That's clumsy all right. In a system like that, every server has to know your password. If the network has one thousand users, each server has to know one thousand passwords. If you want to change your password, you have to contact all servers and notify them of the change. I take it your system isn't this stupid.

Athena: My system isn't stupid. It works like this: Not only do people have passwords, services have passwords too. Each user knows his or her password, each service program knows its password, and there's an AUTHENTICATION SERVICE that knows *all* passwords—each user's password, and each service's password. The authentication service stores the passwords in a single, centralized database.

Euripides: Do you have a name for this authentication service?

Athena: I haven't thought of one yet. Do you have any ideas?

Euripides: What's the name of that fellow who ferries the dead across the River Styx?

Athena: Charon?

Euripides: Yeah, that's him. He won't take you across the river unless you can prove your identity.

Athena: There you go Rip, trying to rewrite Greek mythology again. Charon doesn't care about your identity. He just wants to make sure that you're dead.

Euripides: Have you got a better name?

(Pause.)

Athena: No, not really.

Euripides: Then let's call the authentication service "Charon."

Athena: Okay. I guess I should describe the system, huh?

Let's say you want to use a service, the mail service. In my system you cannot use a service unless, ah, Charon tells the service that you are who you claim to be. And you can't get the okay to use a service unless you have authenticated yourself to Charon. When you request authentication from Charon, you have to tell Charon the service for which you want the okay. If you want to use the mail server, you've got to tell Charon.

Charon asks you to prove your identity. You do so by providing your secret password. Charon takes your password and compares it to the one that is registered for you in the Charon database. If the two passwords match, Charon considers your identity proven.

Charon now has to convince the mail server that you are who you say you are. Since Charon knows all service passwords, it knows the mail service's password. It's conceivable that Charon could give you the password, which you could forward to the mail service as proof that you have authenticated yourself to Charon.

The problem is, Charon cannot give you the password directly, because then you would know it. The next time you wanted mail, you could circumvent Charon and use the mail server without correctly identifying yourself. You could even pretend to be someone else, and use the mail server in that other person's name.

So instead of giving you the mail server's password, Charon gives you a mail service TICKET. This ticket contains a version of your username that has been ENCRYPTED using the MAIL SERVER'S PASSWORD.

Ticket in hand, you can now ask the mail service for your mail. You make your request by telling the mail server who you are, and furnishing the ticket that proves you are who you say you are.

The server uses its password to decrypt the ticket, and if the ticket decrypts properly, the server ends up with the username that Charon placed in the ticket.

The service compares this name with the name you sent along with the ticket. If the names match, the mail server considers your identity proven and proceeds to give you your mail.

What do you think of those apples?

Euripides: I've got some questions.

Athena: I figured. Well go ahead.

Euripides: When a service program decrypts a ticket, how does it know that it has decrypted the ticket properly?

Athena: I don't know.

Euripides: Maybe you should include the service's name in the ticket. That way when a service decrypts a ticket, it can gauge its success on whether or not it can find its name in the decrypted ticket.

Athena: That sounds good to me. So the ticket looks something like this:

(She scrawls the following on a pad of paper:)

```
TICKET - {username:servicename}
```

Euripides: So the service ticket contains just your username and the servicename?

Athena: Encrypted with the service's password.

Euripides: I don't think that's enough information to make the ticket secure.

Athena: What do you mean?

Euripides: Let's suppose you ask Charon for a mail server ticket. Charon prepares that ticket so that it has your username "tina" in it. Suppose I copy that ticket as it whizzes by on its way across the network from Charon to you. Suppose I convince my insecure workstation that my username is "tina." The mail client program on my workstation thinks I am you. In your name, the program forwards the stolen ticket to the mail server. The server decrypts the ticket and sees that it is valid. The username in the ticket matches the name of the user who sent the ticket. The mail server gives me your mail...

Athena: Oh! Well that's not so good.

Euripides: But I think I know a way to fix this problem. Or to at least provide a partial fix to it. I think Charon should include more information in the service tickets it produces. In addition to the username, the ticket should also include the

NETWORK ADDRESS from which the user asked Charon for the ticket. That gives you an additional level of security.

I'll illustrate. Suppose I steal your mail ticket now. The ticket has your workstation's network address in it, and this address does not match my workstation's address. In your name I forward the purloined ticket to the mail server. The server program extracts the username and network address from the ticket and attempts to match that information against the username and network address of the entity that sent the ticket. The username matches, but the network address does not. The server rejects the ticket because obviously it was stolen.

Athena: Bravo, bravo! I wish I had thought of that.

Euripides: Well that's what I'm around for.

Athena: So the revised ticket design looks like this:

(She scrawls the following on a chalkboard:)

```
TICKET - {username:ws_address:servicename}
```

Athena: Now I'm really excited. Let's build a Charon system and see if it works!

Euripides: Not so fast. I have some other questions about your system.

Athena: All right. *(Athena leans forward in her chair.)* Shoot.

Euripides: Sounds like I've got to get a new ticket every time I want to use a service. If I'm putting in a full day's work, I'll probably want to get my mail more than once. Do I have to get a new ticket every time I want to get my mail? If that's true, I don't like your system.

Athena: Ah... Well I don't see why tickets can't be reusable. If you get a ticket for the mail server, you ought to be able to use it again and again. For instance, when the mail client program makes a request for service in your name, it forwards a *copy* of the ticket to the mail server.

Euripides: That's better. But I still have problems. You seem to imply that I have to give Charon my password every time I want to use a service for which I don't have a ticket. I log in and want to access my files. I fire off a request to Charon for the proper ticket and this means that I've had to use my password. Then I want to read my mail. Another request to Charon, I have to enter my password again. Now suppose I want to send one of my mail messages to the print server. Another Charon request and, well you get the picture.

Athena: Uh, yeah, I do.

Euripides: And if that weren't bad enough, consider this: it sounds like when you authenticate yourself to Charon, you send your secret password over the network in cleartext. Clever people like yours truly can monitor the network and steal copies of people's passwords. If I've got your password, I can use any service in your name.

(Athena sighs.)

Athena: These are serious problems. Guess I need to go back to the drawing board.

Scene III

(The next morning, Athena catches Euripides at the coffee area. She taps him on the shoulder as he fills his cup.)

Athena: I've got a new version of Charon that solves our problems.

Euripides: Really? That was quick.

Athena: Well, you know, problems of this nature keep me up all night.

Euripides: Must be your guilty conscience. Shall we repair to yon small conference room?

Athena: Why not?

(The two move to the small conference room.)

Athena: I'll begin by stating the problems again, but I'll invert them so that they become requirements of the system.

(Athena clears her throat.)

Athena: The first requirement: users only have to enter their passwords once, at the beginning of their workstation sessions. This requirement implies that you shouldn't have to enter your password every time you need a new service ticket. The second requirement: passwords should not be sent over the network in clear text.

Euripides: Okay.

Athena: I'll start with the first requirement: you should only have to use your password once. I've met this requirement by inventing a new network service. It's called the "ticket-granting" service, a service that issues Charon tickets to users who have already proven their identity to Charon. You can use this ticket-granting service if you have a ticket for it, a ticket-granting ticket.

The ticket-granting service is really just a version of Charon in as much as it has access to the Charon database. It's a part of Charon that lets you authenticate yourself with a ticket instead of a password.

Anyhow, the authentication system now works as follows: you log in to a workstation and use a program called `kinit` to contact the Charon server. You prove your identity to Charon, and the `kinit` program gets you a ticket-granting ticket.

Now say you want to get your mail from the mail server. You don't have a mail server ticket yet, so you use the "ticket-granting" ticket to get the mail server ticket for you. You don't have to use your password to get the new ticket.

Euripides: Do I have to get a new "ticket-granting" ticket every time I need to get to another network service?

Athena: No. Remember, we agreed last time that tickets can be reused. Once you have acquired a ticket-granting ticket, you don't need to get another. You use the ticket-granting ticket to get the other tickets you need.

Euripides: Okay, that makes sense. And since you can reuse tickets, once the ticket-granting service has given you a ticket for a particular service, you don't need to get that particular ticket again.

Athena: Yeah, isn't that elegant?

Euripides: Okay, I buy it so far... As long as you didn't have to send your password in cleartext over the network when you got the ticket-granting ticket.

Athena: Like I said, I've solved that problem as well. The thing is, when I say you have to contact Charon to get the ticket-granting ticket, I make it sound as though you have to send your password in cleartext over the network to the Charon Server. But it doesn't have to be that way.

Here's really what happens. When you use the `kinit` program to get the ticket-granting ticket, `kinit` doesn't send your password to the Charon server, `kinit` sends only your username.

Euripides: Fine.

Athena: Charon uses the username to look up your password. Next Charon builds a packet of data that contains the ticket-granting ticket. Before it sends you the packet, Charon uses your password to encrypt the packet's contents.

Your workstation receives the ticket packet. You enter your password. `Kinit` attempts to decrypt the ticket with the password you entered. If `kinit` succeeds, you have successfully authenticated yourself to Charon. You now possess a ticket-granting ticket, and that ticket can get you the other tickets you require.

How's that for some fancy thinking?

Euripides: I don't know... I'm trying to think myself. You know, I think the parts of the system that you just described work pretty well. Your system requires me to authenticate myself only once. Thereafter Charon can issue me service tickets without my being aware of it. Seamless, seamless in that regard. But there's something about the design of the service ticket that troubles me somehow. It has to do with the fact that tickets are reusable. Now I agree that they have to be reusable, but reusable tickets are, by their nature, very dangerous.

Athena: What do you mean?

Euripides: Look at it this way. Suppose you are using an insecure workstation. In the course of your login session you acquire a mail service ticket, a printing service ticket, and a file service ticket. Suppose you inadvertently leave these tickets on the workstation when you logout.

Now suppose I log in to the workstation and find those tickets. I'm feeling like causing trouble, so I make the workstation think that I am you. Since the tickets are made out in your name, I can use the mail client program to access your mail, I can use the file service client to access and remove your files, and I can use the printing command to run up huge bills on your account. All because these tickets have been accidentally left lying around.

And nothing can keep me from copying these tickets to a place of my own. I can continue to use them for all eternity.

Athena: But that's an easy fix. We just write a program that destroys a user's tickets after each login session. You can't use tickets that have been destroyed.

Euripides: Well obviously your system must have a ticket-destroying program, but it's foolish to make users rely on such a thing. You can't count on users to remember to destroy their tickets every time they finish a workstation session. And even if you rely upon your users to destroy their tickets, consider the following scenario.

I've got a program that watches the network and copies service tickets as they zip across the network. Suppose I feel like victimizing you. I wait for you to begin a workstation session, I turn on my program and copy a bunch of your tickets.

I wait for you to finish your session, and eventually you log out and leave. I fiddle with my workstation's network software and change its address so that it matches the address of the workstation you were using when you acquired the tickets I copied. I make my workstation believe that I am you. I have your tickets, your username, and the correct network address. I can *replay* these tickets and use services in your name.

It doesn't matter that you destroyed your tickets before you ended your workstation session. The tickets I have stolen are valid for as long as I care to use them, because your current ticket design does not place a limit on the number of times you can reuse a ticket, or on how long a ticket remains valid.

Athena: Oh I see what you're saying! Tickets can't be valid forever because they would then constitute a huge security risk. We have to restrict the length of time for which a ticket can be used, perhaps give each ticket some kind of expiration date.

Euripides: Exactly. I think each ticket needs to have two additional pieces of information: a lifespan that indicates the length of time for which the ticket is valid, and a timestamp that indicates the date and time at which Charon issued the ticket. So a ticket would look something like this:

(Euripides goes to the chalkboard and scrawls the following:)

```
TICKET    {username:address:servicename:lifespan:timestamp}
```

Euripides: Now when a service decrypts tickets, it checks the ticket's username and address against the name and address of the person sending the ticket, and it uses the timestamp and lifespan information to see if the ticket has expired.

Athena: All right. What kind of lifetime should the typical service ticket have?

Euripides: I don't know. Probably the length of a typical workstation session. Say eight hours.

Athena: So if I sit at my workstation for more than eight hours, all my tickets expire. That includes my ticket-granting ticket. So I have to reauthenticate myself to Charon after eight hours.

Euripides: That's not unreasonable is it?

Athena: I guess not. So we're settled—tickets expire after eight hours. Now I've got a question for you. Suppose I have copied *your* tickets from the network—

Euripides: (*Eyes twinkling*) Aw, Tina! You wouldn't really do that would you?

Athena: This is just for the sake of argument. I've copied your tickets. Now I wait for you to log out. Suppose you have a doctor's appointment or a class to attend, so you end your workstation session after a couple of hours. You are a smart boots and have destroyed your copies of the tickets before logging out.

But I've stolen your tickets, and they are good for about six hours. That gives me ample time to pillage your files and print one thousand copies of whatever in your name.

See, the lifetime-timestamp business works fine in the event that a ticket thief chooses to replay the ticket after the ticket has expired. If the thief can replay the ticket before that...

Euripides: Uh, well... Of course you are right.

Athena: I think we have run into a major problem. (*She sighs.*)

(*Pause.*)

Euripides: I guess that means you'll be busy tonight. Want more coffee?

Athena: Why not?

(*The two head for the coffee machine.*)

Scene IV

(*The next morning in Euripides' office. Athena knocks on the door.*)

Euripides: You've got rings under your eyes this morning.

Athena: Well, you know. Another one of those long nights.

Euripides: Have you solved the replay problem?

Athena: I think so.

Euripides: Have a seat.

(She does.)

Athena: As usual, I feel compelled to restate the problem. Tickets are reusable within a limited timespan, say eight hours. If someone steals your tickets and chooses to replay them before they expire, we can't do anything to stop them.

Euripides: That's the problem.

Athena: We could beat the problem if we designed the tickets so they couldn't be reusable.

Euripides: But then you would have to get a new ticket every time you wanted to use a network service.

Athena: Right. That is a clumsy solution at best. *(Pause.)* Ah, how do I proceed with my argument? *(She ponders for a moment.)*

All right, I'm going to restate the problem again, this time in the form of a requirement. A network service must be able to prove that the person using a ticket is the same person to whom that ticket was issued.

Let me trace the authentication process again and see if I can tease out an appropriate way to illustrate my solution to this problem.

I want to use a certain network service. I access that service by starting a client program on my workstation. The client sends three things to the service machine—my name, my workstation's network address, and the appropriate service ticket.

The ticket contains the name of the person it was issued to and the address of the workstation that person was using when he or she acquired the ticket. It also contains an expiration date in the form of a lifespan and a timestamp. All this information has been encrypted in the service's Charon password.

Our current authentication scheme relies on the following tests:

- Can the service decrypt the ticket?

- Has the ticket expired?

- Do the name and workstation address specified in the ticket match the name and address of the person who sent the ticket?

What do these tests prove? The first test proves that the ticket either did or did not come from Charon. If the ticket cannot be decrypted, it did not come from the real Charon. The real Charon would have encrypted the ticket with the service's password. Charon and the service are the only two entities that know the service's password. If the ticket decrypts successfully, the service knows that it came from the real Charon. This test prevents folks from building fake Charon tickets.

The second test checks the ticket's lifespan and timestamp. If it has expired, the service rejects the ticket. This test stops people from using old tickets, tickets that perhaps were stolen.

The third test checks the ticket-user's name and address against the name and address of the person specified in the ticket. If the test fails, the ticket-user has obtained (perhaps surreptitiously) another person's ticket. The ticket is of course rejected.

If the names and addresses do match, what has the test proved? Nothing. Scallywags can steal tickets from the network, change their workstation addresses and usernames appropriately, and rifle other folks resources. As I pointed out yesterday, tickets can be replayed as long as they haven't expired. They can be replayed because a service cannot determine that the person sending the ticket is actually the ticket's legitimate owner.

The service cannot make this determination because it does not share a secret with the user. Look at it this way. If I'm on watch at Elsinore, you know, the castle in *Hamlet*, and you are supposed to relieve me, I'm not supposed to let you take my place unless you can provide the correct password. That's the case where the two of us share a secret. And it's probably a secret that someone else made up for everyone who stands on watch.

So I was thinking last night, why not have Charon make up a password for the legitimate ticket-owner to share with the service? Charon gives a copy of this SESSION KEY to the service, and a copy to the user. When the service receives a ticket from a user, it can use the session key to test the user's identity.

Euripides: Wait a second. How is Charon going to give both parties the session key?

Athena: The ticket-owner gets the session key as part of the reply from Charon. Like this:

(She scrawls the following on a chalkboard:)

```
CHARON REPLY - [sessionkey|ticket]
```

The service's copy of the session key comes inside the ticket, and the service gets the key when it decrypts the ticket. So the ticket looks like this:

```
TICKET - {sessionkey:username:address:servicename:lifespan:
          timestamp}
```

When you want to get to a service, the client program you start builds what I call an AUTHENTICATOR. The authenticator contains your name and your workstation's address. The client encrypts this information with the session key, the copy of the session key you received when you requested the ticket.

```
AUTHENTICATOR - {username:address} encrypted with session key
```

After building the authenticator, the client sends it and the ticket to the service. The service cannot decrypt the authenticator yet because it doesn't have the session key. That key is in the ticket, so the service first decrypts the ticket.

After decrypting the ticket, the service ends up with the the following information:

- The ticket's lifespan and timestamp;
- The ticket-owner's name;
- The ticket-owner's network address;
- The session key.

The service checks to see if the ticket has expired. If all is well in that regard, the service next uses the session key to decrypt the authenticator. If the decryption proceeds without a hitch, the service ends up with a username and a network address. The service tests this information against the name and address found in the ticket, *and* the name and address of the person who sent the ticket and authenticator. If everything matches, the service has determined that the ticket-sender is indeed the ticket's real owner.

(Athena pauses, clears her throat, drinks some coffee.)

I think the session key-authenticator business takes care of the replay problem.

Euripides: Maybe. But I wonder... To break this version of the system, I must have the proper authenticator for the service.

Athena: No. You must have the authenticator *and* the ticket for the service. The authenticator is worthless without the ticket because the service cannot decrypt the authenticator without first having the appropriate session key, and the service cannot get the appropriate session key without first decrypting the ticket.

Euripides: Okay, I understand that, but didn't you say that when a client program contacts the server, it sends the ticket and matching authenticator together?

Athena: Yes, I guess I said that.

Euripides: If that's what actually happens, what prevents me from stealing the ticket and authenticator at the same time? I'm sure I could write a program to do the job. If I've got the ticket and its authenticator, I believe I can use the two as long as the ticket has not expired. I just have to change my workstation address and username appropriately. True?

Athena: *(Biting her lip)* True. How dispiriting.

Euripides: Wait, wait, wait! This isn't such a big deal. Tickets are reusable as long as they haven't expired, but that doesn't mean that authenticators have to be reusable. Suppose we design the system so that authenticators can only be used once. Does that buy us anything?

Athena: Well, it might. Let's see, the client program builds the authenticator, then sends it with the ticket to the service. You copy both ticket and authenticator as they move from my workstation to the server. But the ticket and authenticator arrive at the server before you can send your copies. If the authenticator can only be used once, your copy of it is no good, and you lose when you attempt to replay your ticket and authenticator.

Well, that's a relief. So all we have to do is invent a way to make the authenticator a one-time usable thing.

Euripides: No problem. Let's just put a lifespan and timestamp on them. Suppose each authenticator has a lifespan of a couple of minutes. When you want to use a service, your client program builds the authenticator, stamps it with the current time, then sends it and the ticket to the server.

The server receives the ticket and authenticator and goes about its business. When the server decrypts the authenticator, it checks the authenticator's lifespan and timestamp. If the authenticator hasn't expired, and everything else checks properly, the server considers you authenticated.

Suppose I copied the authenticator and ticket as they crossed the network. I have to change my workstation's network address and my username, and I have to do this all in a couple of minutes. That's a pretty tall order. In fact I don't think it's possible. Unless...

Well, here's a potential problem. Suppose that instead of copying the ticket and authenticator as they travel from your workstation to the server, I copy original ticket packet that comes from Charon, the packet you receive when you ask Charon to give you a ticket.

This packet, as I recall, has two copies of the session key in it: one for you and one for the service. The one for the service is hidden in the ticket and I can't get to it, but what about the other one, the one you use to build authenticators?

If I can get that copy of the session key, I can build my own authenticators, and if I can build my own authenticators, I can break the system.

Athena: That's something I thought about last night, but then I traced the process of acquiring tickets and found that it wasn't possible to steal authenticators that way.

You sit down at a workstation and use the `kinit` program to get your ticket-granting ticket. `Kinit` asks for your username, and after you enter it, `kinit` forwards the name to Charon.

Charon uses your name to look up your password, then proceeds to build a ticket-granting ticket for you. As part of this process, Charon creates a session key that you will share with the ticket-granting service. Charon puts a copy of the session key in the ticket-granting ticket, and puts your copy in the ticket packet that you are about to receive. But before it sends you this packet, Charon encrypts the whole thing with your password.

Charon sends the packet across the network. Someone can copy the packet as it goes by, but they can't do anything with it because it has been encrypted with your password. Specifically, no one can steal the ticket-granting session key.

`Kinit` receives the ticket packet and prompts you for a password, which you enter. If you enter the correct password, `kinit` can decrypt the packet and give you your copy of the session key.

Now that you've taken care of the `kinit` business, you want to get your mail. You start the mail client program. This program looks for a mail service ticket and doesn't find one (after all, you haven't tried to get your mail yet). The client must use the ticket-granting ticket to ask the ticket-granting service for a mail service ticket.

The client builds an authenticator for the ticket-granting transaction and encrypts the authenticator with your copy of the ticket-granting session key. The client then sends Charon the authenticator, the ticket-granting ticket, your name, your workstation's address, and the name of the mail service.

The ticket-granting service receives this stuff and runs through the authentication checks. If everything checks properly, the ticket-granting service ends up with a copy of the session key that it shares with you. Now the ticket-granting service builds you a mail service ticket, and during this process, creates a new session key for you to share with the mail service.

The ticket-granting service now prepares a ticket packet to send back to your workstation. The packet contains the ticket and your copy of the mail service session key. But before it sends the packet, the ticket-granting service encrypts the packet with its copy of the TICKET-GRANTING session key. That done, the packet is sent on its way.

So here comes the mail service ticket packet, loping across the network. Suppose some network ogre copies it as it goes by. The ogre is out of luck because the packet is encrypted with the ticket-granting session key; you and the ticket-granting service are the only entities that know this key. Since the ogre cannot decrypt the mail ticket packet, the ogre cannot discover the MAIL SESSION KEY. Without this session key, the ogre cannot use any of the mail service tickets you might subsequently send across the network.

So I think we're safe. What do you think?

Euripides: Perhaps.

Athena: Perhaps! Is that all you can say!

Euripides: (laughing) Don't get upset. You should know my ways by now. I guess it is mean of me, and you up half the night.

Athena: Pthhhhh!

Euripides: All right, three-quarters of the night. Actually, the system is beginning to sound acceptable. This session key business solves a problem that I thought of last night: the problem of mutual authentication.

(Pause.)

Mind if I talk for a minute?

Athena: (A trifle coldly) Be my guest.

Euripides: You are so kind. *(Euripides clears his throat.)* Last night, while visions of session keys and authenticators danced in your head, I was trying to find new problems with the system, and I found one that I thought was pretty serious. I'll illustrate it by way of the following scenario.

Suppose you are sick of your current job and have determined that it is in your best interest to move on. You want to print your resume on the company's whiz-bang laser printer so that headhunters and potential employers can take note of your classiness.

So you enter the printing command, and direct it to send the resume to the appropriate print server. The command gets the proper service ticket, if you don't already have it, then sends the ticket in your name to the appropriate print server. At least that's where you think it's headed. You don't in fact know that the request is headed for the right print server.

Suppose that some unscrupulous hacker—say it's your boss—has screwed the system around so that he redirects your request and its ticket to the print server in his office. His print service program doesn't care about the ticket or its contents. It throws away the ticket and sends a message to your workstation indicating that the ticket passed muster, and that the server is ready and willing to print your job. The printing command sends the job to the fraudulent print server and the enemy ends up with your resume.

I'll state the problem by way of contrast. Without session keys and authenticators, Charon can protect its servers from false users, but it cannot protect its users from false servers. The system needs a way for client programs to authenticate the server before sending sensitive information to the service. The system must allow for MUTUAL AUTHENTICATION.

But the session key solves this problem as long as you design your client programs properly. Back to the print server scenario. I want a print client program that makes sure the service it's sending jobs to is the legitimate service.

Here's what such a program does. I enter the printing command and give it a filename, the name of my resume. Assume that I have a print service ticket and session key. The client program uses the session key to build an authenticator, then sends the authenticator and ticket to the "supposed" print server. The client *does not* send the resume yet; it waits for a response from the service.

The real service receives the ticket and authenticator, decrypts the ticket and extracts the session key, then uses the session key to decrypt the authenticator. This done, the service runs all the appropriate authentication tests.

Assume the tests confirm my identity. Now the server prepares a reply packet so that it can prove its identity to the client program. It uses its copy of the session key to encrypt the reply packet, then sends the packet to the waiting client.

The client receives the packet and attempts to decrypt it with my copy of the session key. If the packet decrypts properly and yields the correct server response message, my client program knows that the server that encrypted the packet is the real server. Now the client sends the resume job to the print service.

Suppose my boss screwed around the system so that his print server poses as the one I want. My client sends the authenticator and ticket to the "print service" and waits for a response. The fake print service cannot generate the correct response because it cannot decrypt the ticket and get the session key. My client will not send the job unless it receives the correct response. Eventually the client gives up waiting and exits. My print job does not get completed, but at least my resume did not end up on the desk of the enemy.

You know, I think we have a solid basis on which to implement the Charon Authentication System.

Athena: Perhaps. Anyway, I don't like the name "Charon."

Euripides: You don't? Since when?

Athena: I've never liked it, because the name doesn't make sense. I was talking to my Uncle Hades about it the other day, and he suggested another name, the name of his three-headed watch dog.

Euripides: Oh, you mean "Cerberus."

Athena: Bite your tongue, Rip! "Cerberus" indeed...

Euripides: Er, isn't that the name?

Athena: Yeah, if you happen to be a Roman! I'm a Greek goddess, he's a Greek watch dog, and his name is "Kerberos," "Kerberos" with a "K."

Euripides: Okay, okay, don't throw thunderbolts. I'll buy the name. Actually, it has a nice ring to it. Adios Charon and hello to Kerberos.

Appendix D
A Complete Security Policy

The security policy below is currently under development by the author for use at the Purdue University Engineering Computer Network. It contains all of the elements of a security policy described in Chapter 10, as well as some other sections, such as the one on violations and penalties. Much of this policy is based on policies from other universities. Although minor parts of this policy may change before it is finalized, and several parts may not be applicable outside Purdue University, the author feels that the document itself provides a useful example of how to create a security policy.

PURDUE UNIVERSITY ENGINEERING COMPUTER NETWORK POLICY ON ACCESS AND USAGE (September, 1991)

1. Introduction

The Purdue University Schools of Engineering operate and develop the Engineering Computer Network (ECN) to promote their instructional, research, and administrative efforts. The ECN is composed of ten Digital Equipment and Gould UNIX timesharing systems, over 500 Sun Microsystems UNIX workstations, and over 300 Apple Macintosh personal computers, as well as several systems from other vendors. Peripheral equipment includes over 1,200 terminals, over 100 laser printers, over 30 high-speed line printers, several plotters and other special output devices, numerous dial-in modems, and other special-purpose peripherals. These systems are joined together into over 40 local-area networks within the Schools of Engineering. Network connections are also maintained to the rest of the Purdue University campus including the Purdue University Computer Center, as well as to off-campus networks such as USENET, the National Science Foundation network (NSFnet), and the Internet.

The terminology used in this policy tends to reflect that of the UNIX operating system, which is used on the majority of systems within the ECN. However, the policy applies to all computer systems connected to the ECN, regardless of their operating system or manufacturer. As used in this policy statement, the term "user" refers to any person consuming computer resources on ECN facilities; the term "ECN" refers both to the resources making up the network and to the group of staff members responsible for the operation of those resources.

2. Disclaimers

The ECN makes available to faculty, staff, students, and others, computing facilities consisting of hardware, software, and documentation. The use and operation of these facilities is subject to the following disclaimers.

2.1 The ECN accepts no responsibility for any damage or loss of data arising directly or indirectly from the use of these facilities or for any consequential loss or damage.

2.2 Although backups are performed to protect data in the event of a hardware or software failure, the ECN makes no warranty that all data can or will be restored, and accepts no responsibility for any damage or loss of data arising directly or indirectly from the failure of hardware or software, or from human error.

2.3 Because the goals of the ECN are primarily educational in nature, computer systems are generally open to perusal and investigation by users, and security controls may be less restrictive than they would be in other environments. Although every effort is made to maintain adequate system security, the ECN accepts no responsibility for any loss of privacy, theft of information, damage, or loss of data arising directly or indirectly from the absence or failure of system security protection mechanisms.

2.4 The ECN makes no warranty, express or implied, regarding the computing services offered, or their fitness for any particular purpose.

3. Access to ECN Facilities

When applying for access to ECN facilities, a valid University identification card must be presented. Students may also be required to present a current class schedule.

3.1 The facilities of the ECN are made available to the faculty, staff, and students of the Schools of Engineering, generally without charge. Facilities may also be made available to student organizations and faculty and staff of other Schools by special arrangement.

3.2 Only properly authorized persons may access ECN facilities; proper authorization is provided by ECN staff members or their designates in the form of an account issued in the name of the authorized person.

3.3 A user may not permit any other person, including other authorized users, to access ECN facilities through his or her account.

3.4 Those persons who have been issued keys, access cards, or combinations to obtain access to ECN facilities may not use these items to allow other persons to access the facilities. Keys, access cards, and combinations may not be loaned or given to others.

4. User Rights and Responsibilities

A user of the Engineering Computer Network has the following rights and responsibilities.

4.1 To enable the ECN to accurately maintain information about the user of each account, each user is responsible for supplying current information to ECN including school or department affiliation, degree program (undergraduate or graduate), expected graduation or termination date, and University position (faculty, staff, graduate staff, or student).

4.2 The providing of false or misleading information for the purpose of obtaining access to ECN facilities is a violation of University policy.

4.3 Each user is responsible for any and all activity initiated in or on ECN facilities by his or her account.

4.4 Users are responsible for selecting a secure password for their account, and for keeping that password secret at all times. Passwords should not be written down, stored on-line, or given to others. Passwords should never be given out to someone claiming to be an ECN staff member; authorized ECN staff members have super-user privileges and do not need to know individual users' passwords.

4.5 Users are responsible for protecting their own files and data from reading and/or writing by other users, using whatever protection mechanisms are provided by the operating system in use. Most printers and plotters are located in public areas; users are responsible for picking up their output in a timely fashion to avoid theft or disposal.

4.6 Users are responsible for reporting any system security violation, or suspected system security violation, to the ECN immediately.

4.7 Most ECN facilities are made available on an unmonitored basis. It is the responsibility of every user to act in such a manner as to not cause damage to the physical equipment. Accidental damage, or damage caused by other parties, should be reported to the ECN as soon as possible so that corrective action can be taken.

4.8 Users who borrow hardware, software, or documentation from ECN lending collections are responsible for the proper care of that equipment, and for returning it in a timely fashion.

4.9 Users are responsible for obeying all posted signs and placards in terminal rooms, attached to ECN equipment, and displayed in the log-on message of the day.

4.10 Users who are affiliated with the Schools of Engineering may not be denied access to ECN facilities by someone who is not using the facilities for instructional, research, or administrative purposes, or who is not a faculty, staff, or student member of the Schools of Engineering. A user affiliated with the Schools of Engineering has the right to ask this person to relinquish the resource, or to ask an ECN staff member to intervene on his or her behalf.

4.11 Users have the right not to be harassed while using ECN facilities, whether it be physical, verbal, electronic, or any other form of abuse. Harassment should be reported to the ECN.

4.12 Above all, users are responsible at all times for using the ECN facilities in a manner that is ethical, legal, and not to the detriment of others.

5. ECN Rights and Responsibilities

The ECN in general has the right to do whatever is necessary to carry out its responsibility to keep the computing resources operating and available.

5.1 The networked computer environment provided by the ECN is a facility provided to faculty, staff, and students to enable them to accomplish certain tasks required by their roles within the Schools of Engineering and the University. There is an acknowledged trade-off between the absolute right of privacy of a user, and the need of the ECN to gather necessary information to ensure the continued functioning of this resource.

5.2 The ECN at all times has an obligation to maintain the privacy of a user's files, electronic mail, and printer listings to the best of its ability.

5.3 In the normal course of system administration, the ECN may have to examine files, electronic mail, and printer listings to gather sufficient information to diagnose and correct problems with system software, or, with reasonable cause for suspicion, to determine if a user is acting in violation of the policies set forth in this document. The ECN has the right to do this, subject to item 5.2 above.

5.4 In order to protect against hardware and software failures, backups of all data stored on ECN facilities are made on a regular basis. The ECN has the right to examine the contents of these backups to gather sufficient information to diagnose and correct problems with system software, or, with reasonable cause for suspicion, to determine if a user is acting in violation of the policies set forth in this document, subject to item 5.2 above.

5.5 With reasonable cause for suspicion, the ECN has the right to monitor any and all aspects of a system, including individual login sessions, to determine if a user is acting in violation of the policies set forth in this document, subject to item 5.2, above.

5.6 The ECN has the right to alter the priority or terminate the execution of any process that is consuming excessive system resources or objectionably degrading system response, with or without prior notification.

5.7 The ECN has the right to remove or compress disk files that are not related to Schools of Engineering missions and which are consuming large amounts of disk space, with or without prior notification.

5.8 The ECN has the right to terminate login sessions that have been idle (unused) for long periods of time, in order to free resources. This applies particularly to limited resources such as dial-in connections. The definition of a "long period" of time may vary from system to system, depending on resource availability.

5.9 The ECN has the responsibility to provide advance notice of system shutdowns, maintenance, upgrades, or changes so that users may plan around periods of system unavailability. However, in the event of an emergency, the ECN has the right to shut down a system with little or no advance notification. Every effort will be made to give users a chance to save their work before the system is taken out of service.

5.10 The ECN has the responsibility to report any violations of University policy, state law, or federal law pertaining to the use of University computer facilities to the appropriate authorities.

5.11 The ECN has the right to refuse access to any person who has violated the policies set forth in this document, or who has violated the policies of other computer facilities belonging to the University.

6. Proper Use

The ECN facilities are provided for use by faculty, staff, and students in support of the programs of the Schools of Engineering. All faculty, staff, and students are responsible for seeing that these computing facilities are used in an effective, efficient, ethical, and lawful manner.

6.1 Many resources, such as disk space, CPU cycles, printer queues, batch queues, login sessions, and software licenses, are shared by all users. No user may monopolize these resources.

    6.1.1 Users should consume as little disk space as practical, making use of available means for compressing files and archiving unused files off-line.

    6.1.2 Users should not load the system in such a way that others cannot perform useful work, by making appropriate use of batch queues and job priorities.

    6.1.3 Long printer jobs (such as theses) should not be printed during periods of peak printer demand.

    6.1.4 Users should relinquish licensed software when no longer using the license.

    6.1.5 The resources of workstations located in public labs should be respected; jobs may not be run that would interfere with the use of that workstation by the person sitting at the keyboard.

6.2 ECN facilities are provided for academic use (instruction and research) and some administrative uses.

    6.2.1 The license agreements for some pieces of software may specifically restrict the software to instructional use. The ECN should be consulted before using licensed software for research or administrative tasks.

    6.2.2 ECN facilities may not be used for any activity that is commercial in nature without first obtaining written approval to do so. Commercial activities include consulting, typing services, developing software for sale, and in general any activity which is paid for by non-University funds.

6.3 The ECN recognizes the academic value of research on computer security, and the investigation of self-replicating code. However, the use and development of this type of software, if not properly supervised, can inadvertently affect the operation and integrity of ECN systems.

    6.3.1 Users may not intentionally develop or use programs which harass other users of the system.

    6.3.2 Users may not intentionally develop or use programs which attempt to bypass system security mechanisms, steal passwords or data, or "crack" passwords.

    6.3.3 Users may not intentionally develop or use programs that attempt to consume all of an available system resource (memory, swap space, disk space, network bandwidth, etc.).

6.3.4 Users may not intentionally develop or use programs designed to replicate themselves or attach themselves to other programs, commonly called worms or viruses.

6.3.5 Users may not intentionally develop or use programs designed to evade software licensing or copying restrictions.

Users who believe that they have a legitimate reason to use or develop programs in the above categories for research purposes must notify the ECN before developing or using these programs. Special arrangements can be made to provide an adequate environment for conducting the research without risking damage to or impairment of other systems.

6.4 Files owned by individual users are to be considered as private, whether or not they are accessible by other users.

6.4.1 The ability to read a file does not imply permission to read that file. Files belonging to individuals are to be considered private property.

6.4.2 Under no circumstances may a user alter a file that does not belong to him or her without prior permission of the file's owner. The ability to alter a file does not imply permission to alter that file.

6.5 Because this is an educational environment, computer systems are generally open to perusal and investigation by users. This access must not be abused either by attempting to harm the systems, or by stealing copyrighted or licensed software.

6.5.1 System-level files (not owned by individuals) may be used and viewed for educational purposes if their access permissions so allow.

6.5.2 Most system-level files are part of copyrighted or licensed software, and may not be copied, in whole or in part, except as needed as part of an educational exercise.

6.5.3 The same standards of intellectual and academic honesty and plagiarism apply to software as to other forms of published work.

6.5.4 Making copies of software having a restricted-use license is theft. So is figuring out how to "beat" the license.

6.5.5 Deliberate alteration of system files is vandalism or malicious destruction of University policy.

6.6 Game playing, and the development of computer games, is permitted on ECN systems (subject to departmental policies). However, these activities must be limited to "off" periods when demand for system resources is low. Work in pursuit of the goals of the Schools of Engineering has priority over game playing and development.

6.7 Although each user has a right to freedom of speech, harassing or defamatory material may not be sent via electronic mail or posted to electronic bulletin boards and news groups.

6.8 ECN facilities and network connections may not be used for the purposes of making unauthorized connections to, breaking into, or adversely affecting the performance of other systems on the network, whether these systems are University-owned or not. The ability to connect to other systems via the network does not imply the right to make use of or even connect to these systems unless properly authorized by the owners of those systems.

7. Software Copyrights and Licenses

The software used on ECN facilities is operated under license agreements with AT&T, Sun Microsystems, Apple Computer, and others.

7.1 United States copyright and patent laws protect the interests of authors, inventors, and software developers in their products. Software license agreements serve to increase compliance with copyright and patent laws. It is against federal law and ECN policy to violate the copyrights or patents on computer software. It is against ECN policy and may be a violation of state or federal law to violate software license agreements.

7.2 The ECN's UNIX source code license binds each and every user to respect the proprietary nature of the UNIX operating system and its source code. The specifics of the operating system may not be taught, nor may the system or any part thereof (including source code) be moved to, or copies released to any non-licensed site.

7.3 Software in use on ECN facilities, unless it is stored in areas specifically marked as containing copyable software, may not be copied to magnetic tape, hard or floppy disks. Backups are maintained by the ECN; users may not make copies of licensed software.

7.4 Source code for licensed software may not be included in software that is released for use outside the ECN.

8. Violations and Penalties

The disposition of situations involving a violation of the policies set forth in this document, and the penalties that may be imposed for these violations, are as described below.

8.1 Minor infractions of this policy, when likely accidental in nature, such as poorly chosen passwords, overloading systems, excessive disk space consumption, and so on are typically handled internally to ECN in an informal manner by electronic mail or in-person discussions with the offender. More serious infractions are handled via formal procedures:

8.1.1 Infractions such as sharing accounts or passwords, harassment, or repeated minor infractions as described above may result in the temporary or permanent loss or modification of ECN computing privileges, and notification of a student's academic advisor.

8.1.2 More serious infractions, such as unauthorized use, attempts to steal passwords or data, attempts to steal licensed software, violations of University policies, or repeated violations as described in section 8.1.1 will result in the temporary or permanent loss of ECN computing privileges. If the offender is a student at the University, the case will be referred to the Dean of Students office for appropriate action. If the offender is a faculty or staff member of the University, the case will be referred to the head of the school or department by which that person is employed.

8.1.3 Offenses which are in violation of local, state, or federal laws will result in immediate loss of all ECN computing privileges, and will be reported to the Purdue University Police Department for appropriate investigation and action. Offenses of this nature committed by students will be reported to the Dean of Students; offenses committed by faculty or staff members will be reported to the head of the school or department by which that person is employed.

8.2 Penalties for violation of any of the policies set forth in this document, depending upon the nature of the infraction, may be imposed under University regulations, Indiana law, or the laws of the United States.

8.2.1 Section B-2 of the Purdue University *Regulations Governing Student Conduct, Disciplinary Proceedings, and Appeals*, as passed by the Board of Trustees of Purdue University, states, in part

2. Misconduct Subject to Disciplinary Penalties. The following actions constitute misconduct for which students may be subject to administrative action or disciplinary penalties.

a. Dishonesty in connection with any University activity. Cheating, plagiarism, or knowingly furnishing false information to the University are examples of dishonesty.

.....

e. Theft or attempted theft of, or the unauthorized use or possession of, or the unauthorized exertion of control over, or causing damage to property of any kind belonging to the University, a member of the University community, a campus visitor, or a person or agency participating in a University activity.

f. Unauthorized entry or access to, or unauthorized use or occupancy of, any University property including without limitation lands, buildings, structures, telecommunications, computer or data processing equipment, programs, systems, or software, or other facilities or services.

.....

k. Conduct or expression on University property or in connection with a University activity, that is intended to threaten, abuse, or harass a person or group of people on the basis of race, religion, color, sex, age, national origin, handicap, or status as a disabled or Vietnam era veteran.

"Administrative action" means the issuance of an oral or written warning, admonition, reprimand, and/or use of counseling procedures. "Disciplinary penalty" means expulsion, suspension, probated suspension, disciplinary probation, and other educationally sound sanctions.

8.2.2   Title 35, Article 43 of the Indiana Code contains the following:

35-43-1-4 Computer Tampering

.....

A person who knowingly or intentionally alters or damages a computer program or data, which comprises part of a computer system or computer network without the consent of the owner of the computer system or computer network commits computer tampering, a Class D felony.

35-43-2-3 Computer Trespass

.....

A person who knowingly or intentionally accesses: (1) a computer system; (2) a computer network; or (3) any part of a computer system or computer network; without the consent of the owner of the computer system or computer network, or the consent of the owner's licensee, commits computer trespass, a Class A misdemeanor.

In the State of Indiana, a Class D felony is punishable by a minimum of one year in prison and a fine of not more than $10,000. A Class A misdemeanor is punishable by a maximum of one year in prison and a fine of not more than $5,000.

8.2.3   Title 18, Section 1030 of the United States Code imposes penalties of fines and up to ten years in prison for

(a) Whoever—

.....

(3) intentionally, without authorization to access any computer of a department or agency of the United States, accesses such a computer of that department or agency that is exclusively for the use of the Government of the United States or, in the case of a computer not exclusively for such use, is used by or for the Government of the United States and such conduct affects the use of the Government's operation of such computer;

(4) knowingly and with intent to defraud, accesses a Federal interest computer without authorization, or exceeds authorized access, and by means of such conduct furthers the intended fraud and obtains anything of value, unless the object of the fraud and the thing obtained consists only of the use of the computer;

(5) intentionally accesses a Federal interest computer without authorization, and by means of one or more instances of such conduct alters, damages, or destroys information in any such Federal interest computer, or prevents authorized use of any such computer or information, and thereby—

(A) causes loss to one or more others of a value aggregating $1,000 or more during any one year period; or

(B) modifies or impairs, or potentially modifies or impairs, the medical examination, medical diagnosis, medical treatment, or medical care of one or more individuals; or

(6) knowingly and with intent to defraud traffics (as defined in section 1029) in any password or similar information through which a computer may be accessed without authorization, if—

(A) such trafficking affects interstate or foreign commerce; or

(B) such computer is used by or for the Government of the United States;

.....

the term "Federal interest computer" means a computer—

(A) exclusively for the use of a financial institution or the United States Government, or, in the case of a computer not exclusively for such use, used by or for a financial institution or the United States Government and the conduct constituting the offense affects the use of the financial institution's operation or the Government's operation of such computer; or

(B) which is one of two or more computers used in committing the offense, not all of which are located in the same state;

8.2.4 Title 18, Section 2701 of the United States Code imposes penalties of a fine of not more than $250,000 or imprisonment for not more than one year, or both, for anyone who

(1) intentionally accesses without authorization a facility through which an electronic communication service is provided; or (2) intentionally exceeds an authorization to access that facility; and thereby obtains, alters, or prevents authorized access to a wire or electronic communication while it is in electronic storage in such system .....

As defined in Title 18, Section 2510 of the United States Code, "electronic communication" means any transfer of signs, signals, writing, images, sounds, data, or intelligence of any nature transmitted in whole or in part by a wire, radio, electromagnetic, photoelectronic or photooptical system that affects interstate or foreign commerce, ...

8.2.5 Title 18, Section 2511 of the United States Code imposes penalties of a fine or imprisonment for not more than five years, or both, for any person who

(a) intentionally intercepts, endeavors to intercept, or procures any other person to intercept or endeavor to intercept, any wire, oral, or electronic communication; .....

Other regulations and laws may be applied as well, depending on the nature of the offense.

I certify that I have read the *Purdue University Engineering Computer Network Policy on Access and Usage*, and that I understand and agree to abide by all elements of this policy. I understand that upon violation of this policy, the Engineering Computer Network retains the right to deny future computing privileges, and that if warranted, further disciplinary action may be taken by the University, including prosecution under applicable state and federal laws.

Signature: _____   Date: _____

Printed Name: _____   ID Number: _____

Appendix E
UNIX Security Checklist

The checklist below summarizes the information presented in the book, and can be used to verify that you have implemented everything described. It can also be used when installing a new system, to make sure that nothing is forgotten. The sections where each point is described are given in parentheses.

☐ Inform users of good password selection criteria, and use either a proactive password checker or a password cracking program to verify that passwords are secure. (2.1) Password cracking programs and proactive password checkers are available from public software archives. (11.2).

☐ If desired and your system supports it, implement a password generator. (2.1)

☐ If desired and your system supports it, implement password aging. (2.1)

☐ If your system supports it, implement a shadow password file. (2.1) An implementation of shadow password files is available from public software archives. (11.2)

☐ Place expiration dates on all accounts. (2.2)

☐ Carefully control guest accounts, using restricted shells if possible. (2.3)

☐ Password protect well-known accounts that must be on the system; delete well-known accounts that are not needed. (2.4)

☐ Eliminate group and shared accounts, replacing them with groups instead. (2.5)

☐ Avoid placing the current directory in your (and especially *root*'s) search path. (2.6)

☐ Write-protect your startup files and home directory. (2.6)

☐ Codify rules and policies for operating as the super-user. (2.7)

☐ Monitor account security regularly. (2.8)

☐ Set appropriate file permissions on all files. (3.1)

☐ Set your *umask* value to something appropriate such as 022, 027, or 077. (3.2)

☐ If supported by your system, use the sticky bit on world-writable directories such as */tmp*. (3.4)

☐ Do not allow set-user-id or set-group-id shell scripts on the system. (3.6)

☐ Check the modes of all device files. (3.7)

☐ Implement and use a comprehensive backup strategy. (3.8)

☐ Use the `find` command regularly to search for insecurities in the file system. (3.9)

☐ Implement some form of checklist scheme to check the file system for unauthorized modifications. (3.9)

☐ Check the */etc/hosts.equiv* file to ensure it only contains the names of local hosts. (4.1)

☐ Do not allow *.rhosts* files on the system, with the possible exception of *root*. (4.1)

☐ Do not allow *.netrc* files on the system.

☐ Remove unnecessary services from the */etc/inetd.conf* file, and run the remaining services with as few privileges as possible. For example, `finger` can be run as *nobody* (or some other ''regular'' user) rather than as *root*. (4.2)

☐ Check your version of FTP to be sure that it is secure. (4.3)

☐ If you allow anonymous FTP, be sure it is set up properly. (4.3)

☐ Check your version of TFTP to be sure that it is secure. (4.3)

☐ Check your version of `sendmail` to be sure that it is secure. (4.4)

☐ Check your versions of */bin/mail* and */bin/rmail* to be sure that they are secure. (4.4)

☐ Check your version of `finger` to be sure that it is secure. (4.5)

☐ Consider the use of a firewall system to protect your internal network from the outside world. (4.7)

☐ Use ''+:'' instead of ''+::0:0:::'' in the password file when running NIS. (5.1)

☐ Be sure that the NIS map files are writable only by the super-user. (5.1)

☐ Use the `-access` option on all file systems in the *exports* (or `dfstab`) file when running NFS. (5.2)

- [ ] Wherever possible, use the `nosuid` option when mounting NFS file systems. (5.2)

- [ ] When running RFS, use the `-access` option on all `share` commands. (5.3)

- [ ] Implement user id and group id mappings when running RFS. (5.3)

- [ ] If possible, make sure that workstations cannot be taken into single-user mode without providing the *root* password. (6.1)

- [ ] Do not allow untrusted workstations to mount file systems via NFS or RFS with *root* access enabled. (6.2)

- [ ] If your system supports diskless workstations, make sure that the directories on the server that contain client root partitions are accessible only by the super-user. (6.2)

- [ ] Wherever possible, disable any packet monitoring packages in the kernel, and do not provide the ability to rebuild the kernel on these systems. (6.3)

- [ ] If possible, install a version of the PROM monitor that either does not provide or at least password-protects the commands to examine and change memory contents. (6.4)

- [ ] Make use of any access control mechanisms provided by the operating system and window system to prevent theft of workstation display contents. (6.5)

- [ ] If your system provides the capability, designate all public and network terminals as "insecure" in the *ttys* or *ttytab* file. If desired, designate the console terminal as insecure as well. (7.1)

- [ ] Disable message permission using the `mesg` command if you are using a terminal with block mode transmission features or remotely programmable function keys. (7.1)

- [ ] If your system provides the capability, install dial-up passwords on all modem ports. (7.2)

- [ ] Consider the use of dial-back modems or dial-back software. (7.2)

- [ ] If supported, enable passwords on terminal servers. (7.3)

- [ ] Use separate logins and passwords for each system that accesses yours via UUCP. (7.4)

- [ ] Make sure that the file */usr/lib/uucp/L.sys* or */usr/lib/uucp/Systems* is owned by *uucp* and mode 600. (7.4)

- [ ] Define permissions for all remote systems logging in via UUCP using the *USERFILE* and *L.cmds* or using the *Permissions* file. (7.4)

- [ ] Learn how to detect attacks, and watch your system regularly. (8.1)

- [ ] Develop written procedures describing how to respond to an attack. (8.2, 8.3)

Index